The Shape of Sunday

AN INTIMATE BIOGRAPHY OF

Lloyd C. Douglas

BY VIRGINIA DOUGLAS DAWSON
AND BETTY DOUGLAS WILSON

━━━━━ ILLUSTRATED ━━━━━

HOUGHTON MIFFLIN COMPANY BOSTON
The Riverside Press Cambridge
1952

Library of Congress catalogue card number: 52-11451

The Riverside Press
Cambridge, Massachusetts
Printed in the U.S.A.

FOR

HOWARD AND WEARY

AND FOR

ARTHUR, JOHN AND DOUGLAS

Foreword

WHEN LLOYD C. DOUGLAS died in 1951 he had just
finished the first half of his memoirs. The last lines he wrote
for publication were: "The second volume will deal with my
memories of life in the ministry and as a novelist. I shall begin
at once on Volume II. I hope to meet you there."

My sister Betty and I went about the sad task of going
through our father's things. All the household effects had
been disposed of at the time of Mother's death in 1944. His
belongings had dwindled to the books he loved most, his chair
and table, his paperweight collection, and the contents of his
files. In turning over these last, the carefully preserved records
of the years, we felt the appeal of that one sentence: "I hope
to meet you there."

"We couldn't possibly do it," we told each other as we
leafed through the yellowed pages of old scrapbooks and peered
at the newspaper pictures of the young Reverend Lloyd Cassel
Douglas, solemn above a high clerical collar. His face was thin
and intense, his lips sternly set. That young man was a stranger
to us. Lloyd had told us stories of the days when he was just
out of theological seminary and called to his first church, but
they were funny things that had happened to an unsure, anxious
young preacher; embarrassments and errors that were comic
when he remembered them for us after the years had softened

their pain. But it had all happened before we were born or were too little to notice and we felt only regret that our father had not lived to finish his story himself.

We went on with the work of gathering together everything we had left of him. "Do you remember when?" got to be the opening phrase of all our talk. "Let's write that down before we forget it." We did it for ourselves at first as a sort of necessity to keep as much as we could of two people who had made our childhood such a vivid happy time to look back upon.

We each had a big box of letters written to us by our father when he was away on trips, or we were at college or in our own homes. We read these aloud to each other and found them fresh and amusing—too good to put back on the shelf. Gradually the material piled up. Other people had Douglas letters and stories about him to tell. We began to realize that perhaps, after all, we could help him "meet you there."

There are no relatives left to check with us: grandparents, aunts, uncles, all are gone. This picture of Lloyd C. Douglas is drawn from our memories. For the most part it is a child's-eye view, and our beloved parents would probably be astounded at the trivial things which stuck with us and grieved at the important principles which made no impression on us at all.

As for the years before Betty and I came on to the scene, all is mystery. Once in a while our parents drew aside the curtain and allowed us a fleeting glimpse of themselves as a young couple; but glimpses of them sitting close together on the back steps shelling peas, or leaving the dishes unwashed on the dining-room table when they ran out to skate on the Race do not add much to the vital statistics in a serious study of a man's life and work.

And so this cannot be a serious study of the life of Lloyd C. Douglas because he was not like that with his daughters, or even with himself. He often complained he was two people: one going through the motions of living a conventional life of an ordinary citizen, the other standing by smiling at his own antics and people in general. It was the last one we knew best.

We want to make this his book as much as possible, but since we are telling what we saw and heard it is necessary that we be continually present. We will try to keep in the background lest the reader ask, "Whose life is this anyway?"

In writing this book my sister Betty and I have pooled our experiences and our energies. For the sake of clearness I am doing the telling, but it is most often she who is remembering. She was always the ear, the sitter-at-the-feet, the buoyer-up in time of disappointment. Here is the way our father described her in a letter to a friend: "Betty Douglas Wilson is one of the most lovable and interesting people of my acquaintance; indefatigable, relentless, with the industry of an ant and the transparency of glass. While her criticisms have never been very valuable due to an excess of filial loyalty, she has made many a good suggestion."

As for me, I can find no direct quotation of his, putting my character into a nutshell, except for one paragraph apologizing for some social omission of mine which ends, "You know what a rattlebrain she is."

Now that I have made for my sister and myself all the explanations traditional in a Foreword I must include one more. So far I have carefully spoken of our father as Lloyd or Father, or used "he" to the point of confusion. This cannot continue. If it sounds foolish for two grown women to speak of their father as "Daddy" the reader must bear it, for that is what we always called him. Father sounds much more dignified, but he was never that with us, and although on occasion we called him Lloyd (and he loved it) it comes unnaturally. His relation to us was easy and companionable, but always running beneath is the remembrance of early obedience; impudence in the young was a thing our father would never tolerate. Since in these remembrances we are trying to bring back the atmosphere of our childhood, "Daddy" it must be.

We wish to express our warmest gratitude to those long-time friends who allowed us to quote from their letters and told us invaluable stories: Mr. and Mrs. Shirley Smith, H. H. Seeley, Burton Garlinghouse, Mr. and Mrs. James Van Vechten, Mrs. Robert Craig, Jr., Mrs. Thomas A. Peabody, Mr. and Mrs. Glen Hersman, William E. Billings, Miss Mary Young, Mrs. William Kirkwood, Dr. Leland Chapman, Miss Marion H. Hunt and Houghton Mifflin Company, especially Hardwick Moseley.

We are grateful also to those many friends who told us what they remembered of Lloyd C. Douglas and helped us build up a picture of the real man.

VIRGINIA DOUGLAS DAWSON

June 1952

Contents

Illustrations

following page 68

The Shape
of Sunday

I

The Shape of Sunday

MONDAY WAS ALWAYS a fine day in our household. Daddy would come whistling down to breakfast in his oldest clothes. For a man who was generally so meticulous in his dress he could assemble some remarkably disreputable costumes for home consumption. "Begone, dull care!" he would announce loudly from the doorway. "Let joy be unconfined." Safe behind was another Sunday with its last-minute frantic searches, its tension and careful behavior. Next Sunday was too far off to worry about.

In a house where the husband and father has to be in his office at an early hour, breakfast is apt to be a hasty affair. But with us, especially on a Monday, it was one of the three most leisurely meals of the day. True, Betty and I had to scramble off to school as usual, and it was a struggle to tear ourselves away from the highly entertaining company of our parents to face the tedious world of arithmetic and spelling; but on Monday we could count on the atmosphere of unbuttoned relaxation being in effect when we got home.

It would seem that they, the parents, had hardly moved since we left them. Still with their heads together talking they had frittered away the time in our absence. Mother had caught up with her mending, Daddy had covered a few pages of manuscript paper with sermon titles. Handsomely ornamented capital letters and margin decorations testified that much thought had been expended, but little accomplished. They willingly admitted it. "Oh dear," Mother would wail. "I've forgotten to order the groceries. What will we have for dinner?"

Monday was like that.

Tuesday the week began, the ordinary work of the minister. Daddy's calendar was dense with committee meetings and church affairs. He always considered it important to be mixed up in civic things too. Then there were visits to be made; people were born, married and buried. At any time of the day or night a call might come from a parishioner who needed pastoral comfort.

But always the days of the week moved on toward the one big event—Sunday.

In spite of the relief he felt when it was over, the Sunday Service was the part of his job Daddy loved best. It was always a great challenge to him. By the middle of the week the title of the sermon had to be in the hands of the printer. That was easy. Daddy had a knack at thinking up interest-arousing subjects and catch phrases. The sermon subject determined the mood. He and the organist worked out, well in advance, the details of the music and congregational responses down to the last Amen. It was the actual writing of the sermon which he put off by wondrous means. It was alarming at times to have the clever title gone to press, the choir hard at work on the anthems; all marching together in harmony with the sermon, and that still floating at liberty in the blue.

"What'll I tell the flock?" Daddy would inquire of us at breakfast along about Thursday. Betty and I were so used to this that we took it no more seriously than when he announced the world was going to pot, or that next summer we would all pack up our duds and take a trip around the world.

Mother, ever attentive, would pause in her pouring of the

coffee, put a finger on the glass top of the percolator which was cracked and had a habit of plopping unexpectedly into the cups. "Have you got anything worked out, dear?" she would ask. He would stare glassily into space, signifying that there was something, hidden from us all as yet, but about to reveal itself to him.

By Friday the shape of Sunday was beginning to loom up like a great iceberg in the fog coming steadily toward us. Daddy was apt to come home between engagements and follow Mother about at her work. I remember often seeing him standing at the medicine cabinet mirror minutely examining his tongue, taking out the atomizer and spraying his throat with hollow gargling sounds. The first page of any composition with him represented innumerable trips to the basin to scour his teeth.

On Saturday morning the house was sternly quiet. Even necessary sounds like the clinking of dishes being washed and doors opening and shutting were muffled to the utmost. Betty and I crept up and down the stairs and whispered in our play. If something accidentally fell from our hands Mother would instantly appear—guardian of the silence—her finger pressed to her lips in dismay.

One sound only punctuated the tense hush: the nervous, irregular tapping of the typewriter, now silent, now chattering in a burst of speed. From time to time a Sunday voice from behind the study door would speak long solemn sentences, rising and falling, pausing significantly in question. "Have you forgotten the oil for your lamp?" the startled house would be asked. And sometimes his high yell of laughter cracked out when he thought of something funny which would have the college students rocking the pews on Sunday.

Around four o'clock in the afternoon the study door would be flung open and Daddy would appear: tall, thin, crumpled, carefully moving his aching shoulders. The bridge of black hair that crossed from his part to the other side and usually lay so carefully brushed would now be steamed to a high fluff.

"Bessie!"

Mother would hastily bite off her thread and put down her sewing. "I'm coming." She didn't take her work along on these occasions. When he read to her at night as he so often did (the rumble of his voice sweetened our dreams all through childhood) she sewed, but on Saturday he insisted upon her full attention.

She always gave us a little look as she left the room as though she asked, "Wish me luck." It took a good deal of tightrope walking to come up to Daddy's requirements of a good critic. He needed like air to breathe her approval, he delighted in stimulating questions; but the bearer of unpleasant criticism was apt to have her head chopped off like the messengers of old. Mother often braved him and had the quiet satisfaction of hearing her suggestions incorporated in the final product. But what his anxious listener had most to fear was missing a subtle point and later asking a question which would reveal her inattention.

The study door would shut behind them and the voice begin. It was easy to tell the difference between talk and the sermon. Upstairs in Mother's bedroom, sitting on the floor surrounded by our doll things, Betty and I would quietly continue our play, but time was being marked for us by the voice below going on . . . on. Hearing not the words but the tone we could tell when the end was coming. The voice lowered, slowed, swelled in poetic cadences. Without understanding we felt moved.

On Sunday morning Daddy would come down to breakfast very gay and noisy. He would whip his napkin open with a flourishing snap and inquire if everyone was aware that this was the Lord's Day. All his joviality we met with caution for we knew that underneath he was keyed up to a pitch and controlling his nerves with effort. Mother moved about calm and efficient, but with eye ever alert for his comfort, ironing out small irritations before they arose. Betty and I instinctively felt the tension and made ourselves as small and quiet as possible. After breakfast we hurried off to Sunday School, breathing deeply of the air outside our front door.

At ten we joined Mother in our pew and watched the people pouring down the aisles. At ten-thirty the doors were firmly shut while the organ triumphantly called all to worship. From then on every minute of the Service built up with fine music and rumbling response from hundreds of throats to the mood of the sermon.

There would be a silence after the last notes of the anthem died away and Daddy would rise with great dignity and step to the pulpit. Over the sea of people pressed shoulder to shoulder would pass a rustling, a settling, all their eyes centered on him.

I would ask myself, "Is that my own father standing up there so grave and strange with all these people waiting for him to speak?" Daddy who sat at breakfast in his old bathrobe singing loudly Grandfather Douglas' version of the hymn "Welcome Sweet Day of Rest"—Wah caw swah dah aw rah . . .

He would always begin with some sentence that caught his audience at once: "Last Thursday afternoon about five o'clock two men met down here at the corner of High and Main." From then on he had them until the end.

Even when Betty and I were too small to know what the sermon was about we loved the endings. The stillness over the packed church, the breathless attention was like a great silent applause. We knew it was the most exciting thing in the world to Daddy and because he was our world we pressed against our mother and the three of us in our pew were a little island of ecstasy, knowing that he had done it again.

I read this description in *A History of the Congregational Church in Ann Arbor* by Calvin Olin Davis, and again the excitement of those Sunday morning services swept over me.

Dr. Douglas was one of the most scintillating and brilliant ministers ever to occupy our pulpit. To many individuals he was a platform orator. Facile in speech, powerful in imagery, dramatic in delivery, and quick to utilize a pithy saying or humorous anecdote in order to emphasize a point in his sermon, he made a tremendous appeal to young and old alike, particularly to many University students. Within a short time the auditorium of the church was filled to overflowing every Sunday morning. Scores, if not hundreds of persons often being turned away from the doors because there was not an available seat left in the building.

After church, and the greetings and handshakes were over, we four walked sedately home across the Diagonal Walk which cut the campus, and along the Sunday-quiet streets to our house on Cambridge Road. Two by two we went, Betty and I, our white stockings sagging in thick rings by this time, just in front. Mother and Daddy bowed to friends and sometimes stopped to chat, but among the four of us little was said, nothing of the Service.

When the door of our house shut behind us it was like the shedding of a heavy overcoat. Mother reached up and unhooked the tight button of Daddy's collar, while he, with his chin screwed away from her busy fingers, excitedly questioned her on her reaction. "You thought it went all right? That anthem is a tremendous thing, isn't it? Old man Soandso didn't like that crack I got off about Noah, but I saw his wife smile. She's on my side."

Then he would go upstairs and we would hear him whistling loudly while he took off his long-tailed coat. Betty and I set the table and Mother lifted the dinner out of the fireless cooker. The air all over the house would be moist with the smell of steamed chicken and in the kitchen chicken broth hung in droplets from the ceiling.

The rest of the day was spent in making calls and pastoral duties. There was no evening service then, but the atmosphere remained arid and purified, and when Betty and I undressed for bed at night we didn't feel it necessary to spend much time on prayers since we had been so good all day.

That was Sunday.

These are our first recollections of a coherent nature, when life had settled down to a pattern of days. We lived in Ann Arbor, Michigan. Although previously we had lived in many other towns, Betty and I were too little to recall more than brief glimpses of them, startling in their vividness, but isolated. Ann Arbor seems to be where life started for us. Our father was the minister of the First Congregational Church, a church which sat upon the edge of a great university campus and drew each Sunday streams of frolicking students, sedate professors and their wives, as well as many townspeople.

Ann Arbor in 1915 was quiet in spite of the crowds of students who thronged the streets at the change of the hour, and whooped it up at week-ends. Little went on that was not associated with college life. A one-track streetcar lumbered and squealed its way along the leafy streets where fraternity houses mingled with the homes of faculty. I don't know why this streetcar should have boasted a motorman and a conductor, but it did, and their names were Mr. Love and Mr. Darling. This remarkable coincidence was very useful in college jokes and skits.

The social levels in Ann Arbor were laid upon one's position in the University rather than money. This was fortunate for us. While Daddy's church was not connected with the college in any way, he did have a great many faculty members in his congregation. He was active on the campus and the students enthusiastically accepted him as part of the organization.

"Is your father a professor?" we would be asked by the children at school.

"He's the Congregational minister," we would say proudly.

Every June we were invited to Mrs. Jordan's Party which was given in the Women's Gymnasium and was a very exclusive affair for children of the faculty only.

It was wonderful to have a father who could be counted upon to come forth with a brilliant performance no matter how unimportant the audience. He would be just as anxious to amuse and entertain the child next door as the President of the University. Even the applause of Mother, Betty and me was enough to stimulate him to great heights. Our mealtimes were unforgettable.

When we were small he had special acts that we never tired of. "Do your Society Sneeze, Daddy," we would beg. "Now the Cough . . . now the Society Yawn." They were better every time. "Now please do the Lady with the Caramel once more." This would go on for minutes while he demonstrated the agonizing plight of a very genteel lady at a church tea trying to dislodge a large piece of sticky candy from her upper plate without opening her mouth or otherwise disturbing her dignified demeanor.

"Your father doesn't act very much like a minister," our friends would say.

Any newcomer was a fresh audience: the guest at the table, the plumber who came to fix the pipes. In a book of advice to young ministers which Daddy wrote in 1924 he said:

When the plumber comes to your house, and you know he is in the basement, gouging around in the gloom, among the water pipes, go down and get acquainted with him. Make him talk; and, when you have him going, listen to what he says.

That was Daddy all right. Perhaps the sermon next Sunday would be illustrated with an anecdote featuring a leaky water valve, but it always seemed the plumber learned more than

Daddy did. At least he would hear more. He would go away confused, but bathed in a warm glow of good stories and friendliness.

All during Daddy's life this desire to entertain indiscriminately anyone who crossed his path continued. In the last month of his final illness Hardwick Moseley, a member of Houghton Mifflin Company, was visiting him in Los Angeles. They had been talking books and Daddy, gray and gaunt, was sinking deeper and deeper into his pillows. Hardwick realized Daddy was struggling for breath and too tired to continue. He called for the nurse, and she came in followed by the laboratory man wheeling another cartridge of oxygen to replace the one which always stood at the head of the bed.

This entry of fresh company was like a shot in the arm to Daddy. He propped himself upon one elbow, greeted the surprised delivery man with hails of welcome, told him a funny story and sent him on his way laughing.

In the early Ann Arbor days Daddy had a finger in everything that went on in our house. It was not his forte, but he always felt Mother would be helpless without him. The two of them, in a highly inefficient manner, ran the place. Daddy made the decisions; Mother pretended to carry them out.

Just as he enjoyed praising the tradespeople when they pleased him, he also enjoyed correcting them if their services did not meet with his requirements.

"That's the third time the groceries have been late this week," Mother might complain.

"I'll handle it!" Daddy would say, stalking to the telephone with long indignant steps.

We always hung around to hear these conversations for they would be masterpieces of phrase. He would begin by complimenting the unsuspecting grocer: "Excellent service . . . long satisfied customer . . . lately noticeable change . . . is the store under new management? . . . seriously discommoded . . . reluctant to withdraw our account, but . . ."

Only once did I ever hear a conversation like that which did not bring about frantic appeals for a second chance from the grocer and promises of improved service. That was long after the Ann Arbor days, when we were living in Montreal. A dilatory butcher had called forth a fine stream of Daddy's choicest sarcasm. "Just cancel our account!" was his final snort into the telephone.

"Very well, Mr. Douglas," was the butcher's mild answer.

Daddy came away from the phone highly pleased with the fresh twist to an old situation. "That's Canada for you," he laughed, "business when they feel like it."

We lived in three houses in Ann Arbor, and in all the other houses in other towns where we moved there was one thing to be settled first when viewing the new place—which room was to be Daddy's study? It had to be removed from the kitchen and the doorbells and the household traffic, for our father's nerves were always ready to quiver and his hearing was exceptional. In fact he could hear a faucet dripping in the night even after he had got up and shut it off.

"It's his bent septum that makes him nervous," Mother would explain to us.

Betty and I were very proud that we had inherited his bent septum and our sinus difficulties were cherished along with our sound digestions and Grandmother's walnut chest of drawers.

When we had lived in Ann Arbor about three years the church bought a parsonage on Hill Street and we moved with great excitement to this new house which was bigger and finer than any we had lived in previously. It was old; Mother wouldn't let us walk out on the upstairs gallery for fear it would drop off, but it had an iron fence around two sides of a deep lawn, and the front stairs were made of curly maple. Mother said she never dreamed that one day she would live in a house with a whole stairway of curly maple. A panel in the back hall sagged suspiciously and Betty and I at once began to tap and measure looking for a secret room.

Daddy had at first settled in the downstairs library which, with all its bookshelves, seemed the choicest room in the house for his study. But which was the choicest room was a question he was never quite able to settle to his own satisfaction. He soon realized that the library was too near the kitchen, so he staked off a claim for the entire top floor. It took him all fall to get properly established up there. By that time winter was settling in and the lack of heat at the top level began to be severely felt. Once more he moved all his things, this time to the big spare bedroom, which, in spite of its many advantages, he had rejected in the beginning because plaster was apt to drop off the ceiling in quite large hunks. However, Daddy cleverly repaired the weak spots as they appeared by pasting typewriting paper over them.

An interesting development in the importance of the study in our home is gleaned from this letter which he wrote many years later from Montreal, where he and Mother had crammed their belongings into an apartment, pleasant, but restricting nevertheless.

This is Saturday afternoon late. I am in my study which is so-called because I retire here to write of a Saturday upon my typewriter. When I was young and green and had my way to make in the world I had a large front room in which to do my scholarly research and composition. Now that I am old and famous I have a small coop hard by the kitchen where the pots and pans rattle merrily all forenoon. This afternoon my comfort and blessings were somewhat augmented by the janitor who came up with some kind of a lethal gun to squirt noxious fumes over the water-bugs that infest the bathroom, also adjacent to my sumptuous library. If I were not a person of abundant wit and limpid merriment, capable of laughing off one of the major misfortunes of my life, I should curse the fate that sentences me to this nasty hole to do my work. I am glad I can laugh.

When the furniture was moved into a new house the moving men were always astounded by the Chair. They carried it groaning and grunting up the stairs to the study and continued to regard it with suspicion while setting it up under Daddy's directions. He had seen this Chair advertised in the *Congregationalist,* and from the description decided it was exactly what a writing man needed—a complete study built into one piece of furniture.

I remember seeing him sitting in the monstrous thing all caged around by flying bookshelves, hinged tables that folded away and hovering arms for dictionaries, etc., ready to swing into action. The typewriter made the door that he pulled to after seating himself in the great golden-oak box. It was a voracious-looking piece of furniture that might come alive at any time and close in on its helpless victim. Daddy always seemed lost in it. We took the Chair from town to town until Montreal, where they couldn't get it into the elevator and it fell to alien hands.

The study was Daddy's sanctuary and it was a bold child who knocked at the door. Saturday was a day in itself, reserved for the vitally serious business of sermon writing. But speeches also were written, articles for the paper and for religious periodicals; funeral addresses were composed with such thoughtful care that every word brought comfort rather than grief. And always, always the yearning to write a piece that would be acceptable to some distinguished secular magazine. Dreams of fame? No, merely dreams of being one day recognized by people outside the realm of the church.

In *The Minister's Everyday Life*, the little book of advice to young men in the ministry, he says:

> I hesitate somewhat to speak to you about the business of writing for print. If I thought you were good for a long, tedious disappointing experience in doing your level best, only to have your stuff come back to you again and again with a chilly little rejection slip enclosed, I could advise you more heartily to make this adventure. For the benefit of you who think you are up to that sort of misery, it may be said that here is a wide open door.

It was a day for incredulous rejoicing with all of us the time that door opened a crack and the *Atlantic Monthly* accepted a small article of Daddy's for their Contributor's Club. The dazzling gleam of the other side was brief for two years went past before the *Atlantic* took another piece, but oh! the excitement.

"We've done it!" Daddy shouted. He and Mother clung together while Betty and I pranced around.

Not long ago Betty and I searched through the back files of the *Atlantic* trying to locate that article which was unsigned, of course, and could have been in any of three or four years as far as our memories were concerned. I knew I would recognize it at once for my name was mentioned in the first paragraph. We found it in the 1917 volume. It was called "An Interrupted Homily." This is the way it began:

> Somebody was having a tussel with the knob of my study door. It is not a difficult door to open. I have often felt it was too easy. Doubtless this was my small daughter, Virginia, attempting to turn the knob with one little fist, the other being engaged. A doughnut, perhaps. Verily it is more blessed to give than receive a doughnut in the midst of a pile of books and papers. I resolved to watch Virginia's movements stealthily.

So you see I did go into his study. Yes, I often crept in and approached the Chair and looked at the lovely sharp pencils and pads of white paper; the assortment of erasers, crayons, paper clamps and gadgets that Daddy always surrounded himself with. He would give me tasks to do.

"Now this week I'm going to give you two new words to learn. They are 'soliloquy' and 'idiosyncrasy.' Look them up in the dictionary and then write a little essay for me explaining exactly what they mean."

The second article of his which was accepted by the *Atlantic* Betty and I dug out of the Contributor's Club section of the 1919 volume. It was called "Accidental Salvation." That was his first version of the Parker story—the story of a mean old man who broke a needle off in his foot and thought the missing piece was on its fatal way to his heart. He reformed, of course, under the threat of momentary death. Daddy used that story in sermons and speeches until Mother finally said: "If you tell that Parker story once more I'm going to stand right up and howl."

One time after Daddy told it in a sermon a man came up and charged him with having taken it from an unsigned article in the *Atlantic*.

"You've improved on it, I will admit," the man said.

"Yes, I've worked over it a good deal since I first sold it to the *Atlantic Monthly*," Daddy told him.

Its final appearance was in the little book called *Precious Jeopardy*. By that time it was a Christmas story; after the mean old man had become thoroughly reformed his wife gave him back the other half of the needle for a Christmas present. She'd had it all the time.

Over the years I have always been amazed at my father's resilience to disappointment. At least he never let us see him discouraged or self-doubting. I suppose Mother knew of his dark hours for their two lives were as much one as separate bodies can be; but he seemed to have a marvelous faith that in the end he would have what he wanted, and if not, then it wouldn't have been good for him to have it anyway.

I wonder now when I look back at the hours he spent at the piano if it was not then he fought out his problems and consoled himself. Music meant a great deal to him. When he was happy he would sit down and thunder out "Unfold, Ye Portals Everlasting" until the forks on the table hummed. I remember the forks especially because it was generally just before dinner and when Mother was frying something tantalizing that he really got the portals properly unfolded. "I could eat a man off a horse," he would say when he came to the table.

Many times I have half awakened in the night and heard music in the distance, long deep chords, solemn and yet reassuring. My faith in those days was limited to the absolute belief that Daddy and Mother were downstairs keeping watch, that they loved each other and Betty and me and that they could manage anything difficult that might develop. The music in the night said that and I went back to sleep.

Daddy had put himself through college playing the organ and it was that instrument he loved most. Even when he was playing the piano his long fingers sank deep into the keys and he held the chords ringing like organ notes. He would often go to the church on a weekday afternoon and play to the rows of empty pews. People stopped in sometimes and slipped quietly into a back seat to listen.

One time after a church supper when it was raining too hard to go home he went up to the dark auditorium and amused himself for an hour at the console. When he came down he was surprised to find half his congregation sitting in the dark listening to the preacher play.

He seemed to make up the music as he went along most of the time. When I was little I always thought when my father played the organ it sounded like a prayer and I felt God was listening.

We heard a good deal about God in our childhood. They said He was everywhere and we could believe it; He was certainly everywhere we went. Naturally, being the daughters of the minister we were taken along to many church meetings during the week, and unfailingly to Sunday School and the big morning service. I always thought Daddy spoke of God as though He were sublime, but fixed and rather unapproachable. He seemed on much more friendly terms with Jesus, whom he called by His first name and spoke to directly as though He were quite near at hand and not so apt to go off on a cloud and brood over generalities.

One time when Grandmother Douglas was paying us one of her long winter visits she heard Betty and me having tea with our dolls. Betty was not really the great doll lover I have been making her out, but when the weather was too bad to be doing something more interesting she would settle for a short time and resign herself to my more sedentary play. We had small chairs drawn up around our small table and the assortment of stuffed animals and dolls were seated around.

"Take your baby off that chair," Betty said to me. "That's for Jesus. He said he would come and I'm saving Him that seat."

Grandmother hurried off to Daddy to report on this dreadfully irreverent play that was being carried on by his daughters. Mother told us about it long afterwards.

"What's wrong with that?" Daddy had asked. "I'm glad my children are so friendly with Jesus that He consents to come and play with them."

There was criticism by a few in the Ann Arbor church, and in all the churches where our father preached, that he was not deeply spiritual. "At times Dr. Douglas' audience would spontaneously laugh aloud at some unexpectedly descriptive phrase or witty saying," says Mr. Davis in *A History of the Congregational Church in Ann Arbor*. At that time it was not usual for a minister to be funny in the pulpit.

I don't know what kind of spirituality Daddy had. He had it or he would not have been able to pass it on to so many people. I have never known how he prayed when he was alone.

I think his prayers were very much mixed up with his music. Betty reminds me of the many times he wandered to the piano while he was writing his sermons. He would sound out deep minor chords for a while and then go back to his study. Music was one of the everlasting values for him.

In the 1915 scrapbook we found a newspaper write-up of a Sunday sermon. The end was quoted verbatim.

I used occasionally to visit a little old man who was a philosopher by profession, but taught violin lessons to pay expenses. His studio was located in the midst of a long row of rooms, all devoted to the pursuit of the "Heavenly Maid." At ten o'clock of an open-windowed June morning the wooing was something less than tenderly romantic. Here I used to go to visit the wise little man and pick up nuggets of wisdom.

One morning, having been greeted by his usual horse-hair and rosin salute, I asked, "Well, what's the good news today?"

He removed his fiddle from beneath his chin and parried, "Asked lightly or seriously?"

"Seriously," I replied.

Stepping to a curiously shaped metal device suspended from a silk cord he struck it a smart blow with a padded mallet and said, "There's the good news for today. That, my friend, is A. It was A all day yesterday. It will be A all day tomorrow, next week, a thousand years. A. The soprano next door wabbles abominably, and the tenor over yonder flats unspeakably, and the piano across the hall is out of tune. Noise and confusion all about me. But that is A."

It is a comfort to know that in this world of chance and change with its soul-torturing anxieties, its distressing accidents and its nameless vicissitudes, somewhere, no matter how badly out of tune we are in our effort to play our part in the symphony of life, we know we can go and strike A and get A. That there is a changeless Power of whose wisdom and guidance we may be sure.

2

Sentimental Pilgrimage

WHEN ONE IS a child it is hard to realize that one's parents lived and had all sorts of interesting experiences before one even existed. Their stories seem to be the adventures of two young people without the remotest connection to the father and mother one knows—that prosaic pair who live such uneventful lives.

Mother would tell Betty and me about herself as a little girl and we listened enchanted to her descriptions of the clothes she wore, the toys she played with; even the candies she and her sisters bought on their way home from school sounded like confections far more intriguing than anything we had ever seen. We had a funny old picture of her sitting in a three-wheeled pedal contraption which definitely confirmed our impression that she must have been young a hundred years ago.

As for Daddy, his stories of his childhood had a tang of bitter revolt. They conflicted heavily with our Grandmother Douglas' reminiscences of him as a fine, obedient little man.

"I was never allowed to play," he told us. "When the other boys went swimming I could go along if I promised not to go in the water. My mama was a great detective. 'I know you went swimming, Lloyd,' she would say, 'because you've got your underwear on inside out.'"

Betty and I collected in our imaginations impressions of these two queer, old-fashioned children, growing up in Lutheran ministers' homes, but in towns far apart, coming nearer and nearer to the time when they were to meet—at Wittenberg College in Springfield, Ohio.

Mother was gay, loved parties and, we suspected, flirting. Her parents had been less strict and they had lived in larger towns. When she arrived to begin college she was not the raw country bumpkin Daddy always claimed he was.

We read recently a letter written by Mr. Guy Bayley of Springfield, Ohio, to a friend, describing her thus:

> I recall the day Betty's mother first appeared in Chapel. We filed in each morning as Dr. Weaver checked attendance to that ugly room filled with talk and disorder until old Dr. Ort, with his long face and nose, appeared upon the platform.
>
> This disorder and all talk stopped that morning as a new and beautiful blonde girl pushed her way up the south side aisle. We looked in silence as each of us probably made plans for an introduction, a necessary first step of that day.

In the same letter Mr. Bayley describes his first impression of the young Lloyd Douglas.

> It may have been the very day her dad arrived to spend ten years at Wittenberg when I passed him on the walk to the old dorm, Myers Hall. He was very thin and had grown too fast to become used to his long legs, and was awkward at that young age. His engaging smile and an expression of intelligence, and an altogether something delightful as his eyes met mine caused me to turn and look.

We have a box of pictures which give a sort of record of their college days. One is of Mother in a line-up of young girls in long frilly white nightgowns taken in the college dormitory. Their heads are resting on each other's shoulders and with coy smiles they pretend to be asleep. One of Daddy with his thick black hair parted severely in the middle is taken with the members of the Glee Club. They are all frowning furiously, perhaps because of the high white collars which stretch their necks.

They said they had fun in college. Daddy worked at numerous jobs in the town to earn his tuition, but many of his friends did the same. He belonged to a fraternity which was considered very aloof and clannish. In later years the members explained this by confessing that the room they rented for their meetings had such a reek of escaping gas that they hesitated to allow critical outsiders in. This aloofness extended to girls. They prided themselves on being women-haters.

Mother led a gay social life. She had many girl friends and a wide assortment of beaux. She was in the class one year ahead of Daddy, who had started in the prep school, but the campus was small and doubtless they passed and saw each other many times before they spoke. They talked to us when we were children so much about those years, yet how they met, what they first said to each other, even Betty, the incurable romantic, has forgotten.

The one place where all the students met was on the river, skating. I believe it was there they first spoke, for skating seems to have played such an important part in their romance. In his novel *Forgive Us Our Trespasses*, which Daddy always declared was highly autobiographical, he described the first meeting of his hero and heroine as taking place in winter on the pond.

"Very good ice," she said casually.
"You skate beautifully," said Dinny.
Her slightly raised brows accepted the tribute.
"You should know," she replied.
He held out his hands invitingly.
"Shall we?"
"Why not? I'd like to."

She had hardly consented before they were beginning to drift, crossed hands clasped, in a long indolent roll that inclined their tall lithe forms so far off balance none but the expert could have trusted to it.

"Your father wore a white turtle-neck sweater," Mother told us. "And when his heavy black hair fell down in his eyes he would throw it back with a jerk. I remember the first time he asked me to skate. We crossed arms and glided over the ice away from all the others."

There they are—caught in an old-fashioned picture, slim and young, flying into the distance of fifty-five years ago, but so unreal and unrelated to the parents we ever knew. That gay young couple seemed lost.

In his interrupted memoirs Daddy had reached his college years at Wittenberg and at that point Betty and I were attempting to take over: strange territory, peopled by long-ago lives. There was only one thing for us to do: go to the towns where he lived as a young man, see the places he had told us about, talk to the people who might remember.

I hated to begin this chapter. Yesterday I was writing about things I remembered so well. We were little girls playing on the floor in Mother's bedroom in the Hill Street parsonage. Mother, her lips bristling with pins and her glasses tottering on her nose, was sewing on our cotton summer dresses. Daddy, only his bald spot visible among the jutting arms of the Chair, was pounding out his sermon in the study. Now today Betty and I must be grown women about to set out on a pilgrimage to discover the youthtime of our parents.

We decided to take a trip by car to the towns where we had not been since we were children, or had never been at all, but which had played such an important part in the early lives of our parents. We would go to Springfield and roam about the college campus, we would go on from there to the little town where Daddy had been called to his first church when he was twenty-five and still unmarried, then we would go on to the town where we had been born. We would arm ourselves with our father's scrapbooks of old newspaper clippings in order to know the names of people to question. We bought big loose-leaf notebooks and pictured ourselves busily filling pages with useful anecdotes told us by garrulous old-timers.

In the fall of '51 we met at a mid-point; Betty coming from her home in Las Vegas, Nevada, I from mine in Montreal. Except to zip through, we had not been in Ohio or Indiana since we were very young. The highways were quiet. Corn-stocks stood in the fields and piles of fall vegetables were on sale in front of farmhouses. Green, yellow, orange, red; we had forgotten how beautiful are Ohio and Indiana in the autumn.

This was the country our father had known as a child. Over these same roads his preacher father had driven him in their old buggy. They had crawled along through the mud, we drove on smooth pavement at fifty miles an hour. We were more irked than pleased by these signs of progress. It was our intention to throw ourselves into the past of sixty years ago and there seemed no bridge to cross.

APPLE BUTTER FOR SALE. Betty threw on the brakes and we came to a squealing stop. We didn't remember that we had cared much for apple butter, but it was a sort of tribute to Daddy, who had talked so much about the apple butter of his childhood.

"It's made from an old Amish recipe," said the farmer as he helped us stow six dark-brown jars among the baggage on the floor of the back seat.

We bought apples from him too—red ones that gushed juice when we bit into them. We were still munching them when we drove into Springfield, Ohio, where Wittenberg College is located.

The enterprising and up-to-date look of the buildings and streets rather discouraged us, but we kept on hoping for a clue to what we sought. A sign pointing to the cemetery brought a gasp of pleasure from Betty and she swung the car into the smaller street.

"It was in the cemetery where the college boys and girls did their courting," she said elatedly. "The campus should be on a hill quite near." Now she began to remember things. "The river ran along the edge of the cemetery and it was on the river road they walked. Mother said there was a big rock that hung over the road and she and Daddy always went 'way around it for fear it would roll down on them as they passed under."

When they walked together along the river road Mother was engaged to another man—quite seriously entangled too. "I felt guilty about the time I spent with your father," she told us. "I knew it wasn't right for me to have such a good time with him, but he always made me laugh, and when he talked seriously about the things he meant to do someday I knew he would do them all. I knew he was different."

She told us of how he beaued her friend Nell McGavern about when she came to Wittenberg to visit. "I was really jealous of Nell when she would come home and tell me what a good time she had had with Lloyd. He told her about a novel he was writing and I was hurt that I hadn't ever heard about it."

"Then why didn't you break your engagement and get engaged to Daddy?" Betty and I would ask.

While we were waiting for her to answer Mother would look at Daddy over our heads and their eyes would meet laughing. "Because he didn't ask me," she said.

We spent that afternoon in Springfield driving slowly along the river and walking through the campus grounds. There were not many buildings and they were old. We felt we were seeing the college very much as it had been so long ago.

That evening five of Daddy's fraternity brothers took us for dinner to the country club. They were charming, urbane elderly gentlemen, all prosperous citizens of the town. Through the years they had kept in touch with him, but it was not long until they forgot we were talking about the well-known novelist and began chuckling about their thin, long-legged friend of college days and the wild and foolish times they had had together.

Betty and I were shocked to learn that the young "Doug" had chewed tobacco. When we were children we had shared the secret of his occasional cigars, and in later years he had fringed the edges of his typewriter table with marks of burnt-out cigarettes laid down and forgotten in the heat of composition; but chewing! That sounded like the early America of Frances Trollope's discovery.

"Sure, we all chewed and spit too." The fraternity brothers laughed at our pained expressions. They told us how they used to meet at Poor Jake's after their jobs were done—our father coming from the haberdashery store where he worked evenings—and sit around a table in the back room drinking beer and talking.

"Doug and I were writing a novel," Arthur Todd told us. "It was my plot and Doug was going to do the literary part. It was to be called '25041.' That was the number of the hero who was an inmate at the Ohio State Penitentiary. We couldn't decide whether to bring it out as a book first or let the *Saturday Evening Post* have it to serialize.

"We talked about it for weeks down at Poor Jake's or in the dorm at night, but didn't get much down on paper. Then in the spring we got a leave of absence from President Ort and went to a farm to do some real writing. Well, the fishing was pretty good that time of the year and we didn't get much done on our book.

"That summer I went to visit Doug at his home in Columbia City. He met me at the station and I remember while we were walking to his house he seemed quiet and kind of worried. Then he said, 'You know, Art, I had another fellow here this summer visiting me. He didn't make a very good impression on my folks.'

" 'He didn't?' I was very serious about it. 'What did he do?'

" 'It was what he didn't do,' said Doug. 'He didn't kneel with the rest of our family when we had morning and evening prayers.' "

Mr. Todd smiled at Betty and me. "His folks liked me all right; I knelt. But," he went on, "we still didn't get much farther with our book. Bluegills biting that time of year.

"Our manuscript knocked around for a while and finally got salted away in a drawer of Doug's desk in his room at the old Hamma Divinity Hall. That was after he had gone into the Theological Seminary. One Christmas vacation the old hall burned down. When we came back I went with Doug to look through the wreckage and see if anything of his was worth salvaging. We found what had been his desk. Everything in it was destroyed but the pages of our famous novel. 'Must have been too rotten to burn,' Doug said."

Betty and I said we had understood from Daddy that he never covered himself with much glory in English Composition in college. We have a letter written in 1935 to his friend Tom Peabody of North Manchester, Indiana, in which he says:

> I finished my lecture tour today with an address to the post graduate students in English at Columbia University. I'll bet that if the chubby little German-Lutheran professor who taught English Comp. at Wittenberg had known that his laziest student would someday be telling the P.G.'s at Columbia how to write stories he would have died of laughter.

The fraternity brothers agreed that Doug had not excelled in writing in the classroom. "But he was a whizz at oratory and debates," they assured us. "He wrote all our speeches. He was the class historian, you know."

We knew that. In our father's files we had found the old yellow manuscript entitled "The History of the Class of 1900."

In it each member is briefly and facetiously eulogized, and at last the writer comments of himself:

> Your historian has borne an unenviable reputation. If there is any crime in the calendar of which he has not been accused it must just recently have been discovered. He and Dr. Ort have had many long talks in which the doctor did all the talking. From the time he was accused of putting tar on the chairs in '94 to the time he was thrown bodily out of the Sociology class by Dr. Prince, the record keeper of this class has had nothing but trouble. But it is all over now and the banner of peace waves its silken folds over the corrigible and the incorrigible alike.

On his own admission Daddy did not heap up much of a record in any subject in college. He often told us how he happened to get behind in Calculus. "I felt a draft in class one day," he said, "right here on the back on my neck, and I got up to shut the window. Would you believe it! In that little time they got ahead of me and I never caught up."

When Betty and I came home from school with bad grades our father always consoled us by saying that it didn't run in the family to do well in Mathematics or Science. Betty has a letter from him written to her in 1926 when she was a student at Oberlin College.

> Dearest Bettina,
> It is a very sweet and sensible letter I have from you today. There is, of course, a bit of depression in it due to the milling you have had on account of the bad mark in Chemistry, but you are saying you propose to do your utmost this semester to correct that difficulty, and I believe you will. You need not utterly lose faith in yourself because you have flunked Chemistry. Isaac Newton flunked in Geometry. Many of our brighter boys and girls, who later rode rompingly into fame, were notorious flunkers who got the sack from many colleges. These cases, however, are not to be emulated; for I presume it could be shown that the general mine-run of college failures do not ever arrive

at dizzy peaks of eminence where they can talk of their bad marks with Homeric laughter.

Write us often and tell us how you get along. Don't let your little discouragements get you down and wallow you in the mire. Part of a college education is learning how to face the problems you will have when you emerge from school life. The whole business of living in this world is chock full of nasty little situations brimming with disappointments, drudgery and irksomeness. This is not a very optimistic picture of it, but you will find it is so, I dare say. The recipe for happiness—if there is a recipe—is to insure yourself, so far as you can, against letting a disappointment wallop you too hard. It's all right to have a blue day, cry a little, cuss a little, mope a little; but then it's time to arise and shine. To be happy it is demanded of us that we shall have enough resilience to bob up, smilingly, after we have been beaned. It's pretty good training to make yourself do a lot of things for which you have no special liking—and do them well—just to show yourself you could if you had to.

If, for example, you might be able to pull a good mark in something you half despised, it would give you confidence to believe that, in a tight pinch, you might be able to do something you hated, and do it well—should the time ever come when you were flat up against it.

And all that sort of rot. I know you despise advice. I always did. Whenever any of my elders and betters got to dribbling that kind of drool at me I always put them down for a passel of mouldy old imbeciles.

But after all is said and done a lot of the same junk is true. Strait is the gate and narrow is the way that leadeth unto life, and few there be that find it.

Keep a stiff upper lip and do the best you can. Angles—even right angles—can do no more. Selah.

Lovingly,
DADDY

There must have been good psychology in the letter for after being tutored that semester Betty finally passed her Chemistry with a B. Daddy marveled at that. "B in Chemistry! I don't think I ever got a B in anything. Did you, Bessie?"

"Of course I did," Mother retorted. "I studied hard in college. I was good at Mathematics too."

Fortunately her arithmetic hadn't been the practical kind you use in adding up grocery bills, for Daddy would never have been happy living with someone who could make a column of figures come out twice the same.

In later years newspapers reported him as having carried off many honors in scholarship and more than one university claimed him as a graduate. In 1938 he wrote to his friend Shirley W. Smith of Ann Arbor, Michigan:

> I observe by the Who's Who in the Kiwanis Convention Program that I attended five different colleges. The query now arises: did I get the sack in these schools or was my scholarship of such quality that I quickly absorbed everything they taught and moved on to other seats of learning?

That evening in Springfield the five elderly gentlemen who had been our father's fraternity brothers would not let us go until they had given us a description of our mother. We gathered that Miss Besse Porch had been a lovely girl. They disagreed upon the color of her hair. Was it tawny blond or red? Titian, they decided after some discussion.

"Where'd she get that Southern accent?" they asked us.

"Her father was a Lutheran minister in Louisville, Kentucky, for many years," we explained.

"Oh yes," they remembered. "She was teaching school down in the Kentucky mountains those years Doug was in the Seminary."

We asked them what he had been like when he was a theological student. Surely he hadn't run around then putting tar on the chairs and cutting up as he had during his undergraduate days.

"Well, he sobered down some," they said

Harry Gram, now a sedate judge of the Probate Court of Springfield, remembered an evening when Daddy had officiated in the religious part of the ceremony for their fraternity initiation. "Somebody else was supposed to do it, but couldn't at the last moment," Judge Gram told us. "Doug was a student at the Seminary so we told him he was elected. I remember he opened the Bible and stood up in front of us all. He started to read a few verses from Ecclesiastes. That was all right and we were impressed by the way he read them, but he went on and on. He'd finish a verse and then see one more he thought just too fine to leave out. It looked like we were going to be there all night. Finally I had to put a stop to it. 'For Gosh sake, Doug,' I called out, 'aren't you ever going to quit?' "

"Yes, he must have had to sober down a lot," they agreed shaking their heads sadly. "He went right out of the Seminary into his first church."

The next morning Betty and I left Springfield to drive to North Manchester, Indiana. This was the town where the young Reverend Lloyd Cassel Douglas had been called shortly after being ordained as a minister of the Lutheran Church.

The names of the villages through which we passed that bright October morning, though only tiny dots on the road map we followed, were names we had heard spoken often. Grandfather Douglas had preached in some of these little towns. The stories Grandmother had told us as children had been sprinkled with county landmarks and the signposts brought back memories of rainy afternoons long ago. We passed a little sign pointing to Wahwahsee Lake and remembered that our parents had spent their honeymoon there.

"It was April," Mother said, "and we had the whole hotel to ourselves. It rained every day for two weeks. We tried to pretend we were an old married couple, but when the waitress asked me how my husband took his coffee I began to blush because I didn't know. We hadn't fooled her for a minute, of course."

When Reverend Lloyd Douglas went to North Manchester to take his first church he was unmarried. Miss Besse Io Porch, of Kentucky, was still engaged to another man and their two lives seemed to be rapidly moving apart. "The only time I ever played church politics," Daddy sometimes said, "was to get the father of the girl I loved moved to a more convenient charge for my courting."

As we drove along through the Indiana countryside we talked of them and how they would have laughed had they known that some day their daughters would be tracking down their pasts with such industry. It was midafternoon when Betty saw the sign,

NORTH MANCHESTER
10 Miles

I leaned over into the back seat and rummaged among the suitcases and jars of apple butter to find the 1903 scrapbook. Opening it on my lap I read from the first page:

LITURGIES
Lloyd C. Douglas

This was written in his quick bold writing which never changed through the years. Then below:

> July 4th, 1903
> Have decided to make a scrapbook
> out of this volume in order to make
> it worth shelf room.

(It had apparently been originally a college notebook for the pages under the dry, yellowed newspaper clippings were covered with hasty scrawls on Lutheran Church history.)

If anyone ever chances upon it let him not think that the clippings contained are preserved for any other purpose than as pleasant reminders of special services conducted in various places.

We smiled at that for it sounded a little as though the young man writing it had felt for a moment the breath of his biographers reading over his shoulder. I turned to the second page. Here was a carefully pasted report of the first sermon he had ever preached. He was still a student in the Seminary and was substituting in his father's church.

Lloyd C. Douglas of the Theological Seminary of Springfield, Ohio, preached for his father last Sunday at Flat Rocks, Marquardt and Monroeville. The congregations were large and paid the closest attention to the young minister. Lloyd's manner of speech is calm, deliberate and winning. His hearers followed him closely from beginning to end. All who heard him pronounced his sermon interesting and instructive, and predict a bright future for the young man.

Many years later Daddy donated an organ to the church in Monroeville as a memorial to his parents. He was too ill to attend the dedication, but this is part of a letter he wrote to be read at the service.

The first sermon I ever preached was at Flat Rocks. It was, of course, a very deep and scholarly discourse that nobody in the Flat Rocks church understood very well; and I am not sure that I understood it very well myself. But the farmers gave me a break and pretended to listen, though it must have been pretty rough going for them. It later was my observation that it takes about five years for the average Theological Seminary graduate to unlearn everything the old fellows taught him about sermons; and begin to talk in a language that the average layman understands.

My second sermon that afternoon—at the Marquardt church

—was much more of a success than at Flat Rocks, for I was assisted by a baby. Smack in the middle of my tiresome sermon which had put almost everybody to sleep (for it takes a pretty lively form of amusement to keep farmers awake at three o'clock of a mid-summer Sunday, after they have filled themselves with stewed chicken, noodles, mashed potatoes, gravy, deviled eggs, and apple pie) one of the Marquardts, aged about a year and a half, grew restless, and its devoted young mother decided that what Junior wanted was a drink. According to custom there was a tall glass pitcher of water—(not cold enough to give anyone a chill, but wet enough to slake one's thirst)—standing on the pulpit with a tumbler beside it. So she brought her baby forward, poured the tumbler full, and then she stood for a long time happily watching her son drink all he could hold, after which he blew bubbles into the water, giggling until the whole congregation came awake and gleefully joined in the merriment.

Meantime the young preacher soberly continued with his sermon which—if I recall—was a blow-by-blow account of the German Reformation in 1517, or some similar narcotic.

On the following page of the scrapbook was pasted a bright yellow slip of paper which was the official call to the church in North Manchester.

We, the Council of Zion Lutheran Church of North Manchester, Indiana, hereby extend to you a call to serve as Pastor of said church. Regular Services to begin on or before May 1st 1903. Compensation to be at the rate of $800.00 per annum.

Six signatures were affixed to this document. They were written in pencil and carefully lettered as though the writers had licked the lead and chewed their tongues at the task.

During the rest of the ten miles to our destination I read to Betty accounts of weddings, funerals and church meetings. In those days it seemed the newspapers had plenty of time to comment beyond the mere stating of events. Every detail was flatteringly described and the atmosphere of a little country town of fifty years ago rose from the pages like the scent of pressed flowers.

In all these affairs the new minister had been mentioned as officiating in some capacity. By the time Betty and I reached the outskirt (it was definitely singular) of North Manchester we had so thoroughly identified ourselves with the person of the raw, inexperienced young man that we could easily imagine the excitement and apprehension which must have been his as he got off the train that spring day in 1903 to take over his first charge.

"It's very likely the same station," Betty said as we came upon it. Grass grew between the rails and it did not look as though many trains passed this way. The little town dwindled into fields beyond the tracks, but on the other side of the station a walk led past houses more closely placed toward what seemed in the distance to be the business section.

North Manchester had been a town of twenty-five hundred people fifty years ago. It was twice that now, but the old houses looked as though they had seen that time and more. My eyes followed the sidewalk as we drove along and it was easy to see an intense young man walking there, tall and much too thin, dressed in his heavy, black preacher's suit, carrying in each hand a cheap valise.

"A man in a strange place is judged by his baggage," he told us once. "I bought good bags as soon as I could afford them."

There seemed to be only one business street and we were on it; we came almost at once to the Zion Lutheran Church. It was a pretty church, its corners mellowed with years. We parked the car in front and walking softly, silently to the door found it open. The lower entrance hall led to the Sunday School rooms and so we climbed the wide stairs which brought us to the main auditorium. I felt greatly moved standing there looking down the aisle at the pulpit where my young father had stood so many years ago. I felt frightened for him.

"The first Sunday I preached in my own church in North Manchester," he told us when we were small, "a dreadful thing happened. I had just begun my sermon. It was a warm May morning and the window by the pulpit was open. A sudden breeze came in and blew all the pages of my manuscript over the platform. I would have picked them up but a picture of the new parson presenting his bent posterior to the congregation flashed before me. So I carried on. It didn't matter. I had practised my sermon so many times I could have said it backwards."

Betty and I walked down the aisle and stood behind the pulpit. Here he once stood and there was the window, and there—we could almost see the white squares on the red carpet—lay the scattered pages of the sermon. By now the shadows were beginning to collect in the corners of the church and we decided we had better find ourselves a place to spend the night. "It was the Sheller Hotel where Daddy stayed the first year he lived in North Manchester," Betty said, "but I don't suppose it still exists."

"We could always ask," I said.

We stopped a man on the street before we got back into the car. "Is there a Sheller Hotel in this town?"

"Two blocks down and one to your left," he said.

It seemed surprising to us that the Sheller was still a going concern. It was a rambling old place with porches on two sides. A half-dozen rocking chairs stood tilted against the wall and caught small drifts of autumn leaves. Inside the old man at the desk took us upstairs to a big front corner room directly over the lobby. The bathroom, he said, was down at the end of the hall and around a corner. Everything was clean and freshly decorated, but some of the furniture in our room would have interested an antique dealer.

When the old man had gone we stepped out into the hall

again and walked slowly past the other rooms whose doors stood open as in a private home. We were led to this unusual curiosity by an overwhelming desire to know in which of these rooms our young father had spent so many hours—lonely hours perhaps.

Ours was the best one, we decided, and since Mr. Sheller had been an important member of the Lutheran Church, even a signer of the official call, it was highly probable that the room where we were to sleep that night was the very one they had given to the new minister.

The next morning we told the old man behind the desk downstairs of our mission in North Manchester. He remembered Reverend Douglas as did another old man dozing in a rocking chair by a big window. They nodded their heads. "Yes, Reverend Douglas used to live in this hotel." But to all our questioning that fact remained the only thing they could tell us.

"Well, do you know which was his room?" we asked finally. They didn't know. "Go see Mr. Urshell," they said. "He lived here the same time as Reverend Douglas did."

We started out with our notebooks like detectives. Surely if they lived for months in the same hotel Mr. Urshell would have some vivid memories of our father—amusing anecdotes and conversations to relate. He was the president of the town bank and we were ushered into his private office and invited to sit down.

"Yes, I remember your father very well," he said, when we had explained our errand. He spoke slowly and tipped back in his chair. Betty and I sat perched on the edges of ours waiting for his next words. "We lived at the Sheller Hotel at the same time. I ate at the same table with him. Yes," he mused, "I remember Reverend Douglas well. I used to sit downstairs in the front lobby and hear him walking back and forth over my head talking his sermons to himself."

We told him that we had the same room now, but he was not greatly amazed at the coincidence. "It's been about fifty years since your father lived at the Sheller," he said. "We just celebrated our fiftieth anniversary here at the bank." He took two little booklets done in gilt covers from a pile on his desk and gave us each one. "You might be interested in looking at these." He went on to tell us the history of the Indiana Lawrence Bank and Trust. When we thanked him and rose to go he said: "It's been a pleasure to meet you. I remember Reverend Douglas very well."

Fifty years is a long time. We went on that morning trundling our notebooks and hunting down old people who might be able to paint in some details of that earnest young preacher who had once gone about his work on these quiet village streets, but they could tell us almost nothing. They remembered him well, they said, and told us how many times they had read his books and showed us their copies, pulpy with handling.

"Do you remember any little incidents of his everyday life?" we asked, feeling the question to be vague, but not knowing how to go about drawing them out. They shook their heads. "Go talk to Mr. Billings," they all said. "He's got a wonderful memory."

Mr. William E. Billings had been the editor of the North Manchester *Journal* in our father's time. He was now considered the town historian and had written a book called *Tales from a Hoosier Village*. Betty and I went to see him at his home. He was thin and frail, but spry for an old gentleman. We could see that North Manchester interested him as a relic of the past. "We've got three covered bridges near here," he told us. "Not many of them left in this country."

We talked to him for some time and he told us interesting things about the little town and the Lutheran Church of our father's day. "Fifty years ago the Lutheran Church here was a kind of training ground for young ministers just out of the Seminary," he said. "We used to get them pretty raw and inexperienced. When your father came here he was young and inexperienced too, but there was something different about what he had to say. I've got a little sketch about it in my book." He took it down from the shelf and leafed through the pages. "Here is what I say about Reverend Douglas when he preached his trial sermon here."

That sermon was different from the usual trial sermons that were handed out. The speaker was able to say old things in a new way; he had the happy faculty of mixing poetry with his prose, of adding color to what from others had seemed drab and dull.

"We knew he was too big for us," said Mr. Billings. "We knew he wouldn't stay here long."

Betty and I waved goodbye to the old gentleman standing in the door of his lovely Victorian home. Everywhere we had met the atmosphere of the turn of the century, ivy draped upon faded brick; but the young man in the black frock coat was still a picture pressed between the dry and crumbling pages of the 1903 scrapbook. I picked it up from the seat of the car as I got in. "It looks as though everything we'll ever know about him is right here in this book," I said.

Betty agreed and we drove slowly off, not knowing where to go next. Leaves dropped from old trees as we cruised aimlessly along the few village streets. We passed the old seed-store with its wide stoop for loungers. Here perhaps one sparkling fall day long ago the limp, straw-chewing idlers may have straightened up, touched their caps to a passing figure and mumbled, "Morning, Reverend."

We drove slowly past the house where they said our father and mother had lived, but we weren't able to get much satisfaction from its modern-looking exterior. "It's the same old house all right," they had told us, "but it's been fixed over so you'd never know it; fine new clapboard and a sun porch at the side. Great improvement." The walls of the old house were underneath somewhere, no doubt. That was what we were up against: a wall of years. We felt lonely.

I turned the paste-stiffened pages of the scrapbook in my lap and read aloud newspaper reports of our father's first sermons. It was apparent that he was considered a probationer and the comments were in the tone of a classroom approval. "The address showed careful preparation and was excellently delivered" . . . "The young Reverend shows that he has improved his opportunities." An account of a church meeting ended with these remarks: "He is a young man of prepossessing presence, of genial manners and easily makes friends."

Daddy had told us he lived a very social life when he was a bachelor in the little town. All the church ladies had felt pity for the young preacher living in a bare hotel room and had invited him to meals. Sunday evenings there had been singing parties at homes after the services, and the mothers of young ladies were especially anxious to entertain him.

We wondered if it had come as a shock to them when the North Manchester *Journal* carried this item which we found pasted in the scrapbook:

ENGAGEMENT ANNOUNCED
Rev. Douglas Soon to
Wed a Columbia City
Lady

Word comes from Columbia City that the engagement of Miss Besse Io Porch of that city and Rev. Lloyd C. Douglas, Pastor of the Zion Lutheran Church here, has been announced. The wedding will occur April 7th in the Grace Lutheran Church in Columbia City. Miss Porch is the daughter of Rev. Porch, Pastor of the C.C. Lutheran Church, and is a highly accomplished young lady. Rev. Douglas has been a resident of North Manchester for something more than a year and during that time has made many friends who are glad to extend their congratulations.

That romance had moved quickly in a few months owing to a good deal of maneuvering on the part of the young Reverend.

Besse Porch lived in Louisville, Kentucky; she was engaged to be married and her admirer in Indiana had every reason to consider her a lost cause. One day he received a letter from President Ort of Wittenberg bidding him to come to Springfield to speak of important matters. He had always taken a fatherly interest in Daddy because of his long friendship with Grandfather Douglas. The president received the preacher from North Manchester in his study and questioned him about his work. At last the young man got up to go, feeling slightly bewildered as to why the doctor had sent for him. As he stood at the door President Ort said, "By the way, Lloyd, I have a letter here from Dr. Porch. He says his daughter Besse has broken her engagement."

Daddy used often to tell us this part of the story and as a child I could see the room vividly, even to the old black leather chairs, brown at the cracks like penny licorice.

"We grinned at each other," Daddy said, "and I came back and sat down. 'Louisville, Kentucky, is a long way for a poor preacher to go courting, Dr. Ort,' I told him."

The doctor rubbed his chin and smiled slyly. "Your father and mother still live in Columbia City, don't they? You must run up to visit them frequently?"

Daddy was mystified by this apparently irrelevant remark and merely nodded.

"Well," Dr. Ort went on patiently, "As you know the Lutheran Church in Columbia City has been vacant for several months. Your father has a good deal of influence with the council there. You might suggest to him Dr. Porch as a possible candidate."

Daddy waved that off as an absurd suggestion. "Why would Dr. Porch ever consider leaving his big city church for a little town the size of Columbia City, Indiana?"

Dr. Ort tapped the letter on his desk. "I think he would. He says here he has been in ill health for some months and is anxious to exchange his large and demanding pastorate for a much smaller one."

Then the ball began to roll and church politics were practised. Many solemn old people were influenced to do many serious things, never dreaming that behind it all was the ardent desire of one young man to have one young lady. In a few months the Porch family was installed at Columbia City and Miss Besse began to receive regular visits from an out-of-town gentleman.

"I was going to conduct an elaborate campaign of courtship," Daddy said, "but the first time I was alone with your mother I blurted out the whole thing and asked her to marry me. She said no."

"But why, Mother?" Betty and I howled. "You said you loved him from the beginning."

Mother hung her head. "I didn't want to be a minister's wife," she said. "I wanted to go on the stage."

She had made quite a hit as an elocutionist and people had told her she was wasting her talents on ladies' aid societies and church entertainments. With her looks she should be on the stage, they said.

"My wife has quite a pretty gift for mimicry," Daddy used to say at little gatherings at our house if there was any occasion to mention it. Mother would blush and throw him terrible looks and hasten in confusion to some other subject. But when we were alone he would sometimes get her to repeat some little scene which she had done spontaneously for him. "Show the children how Mr. Blank ushers the old ladies down the aisle," he would say. In a few hovering, grinning bobs Mother could make Mr. Blank himself appear, but she only allowed us a fleeting glimpse and she would be back again, smiling shyly at Daddy's extravagant howls of laughter.

"Just think, kids, you might have had a famous actress for a mother. How would you have liked that?"

At any rate it didn't take him long to persuade her to give

up the footlights for a less glamorous career; the Porches had been in Columbia City only a few months when this item appeared in the paper:

> Miss Besse I. Porch gave a unique Valentine Party last night at which her engagement to Rev. Lloyd Cassel Douglas was announced in a clever manner. The guests were all assembled when Mrs. Clyde Kiern was called to the telephone. Rev. Douglas from North Manchester, after a short parley, announced the news. After congratulations the party went to the dining room where plates were laid for eighteen. Hearts and carnations were the decorations, red being the color.

Several pages in the scrapbook are devoted to accounts of the wedding. Besse was the first of the three Porch girls to be married and it sounds as though her parents did it up properly. Of course, our mother made all her own clothes. "I went to Fort Wayne to buy the goods for my trousseau" (she always called any kind of material "goods"). "There was a beautiful green wool that I wanted for my going-away suit, but Mama said it was much too expensive. I told Papa about it when I got home and he said I could have the fee from a wedding he was going to have that afternoon. I was waiting for him when he came back from the church and he handed me the envelope. I drew out the bills: five dollars, ten dollars, fifteen dollars. Whoever heard of such a big wedding fee? It was plenty for the green wool suit."

Things must have been cheap in those days. The description of the wedding sounds very elaborate: ribbons and flowers and palms, to say nothing of a five-course dinner at the bride's home afterwards. Grandmother Douglas never got over muttering at the extravagance. "They were city folks—the Porches—and nothing was too good for those girls. The Reverend must have been ready for the poorhouse by the time his wife got the three of them married off."

The North Manchester *Journal*'s account of the wedding covers both sides of a page in the scrapbook. It ends thus:

The bride received a great many beautiful and useful presents ["We ate our morning cereal out of cut-glass pickle dishes for years," said Mother.] . . . and the groom was especially pleased over the bag of gold consisting of twenty-two five dollar gold pieces which came from the North Manchester congregation. Speaking of Rev. Douglas the Columbia City Post says, "The groom is the son of Rev. and Mrs. A. J. Douglas of this city. He is a young man of fine attainments and great promise. He owes his success in life largely to his own efforts. He was able to complete the course as a student at Wittenberg College, practically paying his own way. During all his college life he was an exceedingly busy boy, for in addition to keeping up with his studies he was obliged to turn his hand to many tasks. He met with many trials, but these only tended to more fully develop him and better fit him for the duties of life. His bride is also a graduate of Wittenberg College and a young lady of many good qualities of heart and mind."

After a brief wedding tour Rev. and Mrs. Douglas will come to this city where they will at once begin housekeeping.

Betty and I had been very hopeful of unearthing some details of those early days in our parents' married life. That afternoon in North Manchester we drove around and around the block, viewing from every angle the house where they had lived.

They had sat on the back steps and shelled peas, Mother said. "I'd get him talking about the derivation of words and he'd pick up a pea and absent-mindedly shell it. We'd get them done in no time at all if I kept asking him questions."

It seemed disappointing that none of the old-timers we talked to could give us one hint of domestic gossip. We had thrown out many small suggestions in an attempt to stimulate their memories.

"Strawberry jam?" repeated one surprised old lady whose kitchen windows had overlooked the minister's backyard in those days. "No, I don't remember about Mrs. Douglas making strawberry jam." She seemed to think us rather odd to bring up such a trivial subject when she wanted to tell us how her granddaughter had read *The Robe* all the time she was having her first baby and never felt a thing.

It was a trivial question, but we had so little.

"I dried the strawberries on brown paper in the sun," Mother had told us, "I did it just like it said in the recipe" (she pronounced it *receipt* as all good Southerners did), "but they turned out to be hard little bullets and I wasted all that good sugar which we couldn't afford. The jam looked so pretty and red in the jars, but we couldn't eat it. When we moved away we left it all on a shelf in the cellar."

It was little more than two years after his arrival that Daddy accepted a call to Lancaster, Ohio. Other, earlier, calls are pasted in the scrapbook and he has written on them "Declined." Lancaster was a town of ten thousand. The compensation was a thousand dollars a year. That extra two hundred dollars would be useful since the young couple were expecting a baby.

On the subject of moving from one church to another Daddy had this to say in his book *The Minister's Everyday Life*. He calls the two towns Pikeville and Blinkton.

Don't begin at once to patronize Pikeville because only two trains stop there daily, whereas Blinkton has one-man street cars n'everything. You went there as green as grass. These people have done a great deal for you and you must not forget it. Leave them feeling cordially disposed to you. Don't go with a hip, hip, hooray.

Clean out the parsonage at Pikeville with a broom. Go over it with a mop. Finish the job by polishing everything with a silk handkerchief. Some people may be able—have been able, I know,—to leave an empty house a mess, but you must not. If there is a broken window pane in the cellar, mend it. If the movers have skinned the paint off the front steps, repaint them. And thus you are off toward Blinkton with a clear conscience and the people of Pikeville will rise up and call you blessed.

He and Mother had both been raised in parsonages and knew that the ladies of the church are always very curious to see how the departing minister's wife has left the house. They come to bid goodbye with kindest wishes for a happy future, but once the pair are on their way the ladies lose no time in pouring through the empty rooms and examining every nook.

Mother described their departure from North Manchester to us. "We were walking to the station carrying our suitcases and had just got to the first corner when we heard the ladies calling to use. We stopped and they called out again: 'You've left your strawberry jam.' "

"They've found the jam," Mother whispered. "What'll we do?"

Daddy put down his bags and cupped his hands around his mouth. "We didn't have room for it," he called back. "We left it for the next minister."

Betty and I drove out of North Manchester the next morning with no misgivings. Undoubtedly the parsonage had been left spic and span, and the *Journal* had reported:

> Rev. Douglas has been located in this city for the past two years and his resignation was entirely voluntary; he leaves the work here with nothing but the best of feelings on both sides. As pastor his labors have given excellent satisfaction to his congregation, and himself and wife have endeared themselves to the people of this community so that much regret is expressed that they are leaving the place. The Journal wishes for Rev. and Mrs. Douglas a happy home in the Buckeye state.

We were now on our way to Lancaster, Ohio, the town where we had been born.

3

Lancaster Revisited

IT WAS NOT much of a drive from North Manchester to Columbus, Ohio. We had decided to stop there and reserve a room at The Neil House, for our washing accommodations during the past few days had not been very luxurious and we knew nothing of the hotels in Lancaster, thirty-two miles beyond. Leaving Betty in the car to cruise with the traffic around the hotel block, I hurried through the necessary arrangements at the desk and then closeted myself in a telephone booth to call one of the Vorys boys. The Voryses had lived in Lancaster during the time our parents had been there. Mr. and Mrs. Vorys, wise and witty people, had been their affectionate advisers. I had been named for the family. The four sons, Webb, John, Arthur and Pat, had been little boys who were taught their catechism by Daddy. Betty and I had not seen them since our childhood, but we had been brought up on stories of their remarkable family and hoped they would remember something of ours. From time to time we had exchanged letters with the boys, generally at the death of one of their or our parents, and they had more than once written that our father had been a very strong influence in their young lives.

Even so, I dialed the office of Vorys Brothers with some trepidation, hoping that my name spoken by an unknown female voice would register some recognition at the other end on a busy morning. After passing through various operators I heard a man, brisk and impersonal say: "Pat Vorys speaking."

I gulped. "Oh, Pat, this is Virginia Vorys Douglas." I didn't confuse the issue by adding my married name.

The discouraging silence at the other end lasted for one full second and then I heard his hearty greeting. "Virginia Vorys, why hello! You're the one who lives in Montreal, aren't you?"

I rushed with relief into my explanation of how Betty and I happened to be passing through Columbus and how we hoped we might be able to talk to the four Voryses later if they were all in town. "We thought you might be able to tell us some things about the old Lancaster days when our families lived next door to each other."

Pat assured me they could tell us a great many things and that luckily all four of them would be in town that day—even John, the Congressman, who was arriving for the big Taft dinner to be held at The Neil House that night. We arranged to meet at ten o'clock after the dinner and the speeches were over.

I went out to hail Betty on her next trip past and reported my progress. We left for Lancaster feeling optimistic that no matter how little information we gathered there we still had the Voryses in reserve for the evening. If they were as lively as they had been described to us as little children, their stories would be good.

During the thirty-two-mile drive to Lancaster I read aloud from the scrapbook such items as I thought would give us an idea of the kind of town it had been in 1905 and how our parents had got on there. Just as though I were reading from the morning gazette over the coffee cups I began:

> Rev. Lloyd C. Douglas, who recently accepted the unanimous call to the pastorate of the First English Lutheran Church of this city, arrived with Mrs. Douglas on Friday evening and are staying at the Hillside.

The next clipping, dated August 20, is long and full of de-

scriptions, refreshments and the success of an evening. Its
heading reads:

MOST CHARMING
Reception Given By The
English Lutherans

Honoring their new Pastor Rev.
Lloyd Douglas and Wife—Hundreds call
at Church and Greet Them. Splendid
Refreshments Are
Served.

Remembering all the welcoming receptions in later churches
where Betty and I too had stood in the line and shaken hands
with an unending stream of parishioners whose kind words and
beaming faces had passed over us in a blur of eyes, noses and
teeth, we wondered how Mother had held up at the Lancaster
affair. Betty had been born the following January and according
to reports Mother's early months of pregnancy had been distressing at times.

"People always know when the minister's wife is going to
have a baby," she had told us. At any rate the news soon got
around in Lancaster. But she didn't resent all the fussing and
interest her condition caused in the church; she rather liked it.
It had been a considerable handicap to go to North Manchester
and break into the affection of a congregation where for over a
year her husband had been the petted bachelor minister. In
Lancaster they took her for their own at once. There were very
few small children among the families of the congregation and
the prospect of a baby for the new minister and his wife was as
important to the ladies as getting a new stove for the church
kitchen.

As soon as a temporary parsonage was established the visitors
began to come. "We had very little furniture," Mother would
recall, "but you know your father—he's so proud. He would

sneak the chairs in from the other rooms and when no one was watching he would stretch out a long leg and prod the hall rug a little farther into the parlor."

Apparently the ministerial leg was not wholly unobserved for this small item appears in the scrapbook:

> Rev. Lloyd C. Douglas and Mrs. Douglas were made happy when the Ladies Aid Society of the First English Lutheran Church and the members of the Congregation sent to the parsonage a handsome davenport and Turkish carpet.

It seems evident that the Lutheran Church was, when the young Reverend Douglas first arrived, a static congregation of kindly elderly people, not very progressive, placidly content to let the oldsters die and the youngsters amuse themselves on Sunday at diversions outside the portals of the church. But not so the new minister. He wanted young faces in his audience, alert, questioning eyes rather than sleepy *Amens*. A deceptively innocent notice in the scrapbook announces:

WILL ORGANIZE BIBLE CLASS

Rev. Lloyd C. Douglas will organize a Bible Class for young men which will hold its first session on Sunday afternoon at three o'clock. The class will not pursue the regular Sunday School course but will devote its time to considerations of some of the features of practical Christianity which are not generally treated in Sunday School.

Another turn of the crumbling old pages and the headlines leap up in black print:

MEN'S MEETING UNEXPECTED SUCCESS

MEN'S MEETING INTEREST CONTINUES TO INCREASE

REV. DOUGLAS DELIVERS GREAT LECTURE TO LARGE

AUDIENCE OF MEN

Seating Capacity of Church Taxed to

Its Limits

MEN'S MEETINGS TO BE HELD IN TOWN AUDITORIUM

Things begin to crackle around the First English Lutheran Church. The scrapbook fairly vibrates with enthusiasm. Along with the staid accounts of funerals and weddings are reports of Sunday sermons which were headlined as "Splendid" and "Masterful." New members were received into the church. The young minister lectured to town groups and was heard at the opera houses of other small towns in the state.

At about this point in the scrapbook, tucked in among the clippings, are also the stubs of the train tickets which he kept after these short journeys. We found this curious and the fact that he continued to preserve these worthless bits of colored paper for many more years. At first they seemed to be just day-coach seats, then later he traveled farther and slept in an upper berth; years later he blew himself to an occasional lower. When the tickets no longer appear in the scrapbooks one gathers that there was no longer romance left in it for him. "I loathe trains," I've heard him say as he packed up to be off again, but the idea of going to a new place never lost its attraction.

I remember once after I was married he and I were driving in the country and stopped at a crossing to let a fast express whisk by. "Trains are proud things," he said. "I've always been fascinated by them. When I was a boy I used to watch them flash through the little towns where we lived and they seemed to have come from some wonderful place and be on the way to a world that I intended one day to know."

The only way he considered it possible for him to arrive at that world was by his writing. It was his secret ambition and in Lancaster it took a crushing blow. In North Manchester he had written a novel. Every draft of it he had read to Mother and the two of them thought it would take its place among the classics of literature. On one page of the scrapbook among Lancaster items are the names and addresses of four Eastern publishing houses. To them the manuscript was probably sent in prayerful hope. How many trips it made to unreceptive editors we do not

know, but not long after his arrival in Lancaster Daddy decided
to borrow money and bring out the book himself. *More Than a
Prophet* was announced by a small descriptive folder which was
mailed out by the author with an enclosed card whereby one
could send one's dollar to Lloyd Cassel Douglas and receive by
mail the volume which four Ohio ministers highly recommended.

In later years Daddy often expounded on the subject of
bringing out one's books privately. "If no publisher is interested
in your stuff take his word for it that it's no good. Don't try to
bring it out yourself. There lies misery."

In 1941 he wrote on the flyleaf of a copy of *More Than a
Prophet* which his secretary had found in some out-of-the-way
shop:

Dear Marion Hunt:
    I appreciate your efforts to locate this long out of print book.
It was written while I lived in North Manchester, Indiana, my
first pastorate, and published at my own expense. A thousand copies
were printed and nearly half of them were sold.
    For many years, I disliked to have my attention called to the
fact that I had written a book; for I couldn't feel that the project
had been successful. I don't care now. It doesn't hurt any more.
    This book never really accomplished anything: but I thought,
while writing it, that I had hit upon a grand idea. I always think
that when I am at work on a book.
    Again I am back in The Holy Land, working on *The Robe.*
Perhaps this new book will have a wider distribution, but it will
not be written in a more wistful and hopeful mood than *More
Than a Prophet.*

                                        LLOYD C. DOUGLAS
February 17, 1941

Recently Betty and I tried loyally to read the small black
book. It was called a novel, but anyone picking it up for a little
light entertainment would be disappointed to say the least. Its

pages stutter with *dosts, shalts* and *hasts*. Gabriel and Beelzebub converse lengthily while their respective legions stand around casting shade or shine according to which climate they represent.

Webb Vorys told us that night when we all met in Columbus: "Your dad was full of *Paradise Lost* when he first came to Lancaster. He taught our class in catechism and to this day I can't tell where Milton leaves off and the Old Testament begins."

"*More Than a Prophet* was less than a profit," Daddy wrote many years later in Betty's copy. The five hundred books which didn't sell belonged to us and we had them in a big box which we carried around from parsonage to parsonage.

"You should see all the books the Douglases have," said little Connie Smith of Ann Arbor, when she went home from an afternoon playing at our house. "I always thought we had a lot," she told her parents, "but they've got far more. They've got a great big box in the attic all full of books exactly alike and Reverend Douglas wrote them all himself."

The struggling young minister of Lancaster whose dearest hope was to achieve literary fame was plunged into deepest debt. The last payment on the borrowed money was made when he endorsed his first royalty cheque for *Magnificent Obsession* over to the kind friend who had been patient so many years.

In these same months of 1906 his deeply loved young brother Clyde suddenly and tragically died alone in a hotel bedroom in Chicago. His father suffered the last of a series of strokes and died, leaving his mother almost wholly dependent upon him for support. In January the baby Betty was born, adding—along with her charming presence—additional expenses. In the spring the harassed young man was striken with typhoid fever and lay dangerously ill for weeks.

"He got up that last morning and heated the baby's bottle," Mother would tell us and it always hurt her to remember.

A nurse came into the utterly shattered household. The frightened young wife who was running between her husband

and her new baby was barred from the sickroom. When the nurse discovered she needed things for her patient and there was no money she went to the church.

"They had to buy sheets and blankets for us during my illness," Daddy once confessed, and Mother looked away from his face when he told us.

Fierce, unsleeping pride was one of our father's strongest characteristics. It did not ease his sickbed to know each day he was being drawn deeply under the obligation of the wonderfully kind people of the Lutheran Church. In a magazine article many years later he wrote:

> Early in my ministry I was ill for ten weeks with typhoid fever. The church was by no means well-to-do and I had but recently become its pastor. Throughout that illness my salary was paid unreluctantly and in full; the whole congregation standing by with proffers of service and affectionate concern. The wealthiest man in the church sent me a birthday check which paid for the nurse.

In the article he goes on to explain how receiving such kindness means taking on an undischargeable debt.

> The minister constantly realizes that his rewards and distinctions are not offered as definite remuneration for a given amount of work, but as a gratuity in recognition of his influence in the community. This places him in the indefensible position of a charitable object whose obligations to his benefactors are so nebulous that he never knows whether he has fully discharged them.

It was too bad he felt that way. He seemed constitutionally unable to accept favors unless he quickly repaid them in some manner. Mother would say to him, "You're always telling the people to be kind to each other and not expect rewards, and you know how nice it makes you feel yourself when you've done a good deed. Then why can't you accept what other people do for you without rushing around at once to repay them in some way? You never give them a chance to bask in their own virtue."

She got it across to him afterwhile, but it never came naturally. Deep inside there was always a core of pride that rejected material gifts. Perhaps it was the shadow of a bitter little boy who used to stand at the parsonage door and watch the farmers bring in bags of potatoes, apples and coal to keep the minister's family through the winter. He was always more comfortable when he was on the giving end.

The people of the church welcomed their minister back with open arms.

Rev. Lloyd C. Douglas, pastor of the First English Lutheran Church, occupied his pulpit Sunday morning for the first time since he was prostrated with an attack of typhoid fever about three months ago. He has fully recovered and looks well, notwithstanding the serious ordeal through which he has passed. He has lost none of his sermonizing ability and power and beauty of thought and eloquence. The members of the congregation are delighted to know that their young pastor has recovered and was able to address them again.

Under this in the scrapbook is an account of the christening of the baby daughter of Reverend and Mrs. Douglas. Her official recognition had been postponed by her father's illness.

"Why do we have so many spoons with Betty's name on them?" I once asked my mother.

"She got them when she was christened," I was told. "It was the style in those days to give babies spoons."

I chinked sadly through the silver drawer. "There are only about four with my name on them."

"That's because we decided to keep you out of the limelight," Mother said. "We made a mistake allowing Betty to be too much in evidence when she was a baby. She got badly spoiled."

Perhaps their decision to keep me in the background came about after the Sunday when Betty, sitting in church with Mother, called out loudly to Daddy's request from the pulpit that heads be bowed in prayer, "No, Daddy, let's sing."

From now on the pages of the Lancaster scrapbook are filled with closely placed reports of speeches made in Ohio and surrounding states. Reverend Douglas seems to have been on a rather frantic lecture tour. In June of 1907 and 1908 he must have had to rush from one high school commencement to the next in order to get them all made. On the last page a record of all the dates and towns is carefully noted with the amount of the fees and his expenses. Ten dollars was the usual recompense, although occasionally a larger city paid fifteen. Also in the back are pasted the life insurance receipts from the Presbyterian Minister's Fund.

He must have had many sleepless nights worrying about money. Between the lines of his calm words of advice to young ministers written in 1926 one hears the groans of experience.

If your salary will not keep up with you, you may be tempted in an hour of emergency to turn toward certain ways out of your dilemma which will do you small credit. You may resort to selling books, taking orders for magazines, or even pocket your pride completely and sell washing machines or almost anything. . . . But you can't be a merchant and a minister. Either get out of the pulpit or keep away from the market place. The two things will not mix. Neither may your wife peddle soap.

In conclusion you should be made aware of the fact that although your salary will be increased as the years pass your expenses will jump up to meet it. You will never be rich. Make up your mind to it and find your happiness some other way. And if you ever become curious to know exactly what kind of an institution hell is, accumulate a miscellaneous assortment of unpaid bills.

I imagine it was during the years in Lancaster when he was in his early thirties that Daddy began gathering local color for his own personal hell. But knowing him as we did through all his trials and disappointments it seems unlikely he was ever more than fitfully depressed. Mother probably did far more concentrated worrying than he did. His optimism was unquenchable. And Mother too had her absolute faith in him, in his marvelous ability to create something from himself which would save the situation. He never failed her.

Betty and I were a long time getting to Lancaster. Finally we covered the thirty-two miles and arrrived at the town where we had been born. We found it much more difficult to put ourselves back fifty years or see our parents on the streets of this humming little metropolis. North Manchester had been sleepy and vine-covered; even the store fronts seemed untouched by the brush of progress, but Lancaster clicked along busily at the pace of 1951. The corners of the blocks were bitten off by gas stations and red chain stores blazed their bargains on the main streets.

We found the old First English Lutheran Church, but it was locked. We walked all the way around and tried all the doors but it was lunch time and no one was there. We went back and read the minister's address from the bulletin board at the gate. "Let's go to the parsonage," Betty said. "It's the same old one if it's across the street from the Fairgrounds. I remember being taken there for walks."

We discovered the Fair was on that day. We could see small clouds of dust rising under the wheels of some kind of a sulky race in the distance as we parked near the parsonage. We were tempted to go, but remembered our time was short and turned up the walk to the small frame house on the corner.

"Come in, come in," welcomed Mrs. Donaldson, the minister's wife, when we had recited like children who we were and why we had come. "This is a surprise. Why, your father and mother once lived in this house. I believe they say one of you was born right here under this roof."

"I was," I said.

She was a most perceptive woman. She took us into her sitting room and chatted comfortably while we sat side by side on the sofa and stared around at the walls and furniture as though we expected to see familiar pieces from our own old home.

"They say your mother was such a beautiful woman. They tell me how she wore her hair piled on top of her head and received her callers in some sort of a flowing gown they all remember. Too bad so many of the old people are gone. This past winter took so many of our old members. They are the ones who would have remembered your parents."

She took us upstairs and showed us all the bedrooms. I was fascinated by a little stairway which branched from the main one and went steeply down toward the back of the house. I was lured and yet repelled by it. From somewhere many many layers down in my mind a warning came as though a voice had spoken, "Don't go near." I watched Betty as she passed. She was smiling and talking politely and then suddenly her head turned and she veered aside with widened eyes as though she too had heard the voice.

Mrs. Donaldson gave us a few names of people she hoped would be able to recall some tidbits of long-ago gossip. We started off and easily followed her graphic directions since the houses we were to visit were all along the old residential blocks.

That afternoon we sat on many Victorian sofas, under many portraits of ancestors in their Sunday clothes, and heard again and again what a famous man our father had been and how much good his books had done, and agreed that we were very proud to be his daughters.

They remembered him—they remembered him well, but it was the North Manchester experience over again. The young minister with the boyish poet's face had been swallowed up by the fame of the man he later came to be. They remembered his sermons and could even tell us the names and texts of some, but it was the little personal things we wanted to hear. Once or twice we struck through.

"What was he like when he came to call," we asked one old lady. She turned her eyes down and spoke to her hands folded in her lap. "The Reverend Douglas never came inside our house. Our mother had tuberculosis and he was afraid of it." She spoke dispassionately, but Betty and I rushed to the defense of the painfully thin young man whose dry cough became so characteristic that we would have recognized it in Grand Central Station blindfolded. "He was terribly afraid of tuberculosis," we said. "So many in his family died of it. He always thought he must have had it himself when he was in college."

We didn't go on to tell her about his terrible colds and anxiety lest a red fleck appear on his handkerchief. Occasionally a spot of red did appear and he would rush to the doctor. "Preacher's throat," they would say.

The old lady listened politely to our explanations, but at the door she said, "Some people thought his sermons were kind of highfalutin," adding softly, "Wasn't he interested in evolution?"

We smiled. It was old-fashioned the way she said it. We hadn't thought of that old monkey story for years. There had been a time when the word evolution brought to my mind a picture of human-looking monkeys leering down through the trees at a modestly posing Adam and Eve.

"I'm afraid your father and mother were not very happy here," another lady told us. The actual statement, made so matter-of-factly, was shocking. We didn't want to hear that anyone knew they had been unhappy, that it had been so bad. For a moment the very foundations rocked under us.

"Oh they loved Lancaster," we hurried to assure her. "The people here were so kind to them. Daddy always said he found himself in the work here."

She didn't mean that, she said. "We knew they loved the Church, but they had such troubles. They seemed very young and inexperienced. After your father had that long illness and was up and about again he seemed so thin and white. I don't think I ever saw him smile."

Oh, she couldn't have known him at all well. Daddy never could have existed an hour without hearing something funny to laugh at—even if he had to say it himself. We left her and went back to our car feeling quiet and not much like talking. "Let's go back to Columbus," Betty said. "The Vorys boys will be fun."

We were in the dining room, which was a smoky nightclub at that late hour, having our dinner when they came stringing in, peering around anxiously for two women who might conceivably look like the children they had once been. We spotted them more easily since they were four and looked like brothers. Soon the six of us were crowded about our dab of a table and talking our heads off.

Their stories were cheerful and exchanged in our minds the sad figure the old ladies had painted for the humorous, entertaining, never long serious father we had known.

"Your dad made an impression on us that lasted a lifetime," they said. "He had all the youngsters fascinated. Seemed to know how they felt about things. Of course he was lively and kept everybody laughing all the time. We liked that."

Between the four of them they pieced together stories for us of the type that small boys would have remembered. Taken alone, their sketch of his character was more colorful than saintly. One evening, they remembered with especial amusement, there was a particular church supper. "The ladies were clearing the dishes from the tables in the Sunday School room and the rest of the people were standing around in groups talking," they told us. "One old chatterbox got Reverend Douglas cornered by the organ and began telling him some long story which seemed to have no end. He edged away from her onto the organ bench, but she kept right after him, her tongue clacking a mile a minute. He listened and nodded sympathetically, but he began to run his fingers along the keys, quietly at first, then pulling out a stop, then another, making it a little louder, until gradually he got up to full blast, working her with him all the way so that she was yelling at the top of her lungs without realizing it."

"I had slipped on the bench beside him," Arthur said, "and he gave me a funny little wink. Then suddenly with one whisk he managed to push all the buttons in. The innocent little melody went on, but the lady was left up there hollering her head off to the amazed room of people."

They remembered how he loved to play the organ. "One Sunday the lady organist was sick," they said, "and by church time no one had been found to take her place. Everybody was wondering who was going to play for the hymns. Reverend Douglas stood up at the pulpit and gave out the number and we all started looking for the place in the book, worried about who was going to begin first. Then we saw your dad step over the low velvet curtain which was around the choir and the organ. He flipped up his long black coattails and sat down. After the tinkle of accompaniment we had been used to, he made the old songs roar and we sang to shake the roof down."

"When he preached it was the same. There was real drama in the old Bible stories the way he told them, as though it were happening today and we were all there. Once he preached a sermon on David and when he came to the part about Absalom he called out, 'O! Absalom, my son, my son' in such a tragic voice half the audience was in tears."

They told us our father had come to their house the day Betty was born. "He wanted our mother to come and be with his wife, but he didn't quite know how to go about asking. He talked to father all around the bush, but finally blurted out that the baby was definitely on the way. Mother grabbed her coat. 'Well, then why are we standing around here talking?' and she hurried off without waiting to be told more."

"You were the youngest baby I ever saw, Betty," Webb said, "I came home from school that afternoon and they told me my mother was at the Douglases'. Your people lived next door to us in a kind of an apartment. I went over and my mother met me with you in her arms. Even my own children were older when I first saw them; you had just been born.

"Your father slept for a whole day afterwards. The nurse had his bed and he went upstairs to the apartment where some bachelors lived. They had to take the door off its hinges to wake him up."

"Of course Reverend Douglas was solemn in the pulpit," they said.

The Vorys boys thought that their house had been the only place where he could really let down. He even smoked. "Smoking is a filthy, disgusting and extravagant habit," they remembered he used to tell them soberly while he took out a big black cigar and lovingly clipped off the end.

All the things they told us that evening delighted us and seemed no end amusing, but they were not very remarkable. Just the kind of tales every family affectionately recalls. None of it added a dot to the vital structure of a career we were hoping to trace. The record of that was still to be found in only one place—the scrapbooks our father had kept. These volumes began to take on a new value in our eyes.

That night in Columbus after we left the Voryses we opened for the first time the third one, which was started in 1909, and found there in faded old clippings the beginning of a reputation. The towns which reported his speeches were bigger and farther away from home. Articles printed in the *Lutheran Observer* and other church papers appeared more frequently. There were letters of congratulation from men well known in the Synod. To Betty and me there was a kind of thrill to turn the pages and see the gradual struggle from utter obscurity to recognition, even though it was only in the narrow world of Lutheranism.

Then came the plum. This was an official document pasted on a page alone. On the outside was written in Daddy's rapid, confident hand: "Official Call to Luther Place Memorial Church, Washington, D.C. 1909. Accepted." When I unfolded this paper I confess my first thought was to run through the ponderous statements until I came to the part about the salary—"and that your support was fixed at twenty-five hundred dollars a year"— that must have seemed like a fortune to them.

It was a plum indeed. The Luther Place Memorial Church was old and famous. The former minister had been nationally known. Washington was a cosmopolitan city: concerts, art galleries, libraries, clever people, the real world was doubtless to be found there. "We've arrived!" Daddy probably shouted at Mother, and she with more restraint probably thought so too. They arrived so often during the years and found that success had so many anterooms where one sat on a bench and cooled.

The many mundane attractions of the Washington church quite outweighed one unpleasant feature which was openly discussed by the papers of that city, according to the scrapbook. It seemed there had been a division of loyalties following the death of the beloved Dr. J. G. Butler who had been the pastor for thirty-six years. A part of the congregation had broken away, but it was hoped that they could be brought back under a new minister.

"Never engage in a church quarrel," Lloyd Douglas advised young men in theological seminaries, but that was later.

The Washington *Post* reported the situation as follows:

> While a young man in the true sense of the word Rev. Douglas is considered fitted to take charge of a church as important in the religious world as the Memorial Church. Many of the members of the Independent Church which broke off from the Mother Church last February are of the opinion that the installation of a young and vigorous pastor like the Rev. Douglas will tend to unite the bodies again in a common welfare and interest.

A long discussion of the affair in the Washington *Herald*
includes an interview with the newly appointed pastor.

"I know," Mr. Douglas said yesterday, "the circumstances of
the last few months of the church. But I am taking up my pastorate
here with the intention of winning and I am going to win. I am
not going to conduct a school. I am a preacher and I shall be a
preacher in the pulpit and out of it." [The reporter went on to
comment:] Rev. Douglas looks younger than his age, but from the
black hair on top of his head to his clean cut chin and the finely
drawn lines about his mouth there are determination and frankness.

Daddy always had a wonderful ability to gloss over unattrac-
tive features in a thing he very much wanted to do. He either
steadily refused to see them, or else persuaded himself and tried
to persuade Mother that they were a "challenge." Once he began
talking about challenges Mother said nothing more. The issue
had passed beyond her control and she was a master at resignation. It was characteristic of her to move with caution and cling
to the known. It was always her dream to live in one house on a
quiet street, to have a cellar for preserves and an attic where she
could store her wedding dress and her daughters' baby clothes.
I can't imagine her being very enthusiastic about hurtling off to
a big Eastern city to buck a strange new world.

Always when we moved she had to be rooted out of the little
establishment she had set up with such care. She was married to
a restless, ambitious voyager and she went the whole way with
him, but even when they finally arrived at the big house with
the golden doorknobs she was still clutching her original
possessions and trailing ivy cuttings and plants born in a quiet
garden long ago.

Here is a quotation from the farewell sermon which our father
preached his last Sunday in Lancaster. Knowing his gypsy nature
as we did it seems likely he was speaking more for Mother than
himself in the first sentences. When he whips out his own arguments for going he sounds more like the dreamer we knew.

If I were to study only my own peace of mind and personal happiness I should ask for nothing more than to stay here with you as long as I live. But mere personal pleasure is not all. I have received an impressive summons to a field presenting many peculiar and complex problems. Circumstances most strange, and which seem to have the Providential stamp upon them have been frequent in connection with this call. I am going only because I believe it is a part of a program which has been laid down for me.

And so in 1909 Reverend and Mrs. Douglas and children left Lancaster. The newspaper report of the informal farewell after the sermon is interesting in its old-fashioned sentiment.

At the conclusion of his discourse Sunday evening almost the entire audience crowded to the platform in front of the church and shook hands with Rev. Douglas and wife, bidding them goodbye and goodspeed. It was an exceedingly touching occasion and will never be forgotten by those who participated.

4

Away with Ivy and Moss

BETTY AND I did not go to Washington on our sentimental pilgrimage. The years had almost obliterated any traces of the young Douglases in Lancaster—how utterly futile and disheartening it would be to seek their footprints in the national capital after the winds of forty years had passed.

We had lived in Washington until the summer of 1911, about two and a half years. Betty was five when we left. "Can't you remember anything about it?" I asked her.

"I remember seeing a big pool of blood on the pavement where a little girl had been thrown from a runaway carriage," she said. And then when I did not appear to consider this recollection very valuable for our purpose, she added hopefully: "The little girl had been riding with her grandfather."

As for me, I am blank on the subject except for the memory of dreaming in the night of the lions in the national park where we were often taken to play.

In Washington we lived in a house which Mother described to us as being quite unique, a kind never to be seen except in that odd city. It was one of a long row of brown houses all stuck together at the sides. The kitchen was in the basement, dark and dismal even on the finest day. The food came bumping up through the walls on a dumb-waiter to the dining room on the first floor.

No lady could do her own work in that house so we had a

cook, a fat colored mammy whose name was Emily. Emily loved us all dearly and Mother became so devoted to her and dependent upon her advice that when we finally moved away she feared for a while she would never be able to manage her house and children alone. The old black lady had lived all her life in Washington and knew all the intricacies of social deportment. There was a special kind of etiquette which originated in the highest government circles and sifted on down through the layers of society to the lowest of Civil servants.

To our mother, fresh from the back-fence friendliness of Lancaster, it was a cold and baffling experience to stand in the afternoon at the front window and watch through the curtains the ladies sitting in their carriages while their colored drivers came to the door with cards.

The first time Emily brought these to her she looked at them, holding them gingerly between the tips of two fingers. "One corner is folded down; does that mean anything?"

Emily said, "That means her husband wishes he could come too, but he couldn't, honey."

"It wasn't much of a call, anyway," Mother said wistfully.

"Never you mind," Emily consoled her, "some ladies will come and stay for a real chat."

"But what'll I do about these cards?" Mother was still holding them out as if they were a live insect. She told us how Emily laughed with her stomach hopping up and down under her apron.

But after it was all explained about the "at homes" and the courtesy calls she found it all too formidable and retired as much as she could to the company of her small daughters.

Daddy too found during his first months in Washington a hedge of decorum which was difficult to break through. The lives of his congregation touched his only at the church and he discovered that "neighbor" was a small-town word. He began to do some story writing, guiltily, because he felt he was stealing the time and using it for frivolous thoughts. His cousin Edith

Kirkwood, for whom he had always a great admiration, recently sent us this letter he wrote to her in 1910:

Things with us move on without incident or accident worth a story. We are well. The kids are growing more pretty and noisy every day. The weather has been demnition bad. I think I can confide this piece of near-profanity to you since you are a newspaperman and probably have a speaking acquaintance with several kinds of vocabularies. The sun hasn't shone for weeks. Whether the Comet swished her tail in his face and he is in a pout, or is merely taking a much-needed vacation, I have not learned. It has rained steadily for thirty-six hours without stopping for fuel or passengers. I have spent the day at home—the first since arriving in this place—working on a yarn which I hope somebody may need in his business—at about a penny a throw.

Lately, I have revived an old slumbering passion for writing yarns. Not long ago I sold a small ornament off my desk to Eddie Bok and the sight of that check, with its beautiful corrugated edges,—albeit it was not for more than two figures—started up my old trouble; and the gnawing at my vitals (not pronounced with a short *i*) has compelled me to scribble some more. God help the preacher who isn't content to stick to his parish duties! He standeth in the way of becoming a hissing and a by-word, when it is found out on him. I have a lot of old mummies in my ecclesiastical museum who would feel that Hell had opened up its maw (and its paw, for that matter) to embrace me, were the news to out that I had disgraced the profesh and besmirched the cloth by writing fiction. I shall spare them the discomfort by seeing to it that nobody finds out.

I am now on the hunt for a satisfactory nom-de-plume. Nothing like "Percy Fitz-sneeze" or other henglish name will do. Neither will Abraham Mand or any such non-euphonious title cater to my sense of the artistic. If you have any ideas on this subject, let me have the benefit of them.

Write to me. Tell me what you have done lately with your pen and I will tell you what the editor is doing to me with his ax.

We have a small collection of essays and short stories written during the Washington years. On the manuscripts it is not stated whether they were published or not, but it seems most likely they were victims of the editorial axe.

In one short story, "Harold," the author calls himself Lloyd Edgington. That rather fancy book name was actually in our grandfather's family. "Harold" is a story of college life: freshmen get tossed into the creek and pole vaulters break their legs. The hero is a pipe-smoking, debonair man of the world who slings one leg over the edge of the table and drawls cynical wisecracks from the side of his mouth. However, he shows himself at the end of the story to be soft and susceptible within, when the heroine shows up all dressed in "some frilly white stuff" with her hair down her back.

Miss Wayland must have caught me looking at the unbraided end of her hair for she took it in her fingers and twisted it slowly as we talked. Her dimples were deeper than I had ever seen them and her eyes were even darker than I had thought. I am afraid I mangled my story badly in the telling, but, honestly, I couldn't keep my eyes off that plait of gold hair and I knew I had no right to be looking at it that way.

Lloyd Edgington is also signed to a story called, "Maitland House," which is about a man who falls in love with a girl he thinks is blind. Blind girls seem to have been particularly attractive to Daddy. They turn up in several of his books. Blindness is an unfortunate handicap, but can be useful in a plot and so often is curable in the end.

As time went on our parents took courage and stepped from behind the protection of their brownstone front, and began to take in the contemporary scene. What innocents they must have been, coming from the small towns of the Middle West where the neighbors knew what time they raised the blinds in the morning and when their lights went off at night, and the very air they breathed was filtered through the stained glass windows of the church.

In Washington their comings and goings were not so closely supervised. They sat in the peanut gallery and thrilled to famous actors and actresses in the plays of Shakespeare and Ibsen. They went to concerts and lectures and spent long hours in the art galleries. "We had been to college, but we discovered we were very ignorant." From every direction new and revolutionary ideas rushed at them, rocking the solid beliefs they had never dreamed of questioning. They began to read the books and articles of churchmen who were openly criticizing the old theories of religion. They found themselves in sympathy with the new protest against tradition. Not only was religion being held up and examined for mothholes, but in Washington they discovered that all the traditions of American life were undergoing a great change in which only a few scandalizing rumors had ever penetrated the old walls behind which they had been raised.

Together they attended a series of lectures given by Shailer Mathews, an exponent of religious modernism, which left them in a most distressed state of mind. They recognized the reasonableness and were forced to agree with the attack upon the old conceptions, but they heard nothing satisfying which they could grasp to fill the void.

"Daddy became very unsettled in his thinking while we were in Washington," Mother told us.

She found comfort on one subject at least. Dr. Holt's book, *The Care and Feeding of Children*, had been a treasure of information to replace her shockingly old-fashioned ideas on child care. "Sometimes I used to wish we could find a book so sane and satisfying on the Care and Feeding of Faith."

The only record we have of what effect his unsettled state of mind had upon our father's ministry is in the newspaper reports of his sermons and lectures of that time. Before he went to Washington there is but one hint that the old Lutheran dogmas

Lloyd C. Douglas at seven years of age

Lloyd and his brother Clyde at fourteen and eight

Lloyd three years
older and considerably
handsomer

Roe Jones

LCD
and hat
and friend

Besse Porch, at Wittenberg

Bradley

LCD at the beginning of his ministerial career

The too liberal pastor,
in Washington D.C., 1910

"The hat with the plume" —
at Champaign, Illinois

Betty, Besse and Virginia

Portrait of the subject as author — Montreal, 1929

LCD autographs a copy of his greatest novel

The house with the golden doorknobs

John Engstead

Besse Douglas in 1944

LCD at the piano in 1944

were not entirely acceptable to him; on the outside of a printed program of the annual conference of the Synod he has written, "Much ado about nothing."

"There was always too much counting of the tassels on the altar cloth," I remember hearing him once say.

In his inaugural sermon at the Luther Place Memorial Church, the Washington *Post* quotes him as follows:

> I have an abiding faith in the church as a divinely established institution. We are living in a time when it has become the vogue to belittle the church of the living God. Many who are willing to applaud Jesus Christ are as free with their hisses and execrations when His Bride is mentioned. One naturally expects this attitude as the logical position of the world, the flesh and the devil, but the modern attack upon the church comes quite as glibly from the pulpit as from the desk of the secular press.

The text for this sermon was "As ye have heretofore received Jesus Christ the Lord, walk ye in him, established in the faith as ye have been taught." That seems a pretty clear declaration of his stand at that time, and it was on that platform he had been called to minister to the conservative members of the old church; it was the liberal wing which had broken away.

Two years later he was saying from the pulpit:

> The present attitude of the church reminds me somewhat of the old printing press of Benjamin Franklin's down in the National Museum. That battered old pile of junk is worth more in dollars and cents than any press in this city, notwithstanding the fact that any big newspaper press in the city will print more papers in a minute than Franklin's press could turn out in a whole afternoon. But the man who buys it gets an antique. He is not going to print with it, but just look at it. If the church is valuable as only a curio then no pains should be spared to avoid modifications, and signs should be put up to warn tourists from scratching off the moss. But if the church is to serve as an agency for humanitarian and philanthropic service, such as many of us think was its original purpose, a little of the ivy and moss will have to be sacrificed in order to admit the light.

And at a student's conference where he could probably express himself more strongly, he is reported as saying:

> Jesus Christ is the same yesterday, today and forever, but men's conceptions of him will change with the times. Conservative people are often in the wrong. The old-time religion was good enough for our fathers, but it will not serve us adequately now.

The church quarrel gets no further publicity in the news. The two bodies went their separate ways and nothing was done to stir up antagonism on either side. The independents never returned to the fold, but their ranks were filled by new members. A paper reports:

> Rev. Lloyd Douglas is now completing the first year of his ministry at the Luther Place Memorial Church and the reports of the council of the organization show that unusual progress has been made. In active membership the church has entirely regained the ground it lost by the secession of the independents. The same is true of the finances. It is said that few churches in the city have larger congregations than the Luther Place Memorial on Sunday mornings.

Even before he came to Washington, Reverend Douglas had not spent his time straightening candles in the cloister. His sermons had dealt with civic problems and often he used the Bible as authority to plead for a new hospital or an organized charity fund. Now he branched out to comment broadly on social and political issues. The *Post* write-up of a Sunday service states: "He began with a somewhat detailed story of idol-building as narrated by Isaiah, but speedily dropped down into the forenoon of the twentieth century with some down-to-the-minute applications." From there on, according to the report, the sermon lashed out at loan sharks, the clash between the masses and the classes, and a potshot is taken at the new rich, symbolized by him as "The man with the fur collar and the lady with the plumes."

"I never had a plume on my hat until we lived in Champaign," Mother said. "Daddy gave me a beaver muff then too."

The parable of the ten virgins was used as a text to introduce a spirited upholding of Mr. Gifford Pinchot's pleas for conservation of natural resources. "America Faces the Penalty of Prodigality, Says Pastor," the headline read. The paper gives one colume to his outline of the various wastes in the kingdom of nature and another to his neat applications of these examples in the kingdom of the spirit.

How many times in special crises have you been steadied by the sheer fact of your parent's faith? What of your child? Have you squandered your spiritual resources? Is he to glean among the stubble while you reaped and tossed away the golden sheaves?

Across the page from this clipping in the scrapbook is pasted a letter from Gifford Pinchot, Chairman of the Joint Committee on Conservation, dated December 13, 1909. "It is with keen interest that I have read in this morning's paper your sermon yesterday on conservation of resources," he writes, and goes on to express his appreciation.

During these years the Mexican situation was far from settled and Daddy thought it his duty to undertake a spell of military life. Betty and I were always very proud of the fact that he had been a soldier. We have a picture of him standing at the open flap of a tent, squinting into the sun and looking extremely tall and skinny in a tight, ill-fitting uniform. In a letter to Burton Garlinghouse of Akron, Ohio, written in 1942, he described this experience as it appeared in retrospect:

When I was young (we lived in Washington) I was given the post of chaplain to a regiment that turned out every little while to bury some old soldier in Arlington, dedicate a monument, or welcome an envoy. I had not been on a horse since I was twelve— a country horse with a wide experience at the plow, but unfamiliar with polo. The horse I rode in Washington was a tall, lean, irascible beast; an introvert, an anti-social, ungregarious monastic. He hated to be regimented. He seemed to know from the first that I both feared and distrusted him. You should have seen this horse and me high-tailing it down Pennsylvania Avenue informing the public that we were conscientious objectors.

One summer our regiment was encamped for six weeks on the old battlefield of Gettysburg, engaged mostly in night tactics. Among my horse's aversions was a strong antipathy for artillery fire. Sometimes when a big gun went off unexpectedly to us, we fled—over ditches and logs, through swamps and quagmires—until we were practically AWOL.

I had often heard that hard ridden horses got saddle-galls. My horse managed to go through the season without them, but I didn't. In fact I had to go to the camp hospital and have strips of adhesive plaster criss-crossed on my fanny until my rump looked like an old-fashioned, open-faced apple pie. I never thought I would be any good to an army. As a marksman I am not a success.

One Sunday in 1911 it suddenly came over the minister of Luther Place Memorial Church that he couldn't go on preaching any longer. He didn't believe what he was saying, and he didn't know what he believed. "Besse, I'm going to get out of the church," he said to Mother on the way home.

"I was terribly shocked," she told us years later. "He had talked that way before, but this time I felt he really meant it. The first thing I thought was: What will his mother say?"

Not many Sundays later at the end of the morning service he resigned. The Washington *Post* reports:

> To the surprise of his congregation which had no inkling of his impending action Rev. Lloyd C. Douglas, one of the most prominent ministers of this city, resigned his pulpit yesterday and will soon leave Washington to become the Religious Work Director of the Christian Association at the University of Illinois, a position under the direction of the International YMCA.

The pastor's resignation was announced to the congregation at the close of the service and later many asked that he reconsider this action and remain with the church. To these, however, he answered that he believed the field for service at the University of Illinois is larger than that in which he has been working here.

It was a bold move and not made without fear and many misgivings, but the position he was trying to fill in the Lutheran Church had now become intolerable. For some time John R. Mott and other leaders of the YMCA student movement had been pressing Daddy to join them, and the idea of working with receptive, searching young minds was appealing after the uphill struggle of preaching to die-hard conservatives.

Grandfather Porch and Grandmother Douglas were utterly horrified when they heard the news. That Lloyd, so fortunate and promising, having reached the very top in his denomination, could turn his back upon all the honors and prospects and set out upon a new kind of work—"What is it you're going to be doing there, Lloyd?" Oh, inexplicable folly!

The usual farewell reception is recorded in the scrapbook. All is goodwill and regret on the part of the members. However, a small item on another page concerning the Luther Place Memorial Church's efforts to obtain a new pastor states in closing:

> It is no secret in the congregation that a certain element is in favour of a progressive minister, while the larger and dominating portion is strong for a man who will preach in the conservative way.

Lloyd Douglas was now out of the ministry. It was to be a breathing spell, but not an apathetic one. In an article published in the progressive *Lutheran Observer* he writes:

> I used to think that if I could just get out of the active pastorate for a week or two and hie myself away where I wouldn't need

care very much whether my constituency understood my motives or not, and take careful aim and bang away at two or three things that everybody knows need to be ventilated, what a glorious, albeit smellful, event it would be.

From this safe angle then I modestly pull the trigger, fondly hoping that all who are in the vicinity of the target will promptly squeal in order that we may be able to check up on the efficiency of our marksmanship.

This article was written from the safe angle of the new position at the University of Illinois.

5

Live Wire Down at the "Y"

RECOLLECTIONS OF LIFE in Champaign seep up through our memories in a series of colorful though disjointed pictures. Our house seemed always to be full of young men: Oriental mahogany-colored men with white turbans wound above their sensitive faces, awkward country boys and the more self-possessed ones from the fraternities. Bicycles were propped against our front porch. I can remember my father clipping the cuffs of his trousers and climbing on a very tall one to push off in the morning for work. Often he took Betty or me for rides on the handlebars and it looked dreadfully far down to the street rolling under the front wheel.

I half remember and have half been told of a time he wanted to surprise Mother by having my photograph taken. She and Betty had gone back to Louisville, Kentucky, to visit her sister Glen, who had married and was living there, thus continuing the connection with the South which Mother always considered her home. Daddy came home in the afternoon and dressed me himself, being particular about only the top layer. My long white stockings were very baggy and soiled. We rode together on his bicycle all the way to the YMCA building where a student was to take the picture, and by the time we arrived my starchy dress was sadly crumpled and my hair stringing in my eyes. One panty leg (without lace) drooped several inches below my skirt in the picture. When Mother unwrapped it at Christmas time all framed and under glass she was really surprised. Of course she expressed pleasure and enthusiasm enough to satisfy Daddy, but she did say: "How did you happen to put those shoes on the child? Weren't her good ones clean?"

"Oh, yes," Daddy said, "but she wanted to wear the ones with the tassels."

Their lives in Champaign were entirely centered in the activities of the big university. For the first time they could kick up their heels and be a little less dignified. They made friends among the faculty later, but for the first year, at least, most of their time was spent among the students. On Sundays they were asked for noon dinner at one or another of the fraternity houses and Betty and I went too. We remember being hauled around piggy-back and sliding down bannisters with romping young men.

The YMCA building was just off the campus and offered various attractions to the students. There was a big battered-looking lounge furnished in solid mission oak where they could meet; there was a library and a cafeteria, and all sorts of events went on to draw the young men in. Of course religion was the main dish, but it was so spiced up you would hardly know the old vegetable.

It was Daddy's job to get acquainted with as many groups as possible on the campus and interest them in the YMCA activities. Religion was having a wave of popularity in those years. The new approach was a novelty and the young people paused to listen. But whether they would shrug and pass on, or stop to hear more, depended greatly on how much they liked the man who stood at the door. He had to have personality of the live-wire type.

"I went galloping from one meeting to the next fairly sizzling with pep," Daddy told us. Pep was a new word then. His success depended almost entirely upon personal magnetism. He must have had it. One sentence in a newspaper report found in the scrapbook described it this way: "Even when he is speaking to a large group of men it is as though he put a finger on each one and said, 'Come.' " It became the popular thing while he was at the University of Illinois for the young men to say, "I'll meet you down at the 'Y.' "

Mother and Daddy were often asked to chaperone college dances and at first considered this a great compliment. When they became a little more experienced they realized that one by one the other faculty couples would creep away before midnight, and it always seemed that they alone were left to yawn it out until the last weary dancers staggered off from under the sagging streamers of crepe paper. In time they too learned to watch for the right moment of escape, but they always enjoyed the parties. The gaiety, the music, the bright lights and excitement, and all the young people who flocked around them, were a wonderful change from the staid and elderly society they had been used to in the church.

Mother especially loved the new gay life. She made herself two evening dresses and had two pairs of satin slippers, size three and a half. They had rosettes of crushed tulle on the toes and Betty and I used to put them on and totter about admiring their daintiness. Mother was always proud of her small feet and I remember her horror when I, at the age of eleven, was told by the shoeman that I would really have to have a size four.

Mother was never a great mixer; she was shy and apt to think that no one would be particularly interested in anything she had to say. Daddy never forgot her presence and continually turned to her, holding her up as a swimmer supports a weaker one. "What was that story we heard the other night, Besse?" Sometimes she would step into the light, but generally she would say, "Oh, you tell it, Lloyd." With her husband such a professional master of ceremonies, she was content to smile and look pretty and see that the cocoa and sandwiches were not running low.

They held open house on Sunday afternoons in Champaign and sometimes foreign students brought their own food and cooked exotic dishes in our kitchen. When Grandmother Douglas came to visit us she found this the most terrible of all the new conditions she had to face. "Little yellow men down in the kitchen stirring up heathen concoctions, wasting all that good food," she would mutter when she came to get us up from our naps.

Every winter Grandmother paid us a long visit. She came with her old round-topped trunk and Betty and I loved to watch her unpack it. On top would be her dark shawls of various thicknesses, and underneath her best black silk dress and several fine-lace collars carefully wrapped in tissue paper. Always there was a big cloth bag of dried corn and a box of homemade noodles. In the bottom of the trunk were her scrapbooks full of postcards and old-fashioned valentines and poems and stories about little children whose parents had died and left them alone in the cruel world.

When Grandmother first arrived she would have lots to tell us and Daddy would sit at the table laughing at her stories about the farmers and people he had known in Indiana. Grandmother's little fist would pound the table: "So when I saw Doc passing by in his old buggy I just went to the window and poured all those pills out on the snow. They didn't do me a particle of good. I cured myself with camphor and olive oil."

After she had been with us a few weeks Daddy would begin to tire of her bossiness. He would turn her over to Mother as much as he could: Mother's long-tried patience never broke the bounds of politeness. At the table Daddy would become more and more impatient with Grandmother as her visit lengthened. She never stayed out its full term. Generally on a wave of a big row she would lay all her things back in her trunk, clamp her home-decorated hat on her head and be off.

The new religious-work director had his headquarters at the University of Illinois, but he traveled to the campuses of surrounding colleges and State universities to conduct religious meetings among the men students. These were called Friendship Campaigns and the pages of the scrapbook for those years are solid with reports of their success. The students and faculty responded with enthusiasm to the kind of religion Lloyd Douglas described to them. He had now abandoned all loyalty to creeds and dogmas and urged his audiences to be tolerant of other men's religions. "Jesus is but one of a group of great prophets," he told them. "If the Virgin birth proves a stumbling block to a man's acceptance of Jesus, let him accept the facts he is sure he can understand and appreciate and let his faith do the rest."

Most of his emphasis to the students was laid upon the practice of everyday religion. In the *Daily Illini* each week appeared his Sunday Sermonette which preached a homely kind of theology: gratitude to one's parents, honor in the classroom, politeness to the faculty, loyalty to the institution, integrity in one's daily life. In simple, little one-hundred-word essays he treated during his three years in Illinois nearly every side of a student's experience. And always he urged them to go to church.

> Any student who will spend all Sunday forenoon reading the supplements of the Sunday paper and then explains that he doesn't go to church because the sermons are not intellectually stimulating should take some steps toward developing his sense of humor.

The college magazine *The Siren* published a series of Pen Portraits of Prominent People. These were unsigned but everyone knew who handed out that mixture of noble endeavor and comic relief. They sketched various characters popular on the campus from the president down to the baggage man, Johnny O'Byrne, who rated a special poem in his honor.

Here's to friend Johnny O'Byrne
Of the swift moving baggage concyrne.
Who at every vacation
Totes trunks to the station
Re-toting them on their retyrne.

Oh, grads, of years hoary and styrne
If forgetting all you did lyrne
While here in Champaign
May your memory retaign
The trunk wizard Johnny O'Byrne.

During the summer when the campus was a quiet leafy park
and Champaign dozed, the job of the Religious Work Director
slowed to a standstill. As always, the Douglas income was
urgently in need of funds and to supply them Daddy began
Chautauqua work, which he always declared he loathed, but
which he returned to for many years. The circus type of life
during the hot summers of Ohio, Indiana and Illinois was grim
and at times cruelly wearing, but undoubtedly the attractions of
the Big Show had a fascination for him.

In those days Chautauqua was an immensely popular institution. The small towns of the Middle West were almost
entirely cut off from the entertainment world and when Chautauqua came, after weeks of posters announcing its program, the
people shut up their shops, put on their Sunday hats and went
to every lecture, concert or dramatic performance that was
offered. The farmers put the kids in the wagon and came to
town.

Recently we wrote to Mr. James Hamilton, now of Ormond,
Florida, for a few details about a summer he spent as a singer on
a circuit of which Daddy was superintendent. He says:

Chautauqua in those days was run along the same lines as the
Civic Music Association of today. They brought to the small towns
and villages such personalities as William Jennings Bryan, Dr.

Parkes Cadman and others; also many attractions such as bands, dramatic sketches and singing groups.

Doug was superintendent of our outfit. It was his job to over-see two college boys who acted as tent men and general flunkies, introduce the attractions and keep everybody happy. It was also his job to sell the Chautauqua for the following season at two bucks per person and seek out homes which would put up the talent for the night for nothing. You can imagine how much money we were pulling down.

We would sing in each town for a week—the Chautauqua was a one week affair—and then move on to the next place.

After the show we would go to the village restaurant for water-melon, coffee, etc., and listen to Doug tell stories at which he was a past master.

In later summers Daddy was billed as an attraction in his own name and finally wound up triumphantly with an invitation to lecture at the main stamping ground in Chautauqua, New York; but in the beginning he served his apprenticeship as tent man and general smoother of rumpled personalities. Of course he had been thoroughly trained for this in his pastorates. Every minister knows that a not unimportant part of his duties includes being a sort of super janitor for the church properties.

In his book *The Minister's Everday Life* Daddy says to young aspirants to the pulpit:

While you are ambling through your homily on Sunday night some of your parishioners whose upturned gaze indicates a state of holy contemplation of your sidereal remarks, may not be indulging in pious reflections at all. They are looking at an elec-trolier in the ceiling in which four lamps are burned out—the same four which were missing last Sunday. Indeed they are same four lamps which were deceased six months ago. It is not your fault of course—you are not the janitor—but it comes to the same thing as if it were. It is your fault if the church steps are icy and somebody breaks his neck thereon. If the clock is ten minutes slow or the linen collars on the choir vestments dirty it is your fault. It will be a responsibility that you can not shake off even in the years to come when experience, industry and talent may have earned you a position in which you have much more to work with in the way of property.

It seemed to be Daddy's lot in life always to be moiling in such details, when it was his inclination to shut the study door and be alone with higher thought. But he was a capable administrator when forced to it. People who knew him at the University of Illinois seem to remember as well as the religious message he preached the fact that he got the YMCA cafeteria back on its feet financially.

There was one side of his work as a religious director of youth which he always viewed with distaste: his expected attendance at the big evangelistic conventions which were held at summer resorts for students and people who worked with the morals of the young. He considered these emotional orgies harmful and hated to be obliged to participate.

I remember his describing one such affair held at a lakeside camp in Wisconsin. The young men were staging their moral revival on one side of the beach and near enough, so the breeze wafted the sound of their hymn singing across the water, the girls were holding a similar uplift. Every night in the velvety darkness of summer the two camps held their respective confessionals. In a tense ring they sat around their leaders and were urged to tell all and repent. Then, washed in purity and in a highly emotional state, many of the young men crept to a hole in the wire fence where they met such of the young girls as had managed to steal through the trees unseen, and they all scampered off to the village pavilion to gather material for the next night's confessional. It sounded like perfect fun to us, but Daddy always insisted the idea was very wrong and dishonored the purpose of religion.

He had come into the YMCA work with enthusiasm. Its

everyday approach to religious matters had appeared a blessed relief after the liturgical phrases of the Lutheran creed. But in time this jaunty, chatty kind of theology began to irritate him. He disliked the YMCA language. He had a great deal of personal dignity and found it objectionable to be referred to as a "live wire." He came to hate the words "snappy" and "peppy," and the constant talk about "contacting the groups" got on his nerves. He never could say the word "group" without holding the middle like a dog baying at the moon.

In his novel *Forgive Us Our Trespasses* his hero has a brief encounter with a YMCA man. Of course this is fiction, but it describes a certain type of enthusiast who was not uncommon in those days:

> "Hope you'll come down to the Y rooms tonight at seven," suggested Kling. "Just a little informal get-together of the fellows to meet the new frosh. A sing-song, brief devotional service, some short prayers, a few snappy talks; all through by eight."
>
> "Thanks," said Ferdinand graciously, but without enthusiasm.
>
> "That's the spirit," approved Kling. "It makes all the difference later if you begin your college life right."
>
> Ferdinand nodded obligingly, but his acquiescence lacked fervor. Bent on saving a soul from anaemia Kling rose to defend his moral precept. Hands deep in his pockets and rhythmically elevating himself on his toes he dealt seriously with Ferdinand's limp aspirations to make a right start.
>
> "Yes, sir, it makes all the difference you'll find. Down there on Sunnyside Avenue the upper classmen are teaching the new fraternity pledges to smoke a pipe, scorn the barbs, and beat the profs . . . up here we have different ideas. You'll start right, won't you, Brumm?"
>
> "You mean—at a prayer meeting?"
>
> "Well, that kind of a beginning would make for safety," said Kling, slightly accelerating the tempo of his adroit bouncing up and down on his toes.
>
> "I'm pretty well up on prayer-meetings," said Ferdinand. "I've been raised on them."

More and more Lloyd Douglas, pep man down at the "Y," yearned to be back in the quiet dignity of the church. In these years out of the pulpit he had tried to work out a personal faith for his own satisfaction. We were told recently how Daddy used to spend every minute he could spare at the University library reading, how he made friends with Catholic priests and Jewish rabbis and drew them into discussions of their beliefs.

He supplied on Sundays in church pulpits of various denominations and talked earnestly with their ministers. He often returned to the First Congregational Church of Champaign and held long theological discussions with its young minister, Roy Helfenstein. The Congregational Church appealed to him; it was reverent, but simple; it was based on the dignity of a traditional faith, but was adaptable and unbiased.

The summer of 1914 Betty and Mother and I spent at Griswolda, a remote resort on Lake Hamlin across the dunes from Lake Michigan. Daddy came up to be with us during August. I remember only the trails under the pine trees and the blackberry bushes, but Betty has a very vivid recollection of one special day. Everyone always went down to the end of the wharf in the late afternoon to wait for the launch from Ludington to come chugging in with the papers and mail. It was the one time in the day when the camp came together and was a social event.

On this particular day that Betty remembers so well the boat bumped alongside as usual and the skipper threw onto the wharf the stack of newspapers. The top one was black with the headlines: GERMANY INVADES BELGIUM. Somewhere along the line an archduke had been murdered, but that news hadn't registered much in our forest retreat.

In a minute's time the friendly camp had split into two hostile factions. Some of the professors were German and many had spent years studying in Germany. One woman in particular raised her voice hysterically in defense of the Fatherland. Others more gently expressed their decided opinions. Then the people slowly went back to their cottages in little family groups, each gathered about the father holding open the paper.

Mother was distressed and Betty and Daddy excited. The peace was broken. For the rest of August, although the stately pines stood unmoved, the camp was on edge and everyone anxious to get back to town. There was unrest in the air and Daddy wanted to be on the move.

The following spring he was called to the First Congregational Church of Ann Arbor, Michigan. His introduction to that town had been as a speaker at a YMCA rally. The college paper had joyously quoted a letter he had sent them in answer to a request for press data.

> Lloyd C. Douglas, aged 37, able-bodied but not husky. Ran one hundred yards in college but never went to Olympic games in consequence. Member Phi Gamma Delta—worked harder on that than calculus. Also manager of Glee Club which took much time which might otherwise have been squandered on logic. Also managing editor of college paper during which administration it was thought to be a humorous sheet—typographically at all events. Managed to corral degree of AM, meaning in this case "Amused Myself."

His second trip to Ann Arbor was to preach a trial sermon in the Congregational Church. He wanted to be called. It was a congregation which combined Town and Gown and was exactly what he felt he could do best. He came back to Champaign anxiously to await the decision.

In his scrapbook pasted above the official telegram from the church committee and dated hours earlier, is a hip-hip-hooraying one from Wilbur Humphreys, professor of English at Michigan and one of Mother's old beaux. "Pack your trunks," it reads. "Unanimous vote in your favor."

In May we left Champaign and moved to Ann Arbor, where we lived for six years—the longest time we ever stayed in any one place.

6

The Town of Beautiful Trees

ANN ARBOR—HAPPY JOB." These words are written on a sheet of paper on which Daddy briefly jotted an outline for the second volume of his memoirs. Betty and I have pored over these scrawls hopefully, but they are too cryptic to be of much assistance. The six long years in Ann Arbor, packed with events, he sums up in two words—"happy job."

We arrived there in the spring. The house which was being prepared for us was not to be ready until fall. At first we lived in a boardinghouse and then moved to spend the summer in a large mansion whose owners were abroad. Some of the rooms were closed to us and the blinds drawn. We had to be very careful of all the furniture, and also the temperamental colored cook who had been left on guard and considered us squatters.

There were no children anywhere. Betty and I would creep into the darkened drawing room and sit in the great plush chairs which were damp in the cracks and smelled of mildew. Upstairs a beautiful cat lay on the guest room bed, but would have nothing to do with us. Our own dog Romie was living with the Humphreys, for the fearsome cook did not like dogs, and we saw him only on visits.

Ann Arbor dozed under its roof of leaves. The few summer students, serious and mature, went steadfastly about the business of learning, doing nothing to disturb the summer quiet. Daddy welcomed the opportunity to get the feel of the town and church before September when, on one day, the whole place would quicken and spring to clamoring activity.

We moved to the new house on Cambridge Road shortly before college opened. Much of our old furniture had been disposed of when we left Champaign and our parents had bought many new pieces in August at Mack's big sale. It was exciting to see the strange new things being carried into the new house, but also wonderful to see again after so many months the big old brass bed with the loose knobs being set up in Daddy's and Mother's room and the curly-maple bedroom furniture with which they had started housekeeping.

The moving men struggled in with the upright piano—friend of the old days, and the tall, bulging Victrola. Betty and I also eyed with recognition a long blanket box which was installed in the guest room. Betty tells me this was actually a rough box for a coffin which Mother had upholstered with old quilts. It was to this abominable piece of furniture we were always led by our father when we were to be spanked—I for telling lies, Betty for her many varied and colorful sins.

By September we were all settled: the books on the shelves, the curtains made and hanging at the windows, the dog restored to us; and Daddy prepared to meet the onslaught. Then one day the skies cracked and the shouting, whooping students began to pour in. Overnight Ann Arbor became a town of young people. I shall never forget the autumns there: millions of red and yellow leaves drifting lightly down, blanketing the ground, lying deep in the gutters for children to scuffle on their way home from school. Everything was tinged with an orange haze. On Saturday afternoons for miles around the air vibrated with the intense excitement concentrated on the football game at Ferry Field. From time to time like distant thunder we could hear the great roar, "Misshh-i-gaan. Misshh-i-gaan." Sometimes we would hear bloodcurdling war whoops and rattling wheels. Rushing out we would see a rough farm wagon passing the house with half-naked boys streaked with red paint leaping around it like wild Indians—Michigamua initiation.

The town was built around the sprawling campus with its many-styled buildings, softened into harmony by their drapery of vines. To get any place (our church) we crossed the campus by the Diagonal Walk, passing under the Engineering Arch where often in the fall one saw freshmen, their trousers rolled up, scrubbing the stones under the imperious direction of the wicked sophomores.

That first year was one of adjustment and settling. Everyone in the church was friendly and anxious to make things go. The students flocked to the Sunday Service with more and more enthusiasm and the new regime carried on much in the way it had always gone under the greatly revered and often quoted former pastor, Reverend Carl Patton. It was a big friendly church—a congregation of families. The students felt the paternal atmosphere and were drawn to it. Before the Sunday Service began the members stopped in the vestibule to chat before allowing themselves to be led to their pews by the pleasantly chatting ushers. It was a cheerful, social gathering and about as reverent as a good old church supper.

The choir was made up of boys—mostly children of the members. It was considered a great feeder for the church, for what parents would not come to see their sons, innocent and lovely, dressed in solemn vestments, standing in the choir box lifting their little voices in sacred song? The innocence did not often hold during the length of the service: notes were passed, whispering and giggling broke out from time to time, and not infrequently a silent writhing convulsion seemed to pass over their entire formation as though an underwater explosion had taken place.

The choir had been highly prized by Dr. Carl Patton. When he had stood in the pulpit preaching and the restless tumult of the boys became noticeably audible, he would snap his fingers behind his back for silence. But Daddy could not take this good-natured attitude; Betty and I could have foretold that from the start. For one thing there was his bent septum to be considered. But above that was the nervous exhilaration with which he laid, each week, his sermon before the people. So much of his soul's fiber had gone into every sentence that any distraction was agony to him. Then too, he came more and more to believe that one small portion of the week—that brief hour and a half on Sunday morning—could surely be set aside for the concentrated worship of God.

However he bided his time. He sat on the platform in the tall spired chair and watched the people stop to greet friends and lean over the pews to exchange gossip with the neighbors. He read the scriptures while the ushers bowed in the straggling late-comers. He announced all the tedious list of church events for the week, what the Ladies' Aid Society were up to and details of the new eggbeater they were selling in aid of foreign missions. But all the time he was forming in his mind how a perfect religious service should move—with quiet dignity and an atmosphere of meditation.

Meanwhile life was full and joyous. There was enough conflict to keep things lively, but the arms of the church took us in. Under the auditorium were the sprawling Sunday School rooms decorated with Bible pictures and branching furnace pipe. There, once a month, were held the church suppers. The food was unsurpassed: home-cooked by ladies with reputations at stake, and served hot from the church kitchen. After the supper, when the grownups fell into heated discussions of church problems, the children crept away in pairs or little groups, careful to avoid much notice, later coming together in shivering excitement to play hide-and-seek or tell ghost stories in the great black auditorium above. I can remember lying with my nose pressed deep into the dusty pew cushion and hearing a sepulchral voice moan, "Where is my golden arm?" or the horrid shriek, "Ivory Soap!"

At home life was also sweet. Cambridge Road curved among the comfortable homes of faculty people. Inside, their houses were apt to be a little cluttered and shaped to the human figure. Books lay open upon tables, and dust was not flicked away the very day it settled. Across the street from us lived the Karpinskis (Mathematics) and their six children, and the Boyntons (Architecture) and their three and at the corner the Riggses (Engineering) and their big family welcomed the neighbors into the garden. "Get out of the trees," Professor Riggs would call in his lovingly remembered impedimented speech. "If you want cherries come to the house and ask for them."

Betty and I soon got to know all the neighbors. It took longer for Mother and Daddy, but when spring came and the men stepped out to putter in the bulbs or stroll about smoking their pipes, nodding acquaintances stopped to chat. "Why don't you and your wife step over when you get the children in bed?" People rarely had real parties; they just left the door open and stayed home.

Daddy and Professor Boynton took to each other on a wide range of subject—one of them fishing. Their idea of fishing was to drive to one of the small lakes around Ann Arbor, rent a boat and row out to a spot where they could continue their conversation without interruption. Of course they took their fishing tackle along, but not often did they come back with anything but colds and mosquito bites. They were generally plagued by foul weather. One time they came home drenched and disgruntled at the end of the first day of what had been planned to be a three-day camping trip. The rain had not been the ordinary variety—much more penetrating. They had managed to get their tent up and a little fire going, and had put a can of beans on to heat. As they huddled dismally over the fire trying to shield it from the rain, the can had suddenly exploded from some mysterious chemistry within and shot beans to an astonishing distance.

It must have been a very large can, for as they described it to us there was no part of their encampment which escaped. "I had two in my hatband," Daddy said.

Many years later Daddy wrote to Mary Peabody of North Manchester concerning another expedition he took with a professor in Ann Arbor.

May 6 1942

No— I don't think there is anything so peculiar about falling off a bicycle. I wonder that so many of our better people contrive to stay on as well as they do. When we lived in Ann Arbor (I was invited by a genial old Professor, who owned a country week-endish sort of cottage, to bicycle out there with him and spend the day. I rented one. I don't believe the better ones are for rent. The machine I got was substantial enough: I know it weighed more than I did, and on the several occasions when it fell on me I couldn't help observing what a really durable thing it was.

After we left the asphalt and wobbled off onto a sandy road, with two deep flivver-ruts running parallel and a large crest of soft sand in the middle; and on either side of the ruts, great clumps of thistles, unkleberry weeds, stinkwort burrs, and a new kind of imported nettle known as the Undetachable, I began to view my holiday in the country with an anxiety that had in it just a trace of distaste. The old man rode on ahead, skillfully piloting his vehicle in one of the ruts. He had an authentic talent for it; I could see that. I daresay it would not have bothered him to have done a trip on a tight-rope across Niagara. He didn't look around to see how I was getting on or off, but moved gracefully up the road, minding his own business. I was grateful for this. As his Spiritual Advisor, and Moral Shepherd, I might have been embarrassed had he hovered near me with solicitude. With fine courtesy, he kept far ahead, and whenever I had a little accident (at first caused by the machine scooping itself sideways in the sand and piling its bulk over me) I could speak to my borrowed bicycle in whatever language seemed suitable to the occasion. I learned to swear that day. Now and then during my youth, I had used strong terms to express my emotion, but—by comparison—all my previous comments on the undesirability of some small misfortune were quite flabby and attenuated stuff.

Falling off on a comparatively level terrain was not difficult and resulted in only minor damages. But, by-n-by the country grew rough. It was pleasant walking up the hills; through deep sand, trudging along-side Satan's Toy; but the trip down the hill (and who would be ass enough not to ride?) was a hazardous adventure. I always knew when we had arrived at the exact bottom of the hill, for the hill and I would reach bottom at the same time.

At length we drew up at the cottage, the Professor a good half hour ahead. He smiled benevolently when he saw me twitching down the lane.

"I'm afraid you've scratched your nose a little," he said. "It seems to have been bleeding."

"It's nothing," I said, nonchalantly. "I sometimes get nosebleed when I exercise."

"Your trousers," he said, "are torn across the knee."

"I like them that way," I said.

"You didn't fall off; did you," he asked, pleasantly.

"What do *you* think," I muttered. "Do I look like a person who would be likely to fall off a bicycle?"

"Yes," said he, soberly.

Daddy also went on fishing trips with Hal Seeley. Mr. Seeley was a business man, prosperous from the very beginning of an unusual career. He and Daddy enjoyed the same kind of humor and after we left Ann Arbor they continued to the end of Daddy's life to exchange letters which make very funny reading.

Uncle Hal had never been what you could call an ardent churchgoer, but out of loyalty to his friend Lloyd he accompanied his wife to morning service as many Sundays as he was in town. One beautiful Sunday morning in early summer he decided to play hooky just for once and have a game of golf. Surely he would never be missed in the congregation—that solid pack of faces; nor did he expect to meet his minister when at noon, shouldering his heavy bag of clubs, he started for home. But that Sunday Daddy had made an after-church call which had taken him several blocks from his usual beat. Mr. Seeley was horrified to see coming toward him, unmistakable, dressed in solemn Sunday clothes and carrying clasped in his hands a little black book, the person he least wished to meet at that moment.

The sinner shot wild glances at the shrubbery and trees, but it seemed unlikely he could hide successfully. The distance between him and his minister was rapidly shortening. He had surely been seen. He shoved the big bag of clubs as far behind as possible and continued on, slinking a little and smiling sheepishly. His weekday, story-swapping pal came sternly toward him, no smile of recognition lighting his features. They faced each other in silence. Then with an expression of grieved reproach Daddy raised two fingers in pontifical blessing. "Benedicti," he intoned and passed on.

During the first years on Cambridge Road the United States was not at war, but the war in Europe was an important fact in our lives. Betty and I ate the crusts of our bread, which in some involved way seemed to help the little Belgian children. We wore white stockings even to school because the new dye in the black and brown ones was inferior to the old German dyes and came off on our legs. All the cartoons in the *Literary Digest* were about Uncle Sam and John Bull and the Kaiser. We could always tell the Kaiser by his pointed helmet and dripping sword. But the pictures were not really funny; the jokes in the *Congregationalist* were much better. Daddy's sermons contained more and more comments on the political situation. He progressed over the months from an attitude of thankfulness that America was not involved in the war to a strong conviction that she should leap in and assist without further provocation.

But we became used to war talk; our family life went on unchanged. In the daytime Daddy was much taken up with church meetings and duties. Mother too was busy with church affairs, but was more at home. We can remember the ladies coming to our house to pack the barrels of clothing to be sent to the foreign missionaries. Everything was mended and cleaned before being folded away in the depths of the barrel. There were clothes for the little children in the families—things that Betty and I would loved to have had—and toys too. I always thought that to be a missionary's child would be most desirable in every way.

In the evenings our parents were almost always home. Often Daddy would read aloud to us all. We loved to hear him read for he could make a story very vivid and the characters stand alive, although he never acted or changed his voice for their parts. Mother read to us too when we three were alone, and could be made to repeat old favorites any number of times. Daddy was always bent upon educating us and steadily enriching the diet.

In the late fall the Sears, Roebuck catalogue came and we spent evening after evening poring over its fascinating pages. Betty and I would ponder the toys, reading the description of each marvelous article: real-hair doll wigs, tiny cans of playhouse food, little trunks with lock and key. Mother was attracted by galoshes and one year ordered some that came halfway up her leg and fastened with buttons inside a scalloped edge. Daddy concentrated on the food and made long lists for the order blank. "Now these kippered herring sound good. We ought to be able to use a dozen cans. They've got a special kind of sardine without bones, Besse. You ought to like that, and here's cod salted down in a bucket; don't you think I should get two buckets of that?"

Mother was never very fond of smoked fish although she tried hard. "You'd better not work on that grocery list before dinner, dear. After you've eaten perhaps one bucket of salt cod will seem enough."

Daddy liked to look at the pages of hardware too. He loved good tools, although he never seemed to have the proper one for the job at hand. He was always yearning for the day when he could have his own workbench and turn out fine pieces of carpentry. Once he did actually make quite a good doll bed for Betty from a box some medical equipment had come in. It stood up well through many tests of strength—our bulldog, Romie, often chose to push out the long-suffering dolls and climb in himself—but we could never unstick the big paper label on the foot of it which pictured a fine commodious bedpan.

When Mother and Daddy were first married they took a correspondence course in bookbinding. We carried the little tools and heavy press around from parsonage to parsonage for years, but the only book they ever bound was Bulfinch's work on Greek mythology neatly done in green burlap.

Romie, the beloved bulldog who would wait at night until Mother and Daddy were settled reading and then creep back upstairs to our bedroom and snuggle under the covers with us— Romie one bitter day passed to his reward. He was so missed in the neighborhood that the Riggses bought one like him. "I never thought after seven children," said Mrs. Riggs, "that I would get up at night to cover a dog."

For a while we had no animal at all. Then one day the circus came to town and Daddy, who loved circuses, took Betty and me. Mother was sick in bed and could not go. After the main show was over Daddy said: "Now we must find something to take home to Mother for a surprise."

We looked at the colored balloons and whips and funny hats, wondering if they would please her, and then along came a man selling tiny white puppies. Just the thing for Mother!

Betty and I took turns carrying the woolly little dog inside our jackets and when we got home we all rushed up to Mother's room and laid it in her arms. It waddled and tumbled over the humps in the covers in a darling way and Mother said we couldn't have found anything she wanted more. "What kind of a dog is he?" she asked.

Well, we couldn't say, but that didn't matter. "He has a very well-shaped head," said Daddy. "Anyone can see he's a thoroughbred."

We called him Theodore after Daddy's favorite President. Theodore grew and grew, he also ate and ate. Sometimes he would go for long walks and get his own food, bringing home parcels of meat still wrapped in paper and string just as the butcher's boy had left it at some back door.

"Is that really a dog?" the neighbors asked.

It was questionable. Theodore grew larger every day but he never seemed to lose his puppy woolliness. "If he baa-ed I'd say he was a sheep," Daddy said.

People began to laugh at Theodore on the street. Mother said, "Don't you think he would look better if we clipped him? Besides, he must be dreadfully hot with all that long wool."

Her suggestion was considered very sensible and as usual our family acted at once. We all went out to the back yard and Mother held the dog while Daddy worked with the scissors. He began under Theodore's chin and clipped down to his waist. "I wonder if we are doing a good thing," said Mother. "He seems so pink. He may be chilly without any covering at all."

Daddy stood up and surveyed his handiwork. Theodore was indeed a curious sight. Above he was very naked, below he appeared to be wearing some kind of cowboy pants. "This has been a mistake," thundered Daddy. "That dog looks dreadful. Get him a shirt to wear."

For quite a while after that Theodore ran about in an old shrunken blue sweater of Betty's. He was very fond of Daddy and liked to follow him when he went to make church calls. We were happy to take Theodore about with us, but Daddy was much too proud. He didn't like the tone of voice people used when they asked, "Is that your animal?"

Finally we had to give Theodore to the milkman. He stole and became so clever and discriminating in his choice of loot that it began to look as though he were being coached at home.

"I doubt if he was a dog at all," Daddy said to console us. "I'm sure he is much happier on a farm where he can play with other sheep."

In 1917 the United States at last joined the war. The University of Michigan became a scene of dreadful confusion. Many students and faculty men enlisted, and the boys who were left were organized into the Students' Army Training Corps. All was disorder. Conflicting directions were heard from every side. And above all the hysterical scream for patriotism. There were many people of German extraction in Michigan; all were suspect. Daddy became very active in the Liberty Loan Bond drive and went about the state delivering a lecture called "Buy Bonds or Wear Them." He was also on a committee of men who drove through the country around Ann Arbor browbeating the farmers into buying bonds. In later years he often said it was wicked the way they frightened the poor people who still clung to the Fatherland, but at the time they thought they were doing their patriotic duty.

"Somebody is going to put a bomb under our house," Mother would say when Daddy had recounted a conversation with some particularly hard-boiled German farmer.

Mother worked at the Red Cross headquarters on the campus, folding gauze into exact and intricate dressings. By the end of the war she had earned a blue veil and a pin. The veil was most becoming, and even Betty and I, posing in it before her mirror, looked like madonnas of mercy.

In October 1918 the epidemic of influenza struck Ann Arbor. Betty, Mother and I were among the first to come down with it and we were fortunate to get a nurse. She slept in the guest room and Daddy slept on a canvas cot in our unfinished attic with only his overcoat to cover him. Mother was very sick. We knew he was worried about her for when he sat on our beds to play Authors he hardly noticed the way we mispronounced the titles, and sometimes would go off into a long stare at nothing. For a while the doctor came twice a day. It would often be midnight when he paid his second call and when he left Mother's room he would go downstairs and rest on our davenport, while Daddy made coffee and the cheerful smell came floating up the stairs.

The day we went back to school the schools closed—everything closed. People were falling ill at a terrrible rate. The students in army training, closely quartered in makeshift barracks, could not be properly cared for and many died.

We have been given the service our father read at the funeral of one splendid young man who died during this grim scourge which swept the country. The words Daddy spoke so many years ago at the grave of their son are still cherished by the boy's parents.

> . . . and then he stepped out of the ranks to obey another call, proceeding from the abode of those, who like himself, had died in the faith, not having received the promises, but having seen them from afar off, and were persuaded of them, and embraced them. "Wherefor God is not ashamed to be called their God."

One Sunday during this dreadful time the churches were allowed to hold service for their anxious, sorrowing members if all came protected with sterile gauze across their faces. It was an unforgettable experience for the minister of the First Congregational Church to stand before the silent, white-masked audience and pray with them for strength:

> Grant unto us, Almighty God, that when our vision fails, and our understanding is darkened, when the ways of life seem hard, and the brightness of life is gone—to us grant the wisdom that deepens faith when the sight is dim, and enlarges trust when the understanding is not clear.

We have many of the prayers Daddy read during the years of his ministry. They are short and carefully composed; every word is intrinsically the language of the soul. In his sermons he tried to clarify the many uncertainties of Christianity, but in his prayers he spoke the mystic words of faith alone which must surpass understanding.

During the last six months of the war Daddy was chairman of publicity for the YMCA War Fund which was out to raise thirty-five million dollars. His headquarters were in New York City and he spent most of the week there, coming back to Ann Arbor Sunday mornings so late that sometimes his taxi passed members of our congregation on the way to church.

After months of living on the run he got very tired and was apt to drop asleep any old place. One time a lady lecturer came to Hill Auditorium to make a plea for money to help the Belgians. Daddy and several other dignitaries sat on the platform to assist with the program. During her speech the lady paced back and forth before them kicking the short narrow train of her evening gown cleverly behind her heels at each sharp turn. Betty and I had been taught not to giggle at public performances, but some of our little friends, sitting primly with their parents in the audience, were seen to shake from time to time, and let out choked noises which were quickly stifled.

Toward the end of her impassioned speech the lecturer pulled down a large screen and we prepared ourselves to see her lantern slides. The men behind her moved their little gilt chairs to the far sides of the platform and the lights went off. One by one the pictures were jerked across the white screen: the battle-fields, her demolished château, and one, I especially remember, of her grand piano which the Germans had filled with marmalade. The audience sat in the darkness for a long time while the voice droned on, the long stick tapped the screen, and the lantern machine hummed and clicked. Then quite suddenly the lights went on again. We all straightened up, blinking and rubbing our eyes, but Daddy above us on the platform did not stir. There he was painfully extended upon the inadequate little chair. His head was bent back at the neck and he snored softly.

During those months we saw little of him; he came home to

preach and get fresh clothes and then was off again. He described New York to us, the skyscrapers and the huge crowds. "Broadway at night is just as bright as day," he said. "You can easily read a paper on the street at midnight." Betty and I were disappointed when we finally saw Broadway; we could tell it was night if we looked up at the sky.

He would describe to us the docks and the big ocean steamers. "You can't imagine how big they are," he said. "Someday we're all going to get on one of those boats and go steaming down the river out to sea. We're going to foreign lands, kids, someday." We liked best to hear about the animals in Central Park and the marvelous penguins at the Battery. I've never yet seen penguins who could do all the delightful things he told us those penguins could do. Each time he came home he brought us a present; sometimes a book, sometimes just a little metal puzzle, but always something. One time he brought Mother a pair of purple silk stockings and she had them in her drawer for years waiting for something to wear with them.

When the war was finally over our parents decided to have a big second honeymoon. They were deeply in love. Their marriage seemed never to settle into the ordinary kind, but was always a very alive affair. We thought it quite natural to see Daddy take Mother into his arms and hold her for minutes in a long embrace. We thought all married people did that. Daddy was very demonstrative with us too. Mother kissed us only at bedtime, but Daddy needed much more affection. We were very sparing with ours and never realized how he delighted in our rare and spontaneous caresses.

They were going to Detroit for their honeymoon, and Betty and I were to stay with the Wilguses, church members, who lived in a big old-fashioned house which had long vistas of polished floor, deep windows and an odd glassed-in room set on the roof. Gay Wilgus often painted paper dolls for us and allowed us to play with her entrancingly furnished dollhouse. We were as excited about the prospect of our three days as

Mother and Daddy were looking forward to the shows they planned to see and the fancy room they were to have at the Book-Cadillac Hotel.

When all was packed and we had been stuffed with directions on correct behavior, the rattle-bang old taxi arrived and the four of us piled in to go, first to the Wilguses, and then on to the station with Mother and Daddy. Betty and I sat on the little jump seats facing them and off we went in a laughing holiday mood. Two blocks down Cambridge Road when Mother was again saying, "Now do remember to be little ladies—" the taxi door on my side flew open and I fell out.

I don't remember how we got home, but I do remember the pain and concern of my parents. My collarbone was broken, but far worse was my unhappiness at having all our fine plans wiped out in one stroke. The honeymoon was off for us all. Betty stood forlornly in the corner, not knowing what to do with herself in all the confusion, her brown eyes huge and glistening with unwept tears. After the doctor had come and pushed and plastered my shoulder into place Daddy and Betty went downtown. He treated her to a strawberry soda and together they spent the afternoon shopping for toys and food to beguile me during my recovery. They returned laden with parcels. They were very much alike; their enthusiasm always carried them on wild waves of generosity. I suppose that a good part of the money set aside for the celebration in Detroit vanished that day.

Illness in our family was always very seriously regarded. "Call the doctor," Daddy would say at once. Any doctor had a stimulating effect upon him. He felt an inherent brotherhood with them. To every word which dropped from their lips he gave the closest attention. Awe was in his eyes as he watched them go about their bedside performances. They brought out the best in him too; he was never more witty than in their company.

In his last years of illness he came many times to the brink of death, but never too near not to rouse when the doctor came.

Once in the hospital in Los Angeles when he was sinking fast and no one knew what to do, Dr. Leland Chapman leaned over his bed and gravely asked: "Dr. Douglas, have you ever had any allergies?"

The sunken eyelids quivered and slowly opened. "Yes."

"What?" Dr. Chapman leaned nearer to hear.

The weak voice sighed the answer, "Singing commercials."

In Ann Arbor Daddy had occasion to visit the big University Hospital many times. Besides seeing his own parishioners, he visited out-of-town patients whose ministers had written him of them. He became so acquainted with the life of the hospital that he seemed part of the organization. Doctors would call him in when they had patients who were depressed and needed spiritual treatment. His method was different with each one. He offered hope to those who wanted hope, but he didn't believe in being fatuously optimistic with desperately sick people. If they wanted to talk of death he let them. In his book of advice to young ministers he wrote:

> You at twenty-seven contemplate death with such distaste that you imagine everybody else must feel the same way about it. You fancy your best contribution can be made by attempting to distract attention from this mysterious warder of the exit gates of life. "Oh, my good friend, you mustn't be thinking about things like that!" you are tempted to say to your parishioner.
>
> Very sick people do not wish to hear so much about the busy, bustling events of active life. The report of these matters only isolates them still further from our mundane world. They do not greatly care what happened at the last church supper or that there is a new concrete walk in front of the parsonage. If they wish to talk to you about death, go to it with them, and talk as helpfully as you know how on this subject. Do not evade it.

It is a curious thing how many people thought the novelist, Lloyd Douglas, was a medical doctor. The idea persisted even among the reviews of his last memoirs in which he referred many times to his various churches. He wrote with authority on operations, and the hospital atmosphere he so often described in his books was taken from years of first-hand observation. He soaked himself in medical lore for love of it. Often in Ann Arbor surgeons would tell him when they were to perform an unusual operation and invite him to watch.

He said he would not have made a very good doctor. He could not disassociate himself from other people's suffering. And, he often confessed, "I have no talent for accuracy."

But we thought he would have made a splendid doctor. When Betty or I hurt ourselves to a point requiring a bandage Daddy was always on the spot. His sympathy was not lessened because of the gleam of anticipation with which he firmly led us to his medicine cabinet. While we stood with tears on our lashes, but the cut member extended in confidence, he concentrated on the delicate business of wrapping on strips of gauze and plaster. The result was always elaborate, but beautiful.

In 1918, after the war was over, the minister of the First Congregational Church turned his attention back to the details of his Sunday morning service. By this time he had won the affection of most of his congregation. Through sorrow and gladness he had attended them, and in many families the memory of his kindness would outweigh any eccentricities he might demonstrate. He was confident they would support him in his new program. The service was to begin with a period of meditation. The music was to be inspirational during this time and nothing must be allowed to break the mood of it. The doors would be closed at ten-thirty sharp and no one would be admitted until the next interlude, twenty minutes later. At no time were announcements to be read from the pulpit. These would be on separate bulletins to be passed out after church. On the regular bulletin would be printed the responsive readings and the hymns and there would be no need to search about for books or leaf through pages. It was hoped the congregation would get used to the new order of service and co-operate that it might move with simplicity and uninterrupted reverence.

The church music was to be the biggest innovation. The Boys' Choir had gone a few months before. The manner of their going was much more dramatic than the mere statement of the fact. One Sunday, halfway through his sermon, like a bolt from the blue Daddy had broken off in the middle of a sentence and turned around to face the suddenly quiet and surprised youngsters. "I want you all to get out," he had ordered. There was a painful silence over the church while the boys filed out. Betty and I in our pew with Mother bled with humiliation. Next Sunday several families were absent.

He must have had a strong hold on the people that they accepted all his peculiarities with no more than a healthy amount of grumbling. In the book *The History of the Congregational Church in Ann Arbor*, Mr. Davis says:

> It is true Dr. Douglas' views were broad and liberal and he gave only slight emphasis to creeds, but to the thousands who came in contact with him either on Sunday mornings or at other times he was a genuine inspiration.
>
> True, he was responsible for the abolition of the Boys Choir, but his sensitive nature could not brook the whispering and annoyances that sometimes emanated from it while he was preaching. Under his direction there has developed a most beautiful and inspiring order of worship, including musical accomplishments, probably unsurpassed elsewhere.

Daddy had long wished to have Earl Moore, who later became dean of the university School of Music, as his organist and choir conductor. Mr. Moore, though greatly interested in Daddy's ideas on church music, refused to be lured to the position as long as he would have to wrestle with the Boys' Choir.

The morning after their painful expulsion Daddy burst into

Mr. Moore's office. "I want you to take over my music next Sunday," he announced.

Mr. Moore raised his eyebrows into his high, bare forehead. "And the boys?" he queried skeptically.

"They're gone!" Daddy said. "Get something together. A quartet will see us through until June. During the summer we can work out our plans for fall."

The service they eventually perfected was built like a symphony, from the first call to worship of the mighty organ to the last quiet blessing. True to the promise, the doors were closed at ten-thirty and no one was admitted for twenty minutes until the service of meditation was over. The college president arrived late one morning and was kept waiting in the vestibule. After that he was always in his pew on time.

Very quickly the congregation slipped into the mood of the new service and allowed themselves to be benefited from the period of quiet reverence at a time when outside events were a turmoil of anxiety.

Behind the smooth performance of choir, organ and minister were hours of preparation and careful timing. Mr. Moore told Betty and me recently that he and Daddy worked out every step of the service as accurately as a modern radio program, so that one thing flowed into the next without a jarring note. To keep this mood unbroken in the face of any unexpected development Mr. Moore kept under the organ bench Dvořák's biblical songs, and if he received a signal from the minister that something was amiss he held up an indicating number of fingers to Bob Dieterle, who immediately arose and filled in the gap with his beautiful baritone.

"Your father had a highly developed sense of theatre and perfect timing," Mr. Moore told Betty and me. "I consider those years I worked with him the most creative of my life."

Always after the Rotary Club luncheon at the Michigan

Union, Daddy and Earl Moore had a little conference to discuss how things had gone the previous Sunday and review their plans for the following one. One time in 1920 they met as usual and Mr. Moore handed Daddy the program of anthems, hymns and solos which were being prepared by the choir for the next Sunday.

Daddy's eyes ran down the list and suddenly he raised a horrified hand to his head. "Earl! You can't do this to me."

Earl Moore's face expressed complete bewilderment.

"Don't you know," groaned Daddy, "what happens at midnight this coming Saturday?"

Mr. Moore thought and then remembered that at the stroke of twelve that night Prohibition was to go into effect in the United States. The solo he had chosen for Jimmie Hamilton to sing was "Ho! Everyone That Thirsteth."

The Sunday service, after the first twenty minutes of meditation, was built around the sermon. If it was seasonal the music was chosen to fit, if inspirational the music followed the mood. Again the benediction might be quiet, or the congregation sent out on echoes of the triumphant Sevenfold Amen.

Mr. Shirley Smith, a member of the church and intimate friend of Daddy's, wrote to him many years later concerning that particular piece of music. Their correspondence was unbroken from the time we left Ann Arbor until Daddy's death, and the droll exchange of sardonic observations on life make their reading a delight. Mr. Smith wrote:

I think you will laugh indulgently at the thing that most often sends me away from church in an unholy frame of mind: the "Seven-Fold Amen" with which the choir delays our departure after the service is really over. It seems a terrible and tedious waste of time to me. Perhaps the real trouble for me lies in "Seven-Fold Crotchets" of age seventy-three.

LCD replied:

In the event that, after reflection, you should tardily feel some embarrassment over your shocking confession of distaste for the Seven-Fold Amen, I may be able to ease your misgivings by admitting that one of my pet aversions is The Hallelujah Chorus. Over a period of nearly two score years I have heard this thing yelped by all sorts of choirs: professional and amateur, good, bad and worse; and it is my considered judgment (though this is a strictly private admission, never to be uttered outside the Chapter House, and then only in a whisper) that this tiresome opus of the late Professor Handel is, unto me, even as a bad pain in the neck.

Let me recall, from memory, selected passages: Haaaa–le–lu–yah! Haaaaaaa–lee–luu–yah! Ha–a–a–a–leee–luuu–Jah! Luu–jah! Luu–jah! Haa–haa–ha–lee–luu–lee–luu–lee–luu! Lulu! Hallee! OOjah! Ooh–jah! Ann–dee–shall–reign for–ever–ann–devver! Lulu! Hallee! OOjah! For–evver–ann–devver! Ann–dee–shall reign–Lulu–Lulu! Forrrr–evver–Lulu!–ann–Ooojah!–Oojah!–Devvvvv–err! Hallee! Lulu! He–shall! Evver! Lujah! Lujah! Amen! Hallee! Amen! He–shall! Amen–f'revver! Amen–Lulu!

Daddy took delight in the large numbers of students who came to hear him regularly. Some part of each sermon was designed for them and they regarded him with a cheerfulness which at times became almost embarrassing. One Sunday he announced solemnly before the Offertory that for some time the collection plates had included an unnecessary number of pennies. "You can't buy anything for a penny," he said. "Neither can the church."

The next Sunday the students came with sagging pockets. When the collection was taken the ushers had to empty the plates several times during the course of their duties. Everyone knew that in the balcony, especially, something unusual was going on. When at last the collection plates were brought down the center aisle and laid on the altar table they were piled high with coins —pennies, all pennies.

Occasionally the *Michigan Daily* found something on Dr. Douglas which they could leap upon with cries of joy. In a letter to Dr. Leonard Parr, the present minister of the Ann Arbor church, Daddy wrote:

> One time during the first World War I announced on the bulletin board that the next Sunday I would review a book which was then causing a great deal of chatter. It was entitled Will There Be Any Religion Left? The bulletin board read:

> SUNDAY MORNING, MAY 26TH
> HYMN NO. 45
> LLOYD C. DOUGLAS PREACHES
> WILL THERE BE ANY RELIGION LEFT?

I was kidded about it in the Michigan Daily and the quip was copied in many University papers throughout our beaddled land.

Betty and I went back to Ann Arbor on our recent sentimental pilgrimage. We scuffled about through the leaves on the campus trying to ignore all the new buildings which had gone up since our time. One entire morning we spent going through old files of the *Michigan Daily* looking for some doggerel verses which we remembered Daddy had written for the editorial page of the college paper. We came upon them in the 1919 volume. The first one carried this editorial note:

> The above verses with some others which will appear in later issues of The Daily were written by a prominent man of Ann Arbor who is very much interested in student affairs, but who, in his own words, wants "his anonymity preserved."

The series of verses contain advice to freshman in the form of startled observations of the newcomer to the campus, and the wise answers of the old-timer. The subjects amusingly discussed are table etiquette, the little girl he left at home, studying amidst confusion, and words of warning to the overconfident frosh, as for example:

The New-Comer says:

> Last night at nine some friends of mine
> Whom I have met quite lately
> Strolled in to call from 'cross the hall,
> I greeted them sedately.
>
> They seemed inclined to let me find
> The theme for conversation
> So I told all I could recall
> Of High School recreation.
>
> The medal that I captured at
> Our contest in athletics
> The prize I won when we put on
> The amateur dramatics.
>
> I hope that they come back some day
> Their visit was delightful;
> Though I could see they envied me
> They were not one bit spiteful.

The Old-Timer Replies:

> My friend this means you've spilled the beans;
> I shudder at your story.
> No doubt these men will come again
> But when they do, be sorry.

Hereafter when some genial men
Drop in for conversation
Be careful lest you prove a pest
Inviting castigation.

Last year a lad—he was not bad,
Just talkative and flighty
Addressed a loud and merry crowd
On State Street in his nighty.

In 1920 the members of the Ann Arbor church presented Daddy with a car—a Model T Ford. It was supposed to be a surprise but Mother was forewarned and decided to tell Daddy lest the idea be utterly unacceptable to him. Goodness knows he loathed the long treks of sidewalk he had to cover each day in the course of his ministry, and streetcars were always an abomination to him, but her whispered news of an automobile was received with dread and alarm. Would he, so inept at things mechanical, ever learn to drive it? Having done so, would he ever have the courage to set out in the contraption alone, or worse, with the responsibility of his innocent family?

When the committee drove up with the shiny new Ford all these fears were disguised under exclamations of surprise and joy. Daddy walked all around the car enthusiastically exclaiming over every gleaming accessory. Betty and I were wild with excitement and never doubted for a minute that Daddy would soon master all the buttons and levers and cranks.

The men from the church received his profuse thanks and waved the gift to him. "The driving lessons are included too," they said. "Here's George from the shop all ready to take you out now." George sat behind the wheel and beamed. "Just hop in, Reverend; you'll get the feel of it in no time."

Daddy looked at Mother, Betty and me and lifted the corners of his lips weakly.

George said to the committeemen: "Any of you gentlemen want to come along?"

They backed away mumbling of other engagements. "Sorry . . . no, no."

Daddy climbed onto the seat beside the driver with the traditional resolution of all who go for a little spin in a tumbril. The car leaped off with a clatter of tin on tin. We who were left stood in a hushed group at the curb and watched them go. "Don't worry, Mrs. Douglas," said one of the parishioners, "he'll do all right."

Mother's fingers were pressed against her mouth. "It's just that I wonder if he will be able to steer it," she quavered. "He's never been able to run the lawn mower in a straight line."

Daddy took to driving like a duck. George, his teacher, told him he had never seen anyone so quick to pick it up, and Daddy came home from his lessons exhilarated by his new skill. The car was a dream, he said. "She's a humdinger." It was the beginning of his long love affair with automobiles. After that he never walked half a block if he could help it. He always sat at the wheel relaxed and pleased, king of the world.

He learned to be a very good driver and had no real accidents all the many years, although he became involved in hundreds of awkward situations. Of course, the busy little pieces under the car's hood always remained a mystery to him, but he was lofty about that. "Oil burning off the spark plugs," he would say when we called his attention to hot smells coming from the engine. Alarming noises were "hard place on the brush." The worst that could happen was "bands slipping"; then it was time to go in for repairs.

They still tell a story around Ann Arbor about Daddy and his Model T. It happened when the car was new and on one of the first occasions when he had it out alone. The time came when it was urgently necessary to replenish the gas, a dreaded business due to the many obstacles to be avoided surrounding the pump. They didn't have big open gas stations in those days and it was quite a trick to maneuver oneself into a position to connect with the supply. However, Daddy managed it after much churning and backing and came to a stop, pleased with his adroitness. He turned off the engine and leaned back in relief. "Fill 'er up," he said to the attendant.

The man stood admiring and smiling, but did not move.

Daddy smiled too. "I want the car filled up," he said.

Still the pleasant attendant stood.

"Well?" said Daddy, a little edge of impatience in his voice.

"Well?" said the attendant.

"I want some gasoline. You know: gasoline for my tank."

"Sure, I know," said the gas man, "but you gotta get out. You're sittin' on it."

Daddy always considered it the worst of bad taste to show fear. He probably had plenty of it inherited from Grandmother, who was a bundle of clamoring anxieties, but he never showed it. Through the years Grandmother continued to pay us long visits and often she was taken for trips in the car which she entered on each occasion with protests and warnings of doom. When we got stuck in the mud, or on a hill where we had to back down, she immediately wanted to get out. Daddy would insist she stay in the car. They would have a long sizzling argument, but in the end she got out. Then, alone with the faithful Mother, Betty and me, he would go about the business of extricating us from the dilemma, whatever it was, all the time lecturing us seriously on the importance of staying with the ship.

Other car deportment he impressed upon us was never to scream or even gasp or otherwise show emotion in moments of sharp alarm. This distracted the driver as well as being very bad form. So well were these lessons drummed into our heads that had we seen a fast train bearing down upon us while we were helplessly cooped on the track, Mother, Betty and I would probably have sat frozen in terror, but silently being good sports about it.

From time to time Daddy would get into heated battles with men who took exception to some of the remarks he made in the pulpit. These rows were generally carried on through letters to the paper where the scathing phrase could be chosen with loving deliberation. Twice he became thus involved with Professor W. H. Hobbs, an eminent geologist, and the second time—over the virtues of President Wilson—they arrived at non-speaking terms.

One wintry day—but we have a letter from Daddy to Shirley Smith describing it:

> I read with interest your account of slippery streets in Ann Arbor through these mid-winter days and recall some of the adventures I myself had years ago in these circumstances. I remember one day, shortly after having received as a gift our beautiful model T Ford Sedan, when I thought to confer a neighborly favor upon Mrs. W. H. Hobbs.
>
> My relation to Mrs. Hobbs was hardly more than a bowing acquaintance, and as for my relation to her husband—we did not even speak to each other on the street.
>
> But that morning when I saw her standing at the top of Washtenaw Hill waiting for the street car, with the wind whistling an eighty mile gale around her, I drew up at the curb and took her in, and right glad she was too, to accept this favor.
>
> She was in the back seat and I was in the front and we careened down the hill pretty fast. It was very slippery and I was still a green driver. I think it was in front of the dental building where things really began to happen. I remember that we made three complete revolutions before we got stopped down in the neighborhood of George Wahr's Bookstore.
>
> I must say for this woman that she was a very good sport. She did not let out one yelp and I was proud of her. I even went back to speaking to W.H.

Daddy soon discovered that the new car added appreciably to his expenses. Aside from the matter of fuel, a minister could not drive around in a mud-spattered vehicle, certainly not take part in a funeral procession unless his car was as well-kept as the shiny one before and behind. As spring came on and the Ann Arbor streets, many of them unpaved, deposited themselves on the sides of the Ford, this problem became urgent.

One morning in late April, when a funeral was to be held in the afternoon, Daddy decided to wash his car himself. We lived now in the Hill Street parsonage and Daddy drove over the wide lawn and stopped close to the house within easy reach of the garden hose. Mother looked out of the kitchen window from time to time and seemed not unduly skeptical of his activities.

"Saving myself two dollars," he called to her. "And a better job at that. Two dollars a week . . . that's eight dollars a month . . . add that up and what have you got? A small fortune in no time." He whistled and sang as the water ran over the sides of the car and settled under the four wheels in the new spring grass.

At length the job was finished. Daddy went around for the last time putting the final polish on the shining fenders. He called us all out to see the effect and we pronounced it a complete triumph of gleaming perfection. All the time the hose lay softly gurgling water under the car until Mother turned it off.

Then Daddy got in and started the engine. The wheels went around faster and faster, but not an inch did they move. The grass flew out in the first few spins, and then the mud shot up in high sprays and fell upon the car in pieces. Daddy got madder and madder. The end of it was that the garage man had to come and haul the car out of a very deep hole and take it off to be washed. Other men were hired to fill in the lawn and replant the grass.

"A small fortune can be saved in no time," quoted Mother, but not for several weeks until Daddy had calmed down and began to tell the story on himself. Mother would never have thought of teasing Daddy in the heat of his anger. Her entire life was spent catering to his moods and doing as much as she could to ease the tension of his nervous energy. What happened to him was the real thing in her day.

I remember once seeing her take the letters from the mailman and, going through them, come upon a bulky envelope—a returned manuscript. She held it against herself for a minute, looking around as though she were considering hiding it, then sorrowfully she laid it on the table.

"Hop on your bicycle dear," she said to me, "and run down to the butcher's for a nice T-bone steak. Tell him you want a big thick one. Daddy must have a good dinner tonight."

It's hard to say what Mother was like in those days. Her children and her husband seemed to be all she thought about. Her smile was patient and sweet, but I remember another smile that sometimes came over her face, a gamin-like grin that seemed too mischievous for a minister's wife. She had only one vice— chewing gum. She considered it a very unladylike habit and not often indulged, but when she did get a piece of gum in her mouth—wax, she called it, she gave it a most energetic workout.

The first summer of the new car we were offered for the month of August a rustic lakeside cottage belonging to some generous parishioners. The lake was about sixty miles from Ann Arbor and we drove there in our Ford. Behind the cottage stood a regiment of pine trees in close formation and Henry, our chicken, was loath to take his airing under their gloom. This chicken did not play a large part in the vacation—in fact that holiday, as all others in our lives, was unmarked by dramatic events—but we feel sure Daddy would like Henry's story included in his biography for he so often told it himself.

In the spring he had brought home twelve chickens, not with a view to the pot, but as an Easter present for Betty and me. As usual after bestowing live gifts and being properly thanked, he didn't want to see any more of them or be consulted on their

care. The chicks made no hit with Betty, for she had been
mortally paralyzed by the sight of feathers since infancy. So
they fell to me and one by one they fell dead—from the cold or
chicken pip or some complaint unknown. At first I buried them
with elaborate ceremony and tombstones, but toward the last of
their numbers I fear they were laid away in haste. One alone survived—Henry.

Betty and my parents did not grieve much at the death of
the chickens. In fact they awaited Henry's end with undisguised
impatience. But the weather took a turn for the better and he
began to perk up and put on weight. He was a very intelligent
and loving chicken and followed me about like a dog. When
summer came and our vacation was being discussed, the family
was resigned to the fact that Henry must be included in the
plans. On the trip to the cottage Betty and I sat on the back
seat of the Ford; she as far as possible into her corner, I holding
the chicken, enclosed to his neck in a paper bag, in my lap. The
next milestone in Henry's life did not occur until fall and I will
tell it later.

Daddy spent most of his time that August fishing. He caught
some fine specimens and was very critical of the way Mother
cooked them. Somewhere he had heard that the ideal way to
cook fish was to wrap them in layers of corn husks and bury
them in a bed of the embers remaining from a very hot fire,
where they would bake in their own sweet succulence, losing no
drop of flavor.

After one especially fine catch he came home and built up
just such a fire and invited us to a feast which he would put on
himself and which, he promised, would be unequalled in our
experience. He wrapped the fish carefully in the corn husks and
when the fire had died down to a rich red glow he laid them deep
in the embers, adding potatoes in their jackets as an extra delight.
Then, to while away the time, he exerted himself to whip up
our appetites with descriptions of the sensations we would feel
when at last the food was set before us. It was very difficult to

wait. From time to time he would haul out a fish and examine it, or probe a potato, but no change could be seen. An hour crawled by and still the food showed no signs of absorbing more than a superficial heat.

At last Mother stole off to the kitchen and began firing up the wood stove. Daddy went out and put his hand under her chin. "You think you have a very foolish husband, don't you?"

She smiled and put her forehead against his shoulder. "No, I don't."

He kissed her and then went out the back door. "Call me when dinner's ready," he said.

Grandfather and Grandmother Porch came to visit us that summer. Grandmother was a composed, charitable lady who never spoke ill of anyone. This made her company restful, but not as exciting as Grandmother Douglas who lived in a continual storm of protest against the ills of the world. Grandfather was a quiet man with a rare but wonderful laugh. Daddy would turn himself inside out to provoke it, and when at last the old white head went back and the great gurgling roar poured out it was ample payment. He had a big moustache which Betty and I referred to between ourselves as "the shredded wheat biscuit." This had to be kissed twice for each visit.

One day the Geifel family, parishioners from the Ann Arbor church, came to picnic and spend the night. We were quite a crowd when we came to load the two boats with the food for our excursion: four children, four parents and the two grandparents. The boat with the outboard motor held five and the rest sat behind in the rowboat to be towed.

We crossed the lake, navigated a small channel and had our picnic lunch on a sandy bar on Bass Lake. The sun was broad in the west when we piled back into the two boats and started for home. It was in the narrow channel that the Evinrude began to complain and show signs of exhaustion. It hiccoughed along a bit farther and then sighed and died.

Daddy and Mr. Geifel took turns hauling at the wheel and

fussing with the little oil cups and whatnot, while we all watched anxiously. There was plenty of fuel; something vital was wrong and they soon admitted their defeat. The heavy oars were fitted into the locks of the motorboat and we started off for the long pull home, still towing the rear load. The four oars rose and fell but never in any kind of rhythm. Daddy always seemed to be leaning forward when Mr. Geifel was leaning back, and the oars whacked each other repeatedly. When Daddy banged his thumb for the second time between the handles, Mr. Geifel suggested politely that he row alone. "It seems difficult for two people to keep together," he said rather doubtfully.

"I'll take over when you're tired; just say the word." Daddy leaned back to rest.

Mr. Geifel struggled and panted and sweated and hauled all the way across the lake with his load of ten. At last we pulled up by our wharf.

"Well done, thou good and faithful servant," Daddy cheered. He leaped gaily out and helped us all up with the rugs and hampers. Mr. Geifel climbed painfully to the wharf and stood mopping the back of his neck.

Daddy untied the two boats and stepped into the first. "Wonder what got into that motor? It's been going so well until now." He gave the wheel a casual spin. Sweet and smooth as molasses it purred into life and took off in a wide circle while the rest of us stood on the wharf and looked with our mouths open.

Mr. Geifel, beet-red and still mopping, seemed stunned for a moment. Then he raised his fist and shook it at Daddy out on the lake. "Lloyd Douglas, I'll never go inside your gol-durned church again," he yelled.

When we went back to town in September, Henry, the chicken, had grown to quite a respectable size. We made him a little home of his own in the back yard and a box to climb on. He would stand and pose like the king of the castle.

One morning very early everyone in our neighborhood who slept anything but the sleep of the dead was awakened by a splendid and triumphant crow. It was Henry, coming of age. After that he couldn't leave the idea alone. He would climb onto his box, stretch his neck and let out crows so terrific that the effort would topple him over and he would lie on the ground quite exhausted for a minute.

"This cannot go on much longer," Daddy said. And when one neighbor registered a written complaint it was agreed upon in a family meeting that Henry must be abolished. Naturally we couldn't eat him ourselves; it was decided that young Edward Crittenden should have him. Edward was recovering from a long illness and Daddy had been in to see him from time to time. "Always take a sick child some little gift," he had written in an article on Pastoral Calls.

Edward was delighted to have the chicken and while his mother was away housing it in the woodshed Daddy told him in full the story of Henry, even to describing how Virginia had rocked him every evening in the country before he would go to sleep.

When Mrs. Crittenden came back to the bedroom she beamed at Edward. "Wasn't it kind of Reverend Douglas to bring you that lovely chicken for your Sunday dinner?"

"Sunday dinner?" wailed Charles. "You mean Henry? You mean eat Henry?"

Daddy rose. "I'm afraid I must be going along," he said.

In 1921 the Christian Century Press brought out a book by Lloyd C. Douglas. It was called *Wanted—A Congregation* and was a development of a series of articles previously published in that journal. It was well received by the clergy and the church press, and paid its own expenses, thereby erasing somewhat the memory of that first little novel which had been such a financial sorrow to its author.

Now with a book published and his church running at top capacity, Daddy began to look restlessly across the fence at further pastures. We recognized the signs. He took an interest in strangers from out-of-town churches who came to hear him. Although none of their offers tempted him his sermons were prepared with extra care when he knew of their coming.

That last winter in Ann Arbor we had a young student girl living in our home, paying part of her tuition by helping Mother. Olive Lockwood became one of the family from the first and Daddy's idiosyncrasies were a matter of concern to her as with us. One particular Sunday we were all aware that an out-of-town committee was to be in the congregation, and Daddy was anxious that the service, of which he was so proud, should that day be an example of perfection. Even before the sermon Olive's quick ear heard the heavy banging of a door in the basement of the church. It was the annoying, hopeless banging of the wind. She waited, expecting someone to find it, but it went on, unrhythmic, exasperating. Daddy finally got up to begin his sermon. Olive imagined she could see him bracing himself for the next thud. She slipped out of the church and went around to the side lower entrance, found the loose door but saw that the latch was broken. When she stepped away it swung slowly open and stood for the wind to catch it again. There was nothing for it but that she remain there all during the sermon holding it shut, like the little Dutch boy at the dike.

When she told Daddy about it at dinner that noon he thought it immensely funny. "So you were the doorkeeper in the House of the Lord," he said.

"Well, I hadn't thought of it that way," she answered, "but I've lived long enough in this family to know about Lloyd Douglas' nerves. The Lord might not have noticed the door banging."

Ann Arbor grew very dear to Mother when she saw that Daddy was thinking of leaving. The very things that made him feel dull and captured were what she loved: their friends, the familiar streets, the well-known ways of doing.

Betty and I were happy but we were always ready for a change. Betty, fourteen years old, was deeply interested in all the activities of high school and she and her girl friends were beginning to cast green looks from afar at certain college men who were popular on the campus. The University represented heaven to her. She knew the names of all the fraternities and sororities and which house was which and how they stood in esteem. She tried hard to drill me in the many combinations of Greek letters and sighed over my lack of interest. My friends and I had our own mystic societies. We drew up elaborate constitutions and elected officers, generally coming to battle over them so that a new society had to be formed, omitting the president of the one before.

Mother was so happy with her missionary meetings and her book club and her garden. Oh, indeed it was time we moved.

Daddy said in a press interview some years later: "After six years of living in a University atmosphere I began to think it was time I became associated with people who were actively engaged in the business of living—not just preparing to live it, or preparing others to live it."

Early in 1921 the First Congregational Church of Akron, Ohio, came seeking a new pastor. Mr. R. K. Crawford, one of the committee, wrote us recently an account of their activities at that time.

Well, George Sherman and I reported our findings to the members of the church and we were advised to go to Ann Arbor and hear Rev. Douglas preach the following Sunday. Before the church service Sunday morning we took a walk and interviewed several people on the street as follows: "We are strangers and would like to hear a good sermon. Perhaps you can tell us where to go."

"I certainly can. Don't fail to hear Rev. Lloyd Douglas, pastor of The First Congregational Church. Be sure to go early or you won't get a seat."

We went early and the church was crowded; many were turned away. The sermon was a masterpiece on the parable of the talents. After the service we introduced ourselves to Rev. Douglas and told him why we were there. We made an appointment to call on him at his residence that same afternoon.

Rev. Douglas told us he was receptive to a change. For many years his work had been in a college atmosphere and he was interested in working in an industrial field. We told him that Akron would furnish just the field he had in mind. After a very enjoyable visit, Rev. Douglas took us and his wife, Besse, for a trip in his Model T Ford around the city of Ann Arbor.

We reported our findings and arranged to have Rev. Douglas give a talk at a noon luncheon before the Akron Real Estate Board in the basement of the old Y.W.C.A. Building on South High Street. At this meeting some twenty of our church members were present. Our people were delighted with Rev. Douglas and his fine talk. That same evening we had dinner at the Men's City Club and about fifty church members were on hand to meet Rev. Douglas and hear him outline his plans for the modern church. Our church people were captivated by the personality of Rev. Douglas and his summary of what in his opinion a church should do to justify its existence.

A call was extended and accepted. At a regular meeting of the Board of Trustees dated July 8, 1921, we note the following: "Mr. Crawford read interesting letters from Rev. Douglas which explain his immediate plans regarding coming to Akron and stated that his household goods would arrive at the Parsonage about July 15th."

On the wave of Daddy's enthusiasm and excitement we left Ann Arbor without many backward glances. But in later years he and Mother came to realize what solid happiness they had enjoyed there among the gentle people in the beautiful little town. In the report of the church regarding the resignation of their minister the committee states:

But not only in these more public ways have Rev. Douglas' activities been manifested so effectively. To many of us in times of anxiety and distress, in ways of gentle and loving kindness both he and Mrs. Douglas have ministered to us in most helpful and understanding ways. To those who have had this experience, it perhaps will be more precious and more abiding than the larger things.

In 1951 at the time of Daddy's death his greatest interest in living was concentrated on the building of a little chapel which he was giving in memory of Mother. It was to be at the side and joined to the old First Congregational Church of Ann Arbor where he and Mother had been so happy.

It is now dedicated to both their memories and the inscription over the door reads:

IN MEMORY OF
LLOYD CASSEL DOUGLAS (1877–1951)
MINISTER OF THIS CHURCH (1915–1921)
AND OF HIS WIFE, BESSE IO DOUGLAS (1878–1944)
THIS CHAPEL WAS ERECTED THROUGH THE GIFTS OF
DOCTOR DOUGLAS AND HIS DAUGHTERS
AND IS DEDICATED BY THE CHURCH
TO THE GLORY OF GOD
AND TO THE REMEMBRANCE OF THESE TWO
HIS DEVOTED AND USEFUL SERVANTS
AND OUR BELOVED FRIENDS

7

Rubber City

AKRON, OHIO, when we went there in 1921, had but recently been struck by a most demoralizing business depression. During the war years and until late in 1920 the rubber companies, from which much of the town derived its income, had enjoyed a great prosperity. "The Boom," they called it, sadly remembering the halcyon days. Workers from every part of America and emigrants from Europe had piled into the city to take advantage of the preposterously high wages. Fortunes were made by the big executives and those townspeople who had been wise enough to invest in rubber; even the lowliest mill hands had fat rolls of bills on their hips.

Then suddenly, not many months before we arrived, Akron's boom burst. Betty and I did not realize what was going on, and I don't suppose our parents fully understood for a while. Mr. Hugh Allen described the situation in a paragraph of his book *Rubber's Home Town.*

> Lloyd C. Douglas, the minister-novelist who came to Akron in 1921 as pastor of the First Congregational Church after ten years in University towns in the Middle West, was fascinated by the situation he encountered. He found a noisy, sprawling, industrial city, quite different from the academic quiet he had known.
>
> In his congregation were men from sections of America where educational facilities were poor; as well as technically-trained

engineers, chemists and physicists. A college town had scarcely noticed the depression, but here the unemployed were walking the streets. The depression had hit a one-industry town harder than most, and while thrifty work-men adjusted themselves to the situation, and carried through to better times, hundreds of men had nothing to show for their high wages but a suitcase full of silk shirts.

On the first day of September our family drove into Akron in the old Model T Ford. Daddy had been lecturing for Chautauqua during the summer and Mother, Betty and I had joined him for the last few weeks. We had been staying in farmhouses or small-town hotels where Betty and I had looked patronizingly at the shy villagers, considering ourselves loftily city-bred. Now we goggled at this large metropolis which was to be our home with the pure, drop-jawed gaze of the hick. Not Daddy, of course; he was well acquainted with New York City. But even so, he gripped the steering wheel and attacked the traffic with strained and anxious eyes.

Akron then had a population of more than 250,000. To us it looked, smelled and sounded like a big city. Part of the business section was built upon a steep hill, and it was up this hill, hindered by streetcars and late afternoon traffic, that the Ford jerked and wheezed its way to our new house.

We turned a corner. The bustle and clang of the city did not follow us into this brief eddy. "Here's our church," said Daddy. "And here, next door, is the parsonage." He stopped the car and stretched up his aching arms. Betty, Mother and I, piled round with baggage, parcels and spare coats, peered at our new home speculatively. The church was large, beautiful and covered with a graceful cloak of ivy. The parsonage was a square red-brick house: large, but not very gracefully designed. Behind was a handsome Parish house. The three buildings were set in an emerald lawn and seemed a little island of tranquility around which the ugly city stood, dirty and noisy.

"Well, this is it," Daddy announced. "All out for Akron."

He was impatient to show us everything, especially the Parish House. "Wait until you see the inside of that; no expense has been spared in its equipment. We've got everything we could ask for here."

Indeed, the whole establishment was a very modern and splendid setup. The rooms of our house were large and freshly decorated. Betty and I had separate bedrooms. "Seems a rather dingy neighborhood" was Mother's only criticism.

The district had once been residential, but for some years the trend had been for the well-to-do to move to the west side of town. It didn't take us long to learn what it meant when people said, "We live on West Hill." Nor long to learn that we lived on the wrong side of the railroad tracks. Buchtel College was not far from us, and the homes of some of the old families who had not migrated across the valley, but our particular corner on East Market Street and Union was definitely not a desirable address.

"I think we live next door to a boardinghouse," Mother announced at breakfast a few days after our arrival.

"And across the street from one too," Betty said cheerfully.

When I came home from my first day at school I reported: "The children are all rather dusky-colored. I think they're mostly foreign. It was funny the way they disappeared when school let out; they all just ran down a couple of alleys."

It was a new experience for us. We were in one of America's melting pots. Akron had become a city too quickly. The post office and railroad station were small town and inadequate. The center business street was called Main Street as though they had never expected to have more than one, and its buildings were a collection of run-down relics between large handsome new structures. There in the busy crowds one saw many foreign women shuffling along in felt slippers and shawled heads, their expensive fur coats reminders of the recent money boom.

The First Congregational Church had met the financial crisis by realizing that now, if ever, their members needed a vigorous religious faith. They had launched upon a program of expansion in every field, bravely increasing their expenses. Daddy was very enthusiastic about his new congregation and found at once that they meant to support him with their time and interest as well as money. In his first sermon he said:

> I hope to make this a preaching station of more than local fame, and I expect with my assistants to make the First Congregational Church of Akron one of the best institutional churches in this country.

Also in that first sermon he explained his theories on how a church service should be conducted.

> The general public has not lost interest in religion, but the churches have so feebly presented their message that the public has lost interest in them. When I see their awkward attempts to imitate the theaters and motion picture houses in trying to create interest, I am chagrined.
>
> The churches are not carrying out their mission and that is to be a place of worship. They may do social work, they should do philanthropic work, but their highest duty is that of being a house of worship. When they fail in this they cannot expect the veneration to which they are entitled.

The pages of the Akron scrapbook reveal the activities of a busy and inventive man. There is a copy of the new bulletin which Daddy introduced to the church almost at once. It is handsome and must have been expensive to produce. On the front is a dreamy drawing of the church under the imposing stamp of a round seal. We can remember Daddy laboring far into the night over the construction of this seal. It pictured a ship—the *Mayflower*—sailing before a setting sun, and around it the name of the church and the words, "A City That Is Set on a Hill Can Not Be Hid." Lloyd Douglas meant to put the First Congregational Church of Akron on the map.

He was news from the first. We had barely got the furniture

settled before he was making speeches all over town. "Pastor Gives Early Impression of Akron," a headline reads.

> Rev. Lloyd Douglas told members of the Exchange Club that his impression of the Rubber City was that the body of the community had grown faster than the souls, owing to the unusual material prosperity of the last five years.
>
> He also said that while this present era of economic depression might bring hardship and discomfort to many people and institutions, still the temporary slowing up would have a steadying effect upon the growth of the city and enable it to give more time and attention to its soul.

Daddy greatly enjoyed his association with the businessmen of Akron and very soon a change came over his personality—at least the part he presented to the public. Between a minister and a professor there is not a great deal of difference, both lead dedicated lives to some extent; but between a minister and a businessman there can be an impenetrable wall on weekdays. Daddy tried to overcome this. He developed a brisk, decisive, up-to-date air and informed himself on a range of subjects which had never had his attention previously. In Akron money talked and one might as well come out of the study and listen.

We had never seen much real wealth before. In Ann Arbor some people may have had it—perhaps they traveled farther and oftener—but there had been little display. The standard for importance there had been one's accumulation of academic degrees rather than the number of ciphers to the right of one's bank credit. In Akron we soon felt the importance of money and things. Betty and I were especially impressed. In spite of the depression there were a good many people in our church who were well-to-do and better. We had not been in town long before we were all asked to dine at the home of the Masons, Goodrich tire people, who were very generous supporters of our church.

Mrs. Mason was a lady of great character. She carried her

head at a queenly angle, but nothing in the church was too small or troublesome for her to give her interest and assistance. Her long black limousine would stop at a house where there was illness and she would enter, followed by the chauffeur laden with eggs and fresh produce from the Mason farm. After church on Sunday, he would pile the altar flowers into the car and she would deliver them herself to the hospitals. Mr. Mason was a lovable old man, rather set apart from the world because of his extreme deafness. During all our years in Akron Daddy had only to mention to them a needy case and Mrs. Mason would be off making wonderful plans to help some boy through college or pay for someone's expensive medical care.

The Mason house in town was old and rambling and very luxurious. Betty and I had never seen such big rooms, such fine furniture, such deep carpets. The maid who led us upstairs was as stiff as paper. It seemed desecration to put our wraps on the elegant bedspreads. We looked at Mother rather helplessly, but she wouldn't encourage us to express our wonder. "Come girls," she said, when we continued to hang over the wide dressing table gaping at the ornaments of silver and crystal.

At dinner the table was long and there were many guests. Betty and I sat at the center with the grandchildren. Daddy, at Mrs. Mason's right, was very brilliant and entertaining. Whenever he started a story all conversation stopped and everyone listened. About halfway through the elaborate dinner he looked down the table at me and smiled comfortingly. "How are you getting on, Ginger?" he asked.

I had hardly spoken a word since we sat down. I looked at my plate. "I've never seen a chicken this small," I said.

This remark produced a surprising amount of laughter. The grandson, just my age, who sat beside me confided in a low voice, "That's not chicken; that's squab."

Having the parsonage next door to the church made our home a part of the organization to an exciting extent. Later, this began to pall, especially on Mother and Daddy, but at first it seemed an ideal arrangement. Couples who came to the church to be married were brought to our hourse for a more informal atmosphere. Betty and I were often called in to act as witnesses, and if not needed for this we would sit at the top of the stairs and wait for the kiss. Sometimes it was a good smack, but more often just a little silence followed by a burst of relieved laughter.

Being so close to the center of town, we had many transient couples coming our way and Mother's hoard of wedding fees began to grow against the day when she and Daddy would take the long-talked-of trip to Europe. Daddy ran in and out of the house all day and Mother shuttled back and forth between the parsonage and the Parish House where something was always going on. Even in the evening our little closed circle of four was often broken by interruptions from the church. Always the shadow of that busy concern lay upon our lives.

We had not been used to locking our doors with any great care, and one night when we came home from a movie a surprised burglar hastily departed by the back. Nothing had been taken, but after that we realized the necessity of bolting the doors and seeing to every window upstairs and down. An endless stream of jobless men called asking for work or a handout, always with a pathetic story to tell. Sometimes they seemed rather sinister and we took to keeping the house locked all the time, even during the day.

Winter passed and spring came. Betty was having a wonderful time at Central High School. She was just sixteen and had several boy friends. Mother made her an evening dress of red chiffon and when she went to parties she wore a gold ribbon bound round her forehead Pocahontas-fashion. "It's the style," she said.

I had no friends. The one little girl I brought home seemed uneasy in our house and never asked me to hers. My parents began to worry about their thirteen-year-old who moped about in her room and wrote poetry on death and allied subjects.

Whenever one of us was not bursting with the joy of life it weighed upon Daddy very much. He couldn't be happy unless we all were happy. His reaction was to make extravagant plans for a treat, generally in the form of a trip somewhere. That spring he took me with him on many of his high school and college commencement engagements. I remember entering the big crowded auditoriums at his side. "This is my daughter, Virginia," he would say as though I were a very important person. Then I would be led to an empty seat while curious eyes watched.

In many ways it had been a difficult winter for us all and Daddy, since early spring, had been making plans for our summer vacation. "Just think," he would say at breakfast, "only six more weeks until we all pile into the good old Ford and take off for the East. Wait until you get a smell of that ocean."

We were going to spend a month at Gloucester, Massachusetts. Already we had rooms engaged at a seaside boardinghouse advertised in the *Congregationalist*. Betty and I had never been East, and at every meal Daddy would entertain us by describing vividly what was in store for us: the mountains, the wide sandy beaches, the great rolling breakers; and best of all the shows and delights of New York City where we were going first for a few days. Oh, Glorious!

The last Sunday finally arrived. The Ford stood in the drive all packed to go. Daddy's sermon was short and we sat in our pew instructed by Mother not to grin at him every time he looked our way. So many people wanted to shake his hand that Sunday after the service. Betty and I went home and changed into our driving clothes. We wore tweed knickers. Betty also wore a large straw hat decorated with stuffed cherries which rattled loosely from their stems. Mother suggested the hat was not quite right with the knickers but did not press the criticism, seeing Betty's drooping face.

We stood at the window watching the last straggling parishioners leave the church, then saw Daddy come down the steps. One more couple reached out to him and he stopped, but soon broke away and came hurrying across the lawn toward home. The door barely closed behind him before he was out of his steaming coat and vest. It was late June and he was sweltering inside his heavy black clothes. But he did not ask us to wait until he bathed. "I'll get a bath in the hotel," he said, "when we stop tonight. Just think we're almost off."

We were excited, but our excitement was nothing compared to Daddy's. Mother didn't register high flights of enthusiasm easily, but all three of us knew from long experience that his happiness would be pricked if we didn't keep the steam up with a lively display of excitement. We went into our act quite naturally; we had been trained to it. All we had to do was to imagine ourselves Daddy as a little boy if he were to be going to such wonderful places.

The picnic lunch was packed in the car. We stowed ourselves in our accustomed seats and ripped out of town lest some parishioner sicken, or worse, die, before we got away. Akron lay far behind before we dared to stop to eat.

That afternoon we drove many miles and not until dusk fell did we begin to look for a place to spend the night. As always on our trips, when we wanted a village with a nice clean tourist home, such places fell from the course and we seemed to be crossing a vast uninhabited wilderness. At last, tired and hungry, we drove into a small town which had one moldy-looking hotel. We were past being critical. The dinner hour was over but they served us ham and eggs in the empty, fly-specked dining room. "Country ham," Daddy pronounced it, "and home-made eggs." With him everything was always extraordinarily good, unless suddenly some little thing happened and all became extraordinarily bad.

We had a big room with two sagging double beds. Adjoining rooms were not to be had, so Betty and I were with our parents in case of fire. Daddy went down to examine the plumbing at the end of the hall. "I guess I'll have to have my bath tomorrow," he said. "I can't understand that contraption down there."

We all went to sleep at once.

Betty and I were awakened by the sound of heavy rain and flashes of lightning. Mother and Daddy were whispering and he was moving around in the dark room. We were on the ground floor and a door in our room gave on to a paved area which in the night seemed to be some kind of an alley. Daddy was working with the lock and finally got it open.

"Where's he going?" we asked Mother.

"He's going to take a shower," she said.

Dimly we saw him take off his pajamas and step outside. He was gone quite a while. The summer rain smelled fresh, and in the flashes of lightning we could see him prancing up and down rubbing himself with soap. When he stepped back into the room Mother threw him a towel and said: "I have news for you, dear. What time do you think it is?"

"Oh, about midnight," he said.

"It's just half-past nine."

He was momentarily shocked but recovered cheerfully. "Oh, well, that was just a little alley out there. No one could have seen me."

The next morning when we awoke the sun was shining brightly. We looked out of our window. Cars were passing, shopkeepers were rolling down their awnings across the street. Our room opened on to a busy intersection at the very center of the town.

The next day we drove through beautiful scenery; wooded mountains rose from the right of the highway and to the left little streams gurgled over stones. For a while Betty and I looked and raved and raved and looked, but teen-agers get used to the beauties of nature quickly, and in the afternoon Betty became engrossed in a magazine story and I curled up in my corner and went to sleep. Daddy, hearing nothing from us for a little while, turned around and saw. "Ye gods!!" he roared. "Here I drive you girls thousands of miles at great expense to show you country I would have given my right hand to have seen at your age, and what do you do? One reads a magazine and the other sleeps."

Daddy was a strain at times.

The days in New York were a dream. We saw Lenore Ulric in *Kiki;* we saw *The Fool* and *Captain Applejack,* and shivered through *The Cat and the Canary.* Daddy gave us each ten dollars to spend and everything was so equally wonderful that we were still clutching the money when we arrived in Gloucester.

Our first sight of the open sea Daddy planned with dramatic effect. "Just smell it," he told us, breathing deeply of the ozone long before we arrived at the promised view. The odors of the Gloucester fishing business hung heavily in the air at that point and we thought the sea was a bit on the strong side. When at last we drove to the top of a wind-swept bluff and before us lay the great gray Atlantic, Daddy held out his arms. "There," he sighed, "there she is"—for all the world as though he had made it himself and saw it was good.

That was a wonderful summer. Mother and Daddy lay on the sand and Betty and I leaped the rocks in company with a band of youngsters from our boarding hotel. We were at the codfish end of the beach; far down the glistening sand, under great colorful umbrellas, lounged the blasé rich from the big hotels. Once many years later Betty and I spent a week in the hotel which we had once stared at from afar with such glittering envy. It was full of old ladies and was a hideous firetrap.

When we started back to Akron we were all refreshed and ready to tackle what came. I was to enter high school and Betty promised me everything would be different. Mother was resolved to begin a campaign to have us moved to the other side of town. Daddy was planning an attack to be made on Akron itself, for he considered the town sadly lacking in culture. We drove home quickly, barely heeding the scenery, our heads busy with plans for fall.

The First Congregational Church of Akron had always had Sunday evening services. Daddy found this a chore; he preferred to concentrate all his attention on one big service in the morning, and found having to prepare two sermons meant a thinning down of his material. However, the church had been so generous in granting his every request, he felt obliged to continue the custom.

During the second year of his ministry he introduced a gradual change for this evening service. For a while he reviewed worthwhile books, and then announced that he would answer questions which were sent to him during the week. This novelty caught on at once. The questions came pouring in—mostly on religious matters at first. The clippings in the scrapbook report a few of these: "Did Jesus Christ have the Power to prevent his tragedy?" "How do you regard the influence of Roman Catholicism in America?" Then the questions came down to topics of the moment and got a little hot to handle: "What do you think of the soldier's bonus?" "What do you think of the Ku Klux Klan?"

Daddy was not a particularly contentious man, but if his convictions were strong enough he did not step aside. Also, he considered the people of Akron needed to be stirred up to think and declare themselves. On the subjects of the Klan and the veteran's bonus he expressed his opinions in no uncertain terms. In the scrapbook appears a hail of sharp headlines. He was challenged to debates by both bodies and letters to the papers heaped abuse upon him. He received many threatening anonymous letters.

Anxious to placate the veterans and to explain further his objections to their bonus he accepted an invitation to address them at a regular meeting. "The air was cleared," the press reports. The veterans never agreed with him, but they cooled down. A letter to the *Beacon Journal* reads:

Although an ex-soldier and in favor of the bonus I want to say something for Dr. Douglas.

I do not believe that any man in Akron has done more for the soldiers than has Dr. Douglas. He has spent both time and his own money all through the winter getting jobs for the men who are out of work. He has contributed willingly and has demonstrated that he has the spirit of a man and a gentleman.

When this controversy died down the anxious members of the First Congregational Church sank back hoping their minister would keep his fingers off third rails for a while, but they weren't allowed to relax long. Lloyd Douglas was making speeches constantly to civic groups in the city and out. The newspapers seized upon all his critical comments and spread them widely: Pastor Raps This, Pastor Raps That.

The Ku Klux Klan he particularly loved to jab. Once when he was about to make a lecture in the southern part of the state the chairman whispered to him before he rose to speak.

"Don't say anything about the Ku Klux tonight. This district is a hotbed of them."

"Oh?" Daddy was pleased. "Just the place for me to air my views."

He had his say but told us later he got out of town as quickly as possible.

"Now we will surely get a bomb under the house," wailed Mother. "Those men are serious."

A few days after the report of that particular speech came out in the news, Daddy was stopped for speeding. The florid cop was giving him the usual gruff dressing down when he saw on the papers the name of the man he was scolding.

"You the preacher Lloyd Douglas?"

Daddy nodded guiltily.

A wide grin spread over the policeman's face. "Say, I've

been reading in the papers what you've been doing to those Klu Kluxers." He went on to tell at great length just what he thought of them. While he talked he tore up the summons he had been preparing. "Good luck, Reverend," he said, removing his foot from the fender. "And—oh—don't go quite so fast through this zone next time."

Probably the worst thing Daddy said in Akron was when he declared publicly that it was a hick town, and pointed out all the sad deficiencies in civic and cultural affairs. But even then the people only blinked and gulped and admitted it was true. Their self-appointed critic had won their hearts and it seemed nothing he could say angered them for long.

On the question of religion the Congregational Church received a new diet. They had not been totally fundamental before, but the type of homily they were now getting was decidedly liberal. Their minister said:

> You can bear it in mind that I have never asked you to think exactly as I think, but only to THINK. What you thought is not of so great importance in my opinion, as that you should have access to all the facts that I have access to; and after that I am entirely willing you should come to your own conclusions without too much assistance from my quarter.

He introduced them to all manner of new conceptions which seemed heretical to some but were listened to with interest by all. "Lloyd Douglas said what he pleased," Hugh Allen wrote, "wore no man's theological collar, no matter how heavy a contributor he might be. He always made his point clear. Some people grumbled a bit that he should stick to the Scriptures, but he made Christ come alive, showed him as a person you would have liked and admired. He brought people to church who needed it, but saw little of it because usually they were bored. It wasn't a sense of duty which emptied the University Club every Sunday morning."

At the end of our second year in Akron, Daddy received a

call from the First Congregational Church of Madison, Wisconsin. The idea of going back to a small university town was hailed with delight by our family. We still lived in the brick parsonage by the church in the swirl and dust of the city. We had not become sufficiently attached to Akron to view leaving it with any feeling of grief. At any rate Daddy, after considering the question from all angles, and hearing the pleas of his wife and daughters, accepted the call and announced his resignation.

No pulpit could attract me away from Akron except one offering the peculiar nature of this for which my experience seems to fit me.

The Madison church was disposed to offer me a larger salary, but in order that the money feature might cut no figure, I insisted on the same financial basis as my present one.

Then a terrific howl of protest went up. The church claimed that he could not leave them now when all their religious ideas were upset by his new theories. It was his duty to remain and finish what he had begun. He was deluged with appeals from individuals and organizations: the Lions Club, the Rotary Club, the student body of Akron University, the Akron Real Estate Board sent petitions asking that he reconsider his decision. The newspaper printed this notice on its editorial page:

To Lloyd C. Douglas, First Congregational Church
Dear Sir:
Madison, Wis., invited you to come. Akron wants you to stay. You see big opportunities in Madison or you wouldn't consider leaving us.
However, you are not going to get away without an argument. Akron needs men of your ability and energy too badly to stand meekly by and see you leave.

PA AKRON

The situation was awkward. The Madison church had officially received an acceptance of their call and the newspapers there had reported it with enthusiasm. To reverse the decision now seemed undignified, as though it had not been made sincerely in the beginning. But Daddy could not deny the plea put forward by the Akron church: he had brought about a radical change in their religious thinking; many of them were reaching toward the new interpretations, but with feet still on uncertain ground. Their minister had not finished his job. He must stay. The next Sunday he said, as reported by the paper:

> "A week ago I announced the call to Madison and at that time I was sincere in my decision that I intended to accept it. But since then I have received such loving remonstration that I have reconsidered and I am on your hands indefinitely."
>
> The ovation he received after this announcement was one of the most enthusiastic ever recorded in the history of the church. The church was crowded to the doors and the entire congregation stood and applauded.

The following fall we moved to the other side of town. A large public dance hall had gone up on the lot adjoining the church and our nights in the red brick parsonage had been considerably enlivened by the blatting of saxophones and the rhythmic thump of the base viols. The sound had caused our parents acute pain. Betty and I had not objected to the music, but we had seen that its proximity had not lent much dignity to our address.

We now lived in Sunset View. Our neighbors were pleasant suburban people who had gardens and families, quite different from the faceless men and women who scurried in and out of their temporary dwellings on Union Street. Betty and I went to West High School and made new friends. After the great avowal of affection from the church and town at the time of the

Madison call, Mother and Daddy settled down to a deeper appreciation of their surroundings. They became moderately social, went to many dinner parties and gave some.

When Mother gave a party it was a time of great airing and cleaning and polishing. Over the years she had acquired some nice things: linen, silver and china—many of them gifts from grateful parishioners; but hers was a hoarding nature and only for special occasions did these fineries appear. Daddy loved to entertain and took much interest in the menu and choice of guests, but the days of preparation were nearly enough to discourage him. One sound had always afflicted him sorely—the whine of the vacuum cleaner. Generally Mother waited until he was out of the house before she used it, but if a party was expected even his nerves were forgotten in the hubbub.

There was much for Betty and me to do at these times too. Betty was a natural cook and Mother relied on her help in the kitchen. I was given the tedious chores in which I had no interest and required constant supervision. Even our closets and drawers had to be tidied, as though the ladies had x-ray eyes.

At last all would be ready. Daddy would sit down at the piano to play until the first loud peal of the doorbell rang through the house. "Now girls," Mother would whisper, "you stay upstairs and show the ladies where to put their things. And do wait until you hear us go into the dining room before you start trying on their hats."

I had finally, after much hanging about "where the brook and river meet," left my childhood behind me, and Betty and I were again congenial with interests in common. Sighing and moaning took up much of our time. Clothes, boys and the latest popular songs filled our foolish heads and we were the despair of our father, who had always hoped we would be women of firm character.

I remember coming down to breakfast one morning with a newly cut layer of bangs across my forehead. "Now what have you done to yourself?" Daddy demanded. "Why can't you decide how you're going to look and stay that way? This constant altering of your face and hair denotes an alarming lack of stability."

He had very strong views on personality: the firm handclasp, the uplifted head and steady gaze, unhesitating speech—these were outward things he urged upon young people in his commencement addresses. "Face the world confidently," he said. "Indecision is a sign of weakness." We had been taught from childhood to make up our minds quickly and act. None of this head hanging and toe turning for us. March right up to the candy man and say, "I want two cents' worth of that, please." Betty and I still order from a menu after one quick glance down the list. Afterwards we might see some favorite dish we had missed the first time, but we have spoken, it is final.

Daddy, himself, once confessed that he wished he had left the initial C out of his name, but he had begun that way and the C would be there until the end.

We discovered at about this time that it was somewhat of a handicap to be daughters of a minister. The boys regarded our house with awe and when we greeted them at the door they stepped in cautiously and behaved like elderly deacons. We tried to be ready on time, but occasionally Daddy would meet them, lead them off to his study and close the door. The youth trapped thus would be placed in the best chair and his opinions deferred to as though they were a matter requiring serious consideration. "I want to read you a paragraph or two of this article I'm writing," Daddy would say. "Tell me how it strikes you."

When at last the study door opened and the two appeared it might happen that they would be beaming at each other and chatting like brothers, but more often the callow young man would be in a pitiful state of disintegration, dropping things, stumbling, hardly knowing his own name.

"Got a well-shaped head," Daddy would report of him the

next morning at breakfast. "Might amount to something." Doubt would tinge his pronouncement.

We were allowed dates only on the week-ends, and whenever our friends could get their fathers' cars and scrape together enough money they wanted to go to the East Market Street Gardens, the dance hall near our church. Betty and I had been forbidden to go.

"What's wrong with it?" we would wail. "Everybody goes. It just means that we'll be left at home. We'll be unpopular." If one were unpopular, of course, one might as well shave the head, wade into a lily pond and let the mud close over.

Daddy had made the original decision and later discussions were left to Mother. But since our upbringing was their joint effort, with Daddy the final court, we knew she could not be persuaded however much she sympathized and yearned with us. "Your father is a minister," she said, remembering her own girlhood in the manse, "and there are many people in our church who would not approve of his daughters going to a public dance hall. You must be loyal to Daddy. You can do your dancing at the Parish House parties."

We groaned. The Parish House dances were all right, but stumbling over the freshly waxed gymnasium floor to victrola music, or at best some willing but thumb-fingered pianist, compared feebly to the delights of the East Market Street Gardens.

I regret to say that the minister's daughters disobeyed their parents and went to the Gardens.

It was reported at once. Betty was seen. How the church lady who promptly called Mother got her information we never learned, but the faces of our parents that next morning when we came down to breakfast shall never fade from our memories. It was grief they suffered. If they had been mad they got over that during the long night when they lay in their bed and discussed what was to be done. When they confronted us with the accusation their decision was made. We were to have their permission to go to the Gardens. Far better that our morals risk contamination in a public dance hall than that we sneak off and behave in an underhand way.

I wish I could report that we were noble and refused this generous offer torn from our perplexed parents. I wish I could say we never entered again the brilliantly lighted doors of the Palace of Jazz; but we did. We rushed off at the first opportunity and told our friends. "We can go to the Gardens! They'll let us go!" "They" being those two loving people at home who for the time being had become separated from us by their age and our foolishness.

Truth was a thing Daddy set great store by; truth when it took courage to tell it—the Big Truth. But there are thousands of little layers underneath that I spent my youth puzzling over. So often I have heard my father retell childish quips Betty or I had made. The story would emerge colorful and full of details we had not been aware of at the time. Our remark itself would be rephrased until it bore only faint resemblance to the original, and we would be regarded as clever far beyond our years.

I inherited this tendency to beautify the facts. "Ginger is the biggest liar on Earth," my family would proudly say. But when faced with the harsh question, "Did you or did you not?" the Truth was demanded and woe to her who did not know it.

In spite of our parents' increasing social activities and Betty's and my adolescent interests, our family life continued simple and close. Daddy spent whole days at home reading or working on his sermons and articles for publication. Mother made all our clothes and in the evenings under her supervision we hemmed the bottoms of dresses or overcast the seams. "A lady's dress should be as nice inside as out," she told us.

Sometimes in the evening we played bridge, everyone bidding wildly with no regard for the value of the cards in hand. "Double" and "Redouble" we shouted at each other.

Off duty Daddy could never bear to sit about in his ordinary clothes. Mother finally decided the time had come when he should have some decent lounging outfit. For his 1923 Christmas present she made him a suit of a dark green silk. She used a Vogue pattern and labored long over the tailoring. Her mouth was hung with basting threads and again and again she ripped off the collar and lapels and refit them while Daddy stood patiently being pinned. When it was finished you could hardly tell it was homemade. Daddy was delighted with it and wore it at home all the time. It lasted for years. In time it took on a sitting position all its own and when he stood up it didn't.

Sunday was still the big day in our lives. Betty and I always dressed with care for church, since our current beaux often would be in the audience with their parents. Sometimes young men sat in our pew with Mother and us and as noon approached their empty stomachs would gurgle and they would stir uneasily and redden to the tips of their ears.

In Akron the church music, always such an important part of Daddy's Sunday service, gradually changed under his ministry. When we came, the organist was a lady who played during the week at a movie house. Sometimes she forgot where she was and in interludes one instinctively looked up expecting to see wild horses galloping across the plains. Daddy found it hard to keep his face straight watching the deacons pass out the Communion in little short tiptoe steps to the tune of "The Funeral March of the Marionettes."

At his suggestion a choir was installed and a trained church organist found to direct them. Several years later another change was made when Daddy was able to persuade his friend Burton Garlinghouse to come to Akron and take over the church music. He and Burton had been in the same Chautauqua outfit a few summers before and had worked together in great harmony. Burton had also sung in the Ann Arbor church choir under Earl Moore, and music ran in his veins. Best of all he and Daddy appreciated each other's witty remarks and were stimulated to great heights in each other's company.

The summer they had been together in Chautauqua, to enliven

the long, hot programs, grown monotonous from constant repe-
tition, they would sometimes change places: Daddy would be
Mr. Garlinghouse and accompany the lady artists at the piano,
Burton would be Dr. Douglas and deliver the address with all the
correct gestures and a few of his own. They both found this
excruciatingly funny.

In Akron Burton assembled a trained choir, and the service,
developed under Earl Moore, was followed and perfected until
it acquired a nation-wide reputation. Burton composed music to
accompany certain beautiful scriptural passages; he arranged for
male voices an old Czecho-Slovak tune which Daddy had found
and set to words. It was used as the benediction and the service
always ended with this simple, graceful little melody, "May the
Lord Bless You."

The high spot of Burton's choir under Daddy's ministry was
an invitation in 1925 to provide the music for the Council of
Congregational Churches held in Washington, D.C. Daddy's
scrapbook records the success of this engagement. The flattering
report of the Washington paper ends with this comment.

> Dr. L. C. Douglas of Akron, Ohio, led the service. With a
> commendable desire for reverent worship unvexed by the entrance
> of latecomers, orders were given to close all the doors at the
> beginning of the responsive service. Consequently not five but
> five hundred foolish virgins and others clamored vainly on the
> outside, "Lord, open to us," and for half an hour cooled their
> heels in the vestibule the while they grew warmer under the
> collar.

In the summer of 1924 we rented a cottage on Cape Cod
where we could be quiet and undisturbed. Betty and I didn't find
this an absolute necessity to our happiness, but Daddy was
writing a book and as always the most essential thing was silence
throughout the house. The book was *The Minister's Everyday
Life,* from which I have quoted in earlier chapters.

Adapted from a Czecho-Slovak ballad by Lloyd C. Douglas.
Arranged by Burton Garlinghouse.

We rented our cottage from an old lady who had advertised in the *Congregationalist*. She must have been a very pious old lady, for the books we found on her shelves were mostly sermons of long-ago preachers. Mother and Daddy were delighted with the place. It was a quaint old salt box miles away from any human habitation. The beach, a good distance from the house, was sudden and the sinister waves rolled up the incline and gulped hungrily at the feet of courageous waders—us, no one else ever came.

Daddy was at his typewriter all day. Mother, never at a loss for occupation, read books on higher thought or sewed. Betty and I, after exploring the neighborhood and finding nothing but vast expanses of salt marsh, took to sitting on the roof and reading current issues of *Snappy Stories* and other pulpy love magazines. At night several times each week Daddy would drive us to the nearest town to see a movie and replenish our store of corrupt reading matter. Anything to keep us occupied and quiet.

After we departed the old lady who owned the cottage wrote our father a very scalding letter on the low type of literature she had found piled in her attic—not at all the kind of thing one would expect a minister of the gospel to be interested in. She also reported that two of her sofa cushions had been badly faded by the sun.

The next fall Charles Scribner's Sons brought out the little religious book. It had good reviews in the church papers and was put on the reading lists of many seminaries. (It is still there in some.) Daddy considered it quite a success and perhaps felt his literary ambitions were being achieved. In middle age one is apt to compromise with the fiery hopes of youth. I doubt if he gave much house those days to dreams of writing books which would sweep the country in popular appeal.

All these years, in fact, as long as we could remember, he and Mother had been talking about the trip to Europe they were going to make one day. In Ann Arbor it was only a glorious idea, but in Akron the store of fees from weddings and commencements was beginning to bring the project down from the clouds to a real possibility. They read many travel books and were constantly elaborating their plans with each new place they read about.

They decided it was imperative they know French. At least Daddy thought Mother should know French. She was able to apply her fluffy little head to such long tedious books and seemed to enjoy mental tasks of all kinds. Surely a new language would be a snap for her. For Christmas he gave her a set of French gramophone records which guaranteed a fluency in that language if practised diligently and according to the directions.

We would all learn French. Daddy, his plans rushing ahead as usual, gilding the future with the same old rose color which Mother, Betty and I had learned to view with dark glasses, described to us how in no time we would all be chatting like natives. "We'll make a rule," he said. "No English spoken at the table and a fine for offenders."

The first record was naturally very elementary. One followed the written lessons provided and listened to the carefully enunciating voice from the Victrola. "Que . . . que voulez . . . que voulez-vous . . . que voulez-vous ce . . . que voulez-vous ce matin?" By this time we were all rolling in our chairs with wild laughter. The piping foreign voice was funny enough, but the effect it had on our little dog was even more funny. At the first few words his ears stood up, he had stretched his neck and let out one long moon-howl after another.

Because there has been no mention of dogs for some time does not mean we had been without them for all these years. Many had come and gone. The city was a difficult place to keep animals and ours had been stolen or lost before their characters became deeply ingrained in our family history. Earnest, the dog who didn't like French, Daddy had given to me for Christmas. I had been allowed to pick him out myself. Daddy drove me to the pet shop one snowy afternoon and while I went in he waited double-parked on Main Street with cars honking for him to move on. "Now hurry," he told me, "I won't be able to stay here long."

I rushed in and was out again in a few minutes for advice. "Daddy," I said, "the man has only got two dogs in there. One has sore eyes and the other—" "Get the other," Daddy said, "and hurry."

Earnest never learned to enjoy French. In fact, after that first session, the family lessons were abandoned and only Mother kept at it. She was very serious about anything she undertook and considered it a great blot on the character to admit defeat. Daddy quite cheerfully gave up all manner of things if they proved too hard, although one of his favorite remarks to us was: "If a thing is worth doing at all, it's worth doing well."

In the spring of 1925 it looked as though our parents were actually going to Europe. The long mulled-over plans began to arrange themselves in practical order. "I told you I would take you abroad, Besse Porch," Daddy said, "and this summer we're going." It sounded like the real thing. Mother pinched on her glasses and paid attention to the latest itinerary Daddy had laid out.

The house was full of travel folders and booklets put out by the big steamship companies. In the pictures of the rooms of these floating palaces elegant ladies lounged in evening dress, their shoulders draped in long, fringed Spanish shawls.

"What do you kids want us to bring you home?" Daddy asked.

"Spanish shawls," we said promptly. "Like these." We showed him the pictures.

He looked. "I thought those were to hang over pianos," he said. "Well, next time we'll all be going. We'll rent a car and the four of us will roam over France wherever our fancy takes us. Mother and I will know the country like a book by then and . . ." He was off on another of his dream trips. Betty and I listened with practised attention while our eyes slid cautiously back to the ladies in their embroidered shawls.

Mother sewed furiously on clothes for herself, Betty and me. (We were to spend the summer with our Aunt Glen in St. Louis.) At night she sat propped up in bed reading French history to Daddy who lay beside her with closed eyes.

"Are you asleep, Lloyd?"

"No, indeed. The light is a little bright for my eyes. You said 'The Palace of Fountainblue—' "

"Fountainblow," Mother would correct gently.

This always roused him. "The last time I said Fountainblow and you said it was Fountainblue. That's the trouble with French. No matter how you say it, it's always the other way." He would flounce over on his side. "Well, go on—what about the Palace?"

That spring Daddy went about his duties in a happy glow. He preached and tended his flock, but inside his mind was running a brightly colored travelogue. "No souls saved after Easter," he sometimes remarked after a long wearing Lenten season. It was really true that year.

To look back on his enthusiasm, demanding as we found it at the time, it seems more than a little pathetic. Distant lands, foreign ways had always fascinated him. An incredible dream was coming true. The little boy who had sat on the post at the corner of the melon patch and watched the haughty express flick by was as alive as ever. Always, whenever he went to New York, he would hurry to his hotel, leave his bags in his room, and then take a Fifth Avenue bus, riding on top of course, and head straight for the Battery. There he would stand, hanging over the rail, peering down the misty river as far as eyes could carry him . . . out to sea. His heart was on the big boats that sometimes moved slowly past to fade over the horizon.

As time grew nearer there were going-away parties for Mother and Daddy. Night after night they ate baby chicken, baby potatoes, baby peas. Mrs. Schleewee, popular cateress, often served at these dinners. When she knew Daddy was to be there she set his place at the table with the knife and fork reversed and the water glass at the left as she knew he would soon have it. When she passed the chicken she would whisper to him, "There's the thigh, Doctor, the piece you like."

In 1925 going to Europe was not the little hop it is in these days. At least as far inland as Akron it still bore the sound of the Grand Tour. Mother was very nervous about putting such a distance between herself and her daughters, aged sixteen and eighteen. She and Daddy made their wills and explained to us the insurance. Uncle David, Aunt Glen's husband, was made our guardian . . . "in case" . . . Mother would break off in distress at that point and Daddy would go on. "In case anything should happen to us. Nothing is going to happen, but it's sensible to be prepared."

June came. School ended. We all got into the car—a bulging Buick—to drive to Monroeville, Indiana, where Grandmother Douglas lived in her little old house with her wood stove, her clock, her pump and her backhouse. She had strongly opposed the trip to Europe, but her arguments against that were forgotten when she saw Mother with her bobbed hair.

"Oh my!" she flapped her apron.

"Cute, don't you think?" Daddy fondled the back of Mother's shingled head.

Grandmother did not think it was cute and expressed her views off and on during the rest of our visit.

Then it was time to part. Mother and Betty and I drove on to St. Louis, Betty driving and attending to all practical matters as usual in Daddy's absence. Daddy went back to Akron to preach his last sermon, gather up the baggage and leave for New York City where Mother was to join him.

8

All Aboard for Yurrup!

New York City
June 29, 1925

Mᴙ DEAR BABIES,

As you see, I am in the big town, a nice large airy room on
the ninth floor back on the side where our rooms were when
you were here with us two years ago. I have unpacked all the
junk, of whom there are considerable; and have put all Mother's
trinkets in her drawers, and hung up all her pretties in the closet.
Now I have nothing to do but eat, drink and try to be merry
until she comes. I shall be at the station early tomorrow, with
my nose inserted between the bars, watching for her bobbed
head.

I found my way back to Akron from Grandma's the other
night, and spent Thursday, Friday and Saturday at home watching the clock, and occasionally chucking something else into the
luggage. There is a lot of it. Lady Bountifuls from the church
kept sending in more things daily—more socks, soap, matches,
cigarettes, nail brushes, back scratchers, toe-cleaners, cases to
hold dirty linen with my initials in diamonds; boxes to keep burnt
matches in, with little poems on the cover, etc.

Sunday dawned b. & c.* Church well filled. Lots of miscel-

* Bright and clear.

laneous stuff in the service; babies to baptize and members to take in, and a missionary to "commission." She goes to Turkey, where they carry off girls to their harems; but I think *this* girl will be safe.

Noon came and no potatoes, as Ginger says, eh what, Ginger? And the peepul came tearing down to the pulpit to wish me joy. Burton played God Be With You Till We Meet Again at the request of Mrs. M.

Presently it was all over. I drove home in the Ark, changed clothes, took my enormous load of baggage to the station and checked it; thence to Brighton Farm, where we had dinner and the usual line of chatter.

Mr. and Mrs. Mason drove me to the train and presently I was off. Lots of people I knew on the train. Dinner with Mr. Stillman, V.P. of Goodyear.

Got here early, and haven't been out. N.Y. is noisy as ever, and a gladsome sight to one who loves her dearly.

I shall write again when Mother comes. If there are any final questions you want to ask—now that you are out there—wire me; and if it's anything I can take care of at this late hour, I shall do so.

I hope you are to have a fine summer.

New York City
July 1, 1925

Dear Girls,

Mother is buckling on her armor for the fray this bright morning and while I wait, I shall have a word with you.

Yesterday I went to the station an hour early and when her train was called, I told the gateman I was down to meet a sick old lady, so he let me by. I saw her get off the train and come pattering down the platform head up and a most radiant smile. We blocked traffic in that vicinity for awhile. Thence to the hotel where I cleaned her up as well as I could with soap and water. Then we went down town on the Sixth Avenue El to a little eating house on Eleventh Street.

She protested she wasn't hungry; but they brought a plate of pickled cabbage, pickled fish and a lot of other sour snappy stuff, and after she had munched a goodly quantity of it she was ready to eat the chimney right off the building.

We went from there down into the Lower East Side. She knew about a brass shop. She bought about 75 pounds of candle-sticks for me to carry, and then she decided she wanted to ramble around in the dirt, watch the Yiddish, and shop off the push-carts. Usually she goes through the L.E. Side, you will remember, holding up her skirts with one hand and her nose with the other; but yesterday she just waded through everything—rotten bananas, essence of horse, etc., rejoicing—while I came trailing along under the goodole brass, hoping she'd soon get sick of it.

A show last night—a jolly little thing by O'Neill in which everybody went around with dragging heels, looking sad and goddamning each other. The only shocking crime actually committed in full view was the strangling of a baby, but a lot of dark business was hinted at which must have happened while the curtain was down—which, I take it, was just as well.

Then we, being very hungry, had a broiled lobster, went home, played a couple of games of solitaire, in which papa acquitted himself nobly; and so to bed.

Later—

We have had breakfast, over at Drake's. Mother took a taxi from there to go up on Fifth Avenue around 49th sum'mers, to have her pretty head tinkered with as it is dirty and the curl is all out. We are meeting at 2 (I lunch with Sherman of Scribner's) and then we look at the animals in Central Park.

Bessie has consented to do this in a swap promise that I will go on a long bus ride with her up Riverside Drive.

New York City
July 2, 1925

Dear Ickle Childwen,

This is Thursday at 4 pm. Just 24 hours from now we will be moving out for Yurrup.

Yesterday, Mother shopped until the middle of the afternoon while I had lunch with Mr. Sherman. He was very nice and we had a fine lunch which began with some good scotch and closed with claret, in spite of all the good things that are surely to be said in favor of prohibition.

At 3 Bessie and I met at the hotel and loafed for an hour. Then I persuaded her to join me on a bus ride. We went away out to 110th and took another bus back. We stopped at 67th and got off to see the animals in the Park zoo.

Bessie had omitted lunch; and when she saw all the other animals eating peanuts I bought her some on request; but they were so old and tough that she gave them away to whatever birds, beasts and insects like them. I think she got her philanthropic ideas from Ginger's song of love relative to birds, bees, trees and such like natural phenomena.

Bessie went through the animal phase of the trip very creditably, exacting only one condition—that I wouldn't take her into any of the small places where the animals just sit and (s)think.

Well; at length she was pretty well satisfied with the animal show; so we took another bus and came down to 6th and 49th where we had dinner at an Italian place.

Later we saw "They Knew What They Wanted," which is the Pulitzer prize play of the season and is full of much tragedy and some comedy. If there had been as many people in the house as there were naughty cuss words in the play, they would have had to hang out the S.R.O. sign—which they didn't.

And so to bed, after a couple of games of the ancient vice—solitaire.

This morning, after breakfast at Drake's, we took a taxi down to the docks, and went on board the Majestic. A boat guide took us all through. We saw our room and it is very nice. It is on the south side, so we will have sunshine through the day. To attempt to describe the boat is out of the question of course. She is an enormous thing, and like a city. We were all through the kitchens and third class quarters. Almost nobody was on board but the ship's employees.

We were on board a half hour; then went out to the end of the dock and saw a big French liner and a Cunarder towed out and started for Europe, the bands playing and passengers waving to the big crowd of mourners on the piers.

Then we came back and went out to lunch with Mr. Sherman. It was a nice party and Bessie was very pretty and charming. We met a couple other big men at Scribner's at the luncheon place—one of them, Will Howe the "literary critic," was especially fine to meet. Betty will know about him, doubtless, through her dear teachers in English Lit. Then we sat and talked for a couple more hours. Sat until I almost wore out my capacity for sitting.

Mother left me up here at the corner of 45th and 6th Ave., saying she was going to scout around for a sweater. But she will be back presently and we will nap until dinner. Likely we will see the Student Prince tonight.

Mrs. Mason is sick and can't come to see us off. So nobody will see us off. We will just go; and, as I said, nobuddy will see us off. But we will go, anyhow.

(More later. I'm getting sleepy.)

Bessie is back with her new sweater—a peach—and is sprawling on the bed.

I am out to buy tickets for a show.

We will write you a note before we leave tomorrrow.

New York City
July 3, 1925

Dear Girls,

We were at the boat this morning. Had a letter of introduction to the Chief Engineer. Hunted him up. He introduced us to all the main guys and they legged it to find us accommodations. Our chairs are in a fine place on the sunny side Deck B—a choice location—and a cute little table in a fine location in the dining room.

We will go down with our stuff in a few minutes. Greatly enjoyed your breezy letter, Ginger. You are a very thoughtful child to write to Fpappa and Fmamma as they set forth and so forth.

We will scribble a line on the boat after we get started and the pilot will bring it in and mail it when he leaves the boat at Sandy Hook.

On Board S.S. Majestic
July 3, 1925

Bye Bye Babies

Be good children. Next time you hear from us we will be in France.

Oh Boy; it's a grand and glorious feelin'.

Lovingly
DADDY

We're on the way.

On Board S.S. Majestic
July 9, 1925

Dear Girls,

This is Tuesday night and we are getting on toward the end of our journey. Tomorrow is the last day of it; and the next morning we are arriving at Cherbourg about 9 or 10 o'clock.

Our daily program runs something like this: At 8 o'clock (and

eight is an hour earlier, every day) there is a rap on the stateroom door and the steward says, "Your bawth, Sir." So I tumble
out, half asleep; put on my slippers and bathrobe, and go digging
down the alleys, a half mile or so to find me bawth. (The first
morning I got lost and was found wandering around in the
Palm Gardens about 8:30 still looking for it.) Well, I have had
said bawth and am dressing when there is another knock on the
door and "Madame's bawth is ready." Then there is the devil
to pay; for Madame has to be got up. We begin with the
honeyed words which used to incite Bettina to do murder—little
love phrases like: "Woudan the sweet little woman have some
nice get-up a thin?" etc. Failing to get any results by such poor
tactics, we tickle her feet, and tousle her hair. In the end she
yields to entreaty and tumbles out looking wildly about as if
it had just been announced that all passengers must take to
the boats.

Having performed this duty, I go up two decks to *B* (our room
is on D) and walk until I see Bessie sitting in one of our chairs
(also B). Then we take the elevator and go clear down to F,
for breakfast. The dining room is just like a very finely appointed
dining room in a fine hotel.

My breakfast is generally fruit, ham and eggs, griddle cakes
and chocolate. And Bessie eats pretty healthily too, for one so
young and frail.

Then we go up on B and read for a couple of hours, and take
cat-naps and look at the water. There is always lots of water out
here where we are. There's almost more of that than any other
kind of scenery.

Lately we have not been going down to lunch. For there is
bouillon served at 11 and Tea and cookies at 5. With a late
breakfast; it is hard to eat a big lunch. (I just now heard the
man across the corridor wommick a bib-ful. That's what comes
of too much eaty.)

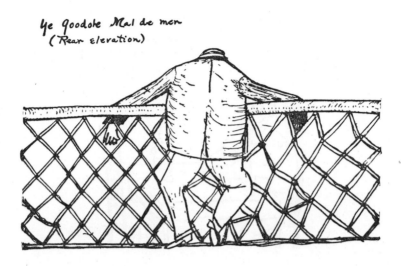

Ye goodole Mal de mer
(Rear elevation)

Generally I stroll up to the Smoke Room about one and have a sandwich and a stein of beer.

All afternoon we parade the deck and read. Dinner at 7, all arrayed in our hard-boiled shirt and the women bare to the waists. Lots to eat at dinner, and a nice little bottle of wine to wash it down.

Then we go to the big "Lounge" and watch the jazzers. About 11 we turn in.

This forenoon I went all through the engineroom and saw all the machinery. It was very interesting.

It has been quite smooth until tonight. There is quite a breeze; and the goodole ship rolls about considerably. Mother has just turned out her light. She has been reading, but apparently thinks she will be better off asleep. I am sitting in my bed writing this; but I too feel that I will be more comfortable lying flatwise.

The Douglas' at dinner
on shipboard
on a rough evening

Wednesday morning.

Mother thought she would be very stylish and have her breakfast in bed. She is sound as a nut; not sick at all; loaded up on frizzled 'am and eggs, and a lot of other stuff; but she will stay in bed awhile. It is a bright, sunny day, and the sea is smooth. Last night it was a wee mite rough.

I have been down to breakfast and filled my pockets with French money. This time tomorrow we will be on French soil, maybe.

I have read a lot of cheap detective stories belonging to the Ship's Library. The Brooks book, "Like Summer's Cloud" was *most* entertaining. I think it was delightful of my babies to send it to us. I read lots of it to Mother while we sat on deck.

I go up now and scout around in the open air. This is the last day. We will keep writing you everytime we stop long enough to limber a pen.

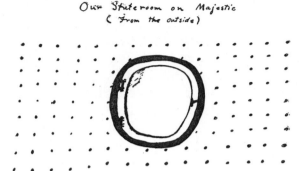

Our Stateroom on Majestic
(From the outside)

In Bed at Hotel Regina,
Paris,
Saturday Night
11:30
July 11, 1925.

N.B.   This letter had better not be read aloud before the
relatives. Bessie has seen it, and offers this suggestion
with her love and kisses.

Dear Girls,
   You may have heard it hinted, a time or two, that Mama and
Papa were thinking some of going to Europe this summer. Well,
we have gone to Europe. And if I were to know tonight that
I would never in all my life see anything more interesting,
fascinating and altogether lovely than Paris, I should be content.
   Bettina is a very excellent driver, but I'll bet my hat she
wouldn't want to do it in this town. No speed limit, at all; and
only an occasional traffic officer. Everybody goes likell and the
fellow with the most nerve gets the right of way. Taxis are so
cheap that you have to go a very long trip to spend a quarter.

There is so much to tell you that I don't know where to begin.

Well, maybe I'd better tell you how we got here. The Majestic sighted land early Thursday morning. Two hours later we came to anchor in the harbor at Cherbourg. Little tenders came out and took us off. We fought our way though customs—a thousand people waving their arms and shouting in 17 different languages.

The game seemed to be something like this: first you locate a porter to carry your things; which you haven't found yet. The porters are all engaged by this time. And you can't find your baggage anyhow. So, the game is to instruct this French porter, who is engaged and too busy to listen to you, to carry your luggage, which you can't locate, to the customs officials, in order that you may answer certain questions put to you in a language you do not understand. It all sounds easy enough perhaps; but before I had accomplished all of the feats I was tired, hot, dirty; and had the general appearance of something that had been fished out of a great disaster.

Safely through the customs, we boarded one of the absurd little trains that lay toasting under the broiling noon, and learned that it was not leaving for an hour and a half. Our tickets had been made out for second-class travel in France. Our agents and several other people had told us that second-class travel in France is quite the same as first-class. Well, whoever started that report is no friend of mine. The French trains all try to carry twice as many people as their capacity. When a train pulls in, great mobs stage a battle to get on. The train is already more than full, but everybody gets on. So far as I have observed, nobody ever gets off of these trains. People are always getting on.

There was a silly little dining-car on the train that hoped eventually to leave Cherbourg for Paris; and we patronized it. A half dozen untidy girls, girded with unbelievably dirty aprons, milled about with huge platters of food which they splattered indiscriminately around among the customers. Some of this nourishment you were expected to get by absorption through your clothing. You sat down before a stack of five heavy dinner plates. Plop! —comes a big spoonful of something soft and gooey on Plate #1 and almost before you have had time to poke about in it with your fork (what the doctors call an "exploratory operation") the plate is whisked away magically, and Blob! —comes a triumphant ladleful of something on Plate #2. You finish on green almonds; but it is hardly worth all the bother one goes to in trying to arrive at the kernel. After you have peeled off the outside and hacked through the shell, and cut your thumb and skinned off the husk, the secret treasure is about the size of a worn Canadian dime and tastes like a little glob of unseasoned summer squash. I do not recommend green almonds except to my enemies.

The train finally started and ran like the very devil once it got going. The country was beautiful—coming through Normandy —quaint old stone houses, with old slate roofs with grass growing through the crevices. Every building had a grassy-slate roof— houses, barns, chicken-coops (low-bridge!) back-houses et al.

The fields were all tiny; and in most of them the people were making hay, which they loaded on donkey-carts or stuffed into huge bags which men and women (mostly women) toted on their backs. Women have equal rights (with the donkeys) in Normandy, to work all day for their fodder. The farm implements were all very primitive; and nobody seemed in a hurry.

Paris was reached about eight-thirty. Paris is a long trip from Cherbourg. Pulling into the station, we put our bags out through the windows and began to howl for a porter. In America we expect the porter to carry our bags to the vestibule of the car, and we leisurely follow him. He puts them on the station platform and another porter carries them to the taxi. But over here you begin shrieking at the top of your lungs before the train stops, for a porter; and if luck is with you (as it always is with us) a tired little man in a blue denim smock who looks as if he had just come in from a hard day's work as a sewer-digger, and needs a hair-cut and about two hundred dollar's worth of dental attention, reaches up for your stuff and straps it all together (four heavy suitcases) and loads himself down till he fairly staggers under it. You pity him; but he doesn't seem to mind the labor. Presently you will tip him about five francs and he will lift his cap and smile.

Taxied to Hotel Regina. Elegant room. If we had the same accommodations at the Waldorf in N.Y. (which is about the same class of hotel) it would cost easily $14 a day. Cleaned up a bit, and started to walk down the street—Rue de Rivoli. (We are directly across the street from one wing of The Louvre). Walked a half dozen blocks and turned in at a beautiful court, The Hotel Continental, and had a really wonderful dinner at a moderate cost.

I have filled my pockets with French money but don't know what any of it is worth actually. I shall receive my change for it in an outburst of simple faith. A franc is worth a nickle. A centime is the 100th part of a franc. A sou is the tenth part of a centime. The sou has a hole in it. You can have enough coin in your pockets, over here, to make you sag on that side—and still not have enough to pay for a shoe shine. (Enough about money.)

Friday morning we went on an all day trip by rubber wagon over the city. Visited Napoleon's Tomb, Sainte Chapelle (an old church dating from the early 12th century) Arc de Triomphe—where the unknown soldier is buried—Notre Dame—and scads of other noted places.

Sainte Chapelle attracted us. It was built by "Saint" Louis—so long ago that it is tumbling to pieces. Paris is well-stocked with ruins, of all sorts. You tramp all day among fallen arches; and find when you get back to the hotel in the evening, that you have a couple of fallen arches of your own.

Notre Dame is quite impressive. But the huge flocks of tourists, scurrying madly through these sacred places, trying to keep up with a chattering guide, lend an atmosphere of contemporaneous worry and care to the ancient shrines. A tired old priest, sitting in a box, at the entrance of Notre Dame, waved a thing over us that looked like a long-handled, gilded whiskbroom, and muttered something that sounded suspiciously like "penny." Holy Church is a good business man and turns an honest penny wherever she can. I said to the guide, who had a nimble wit, "Does he want a penny?" "No," replied the guide, "he doesn't want a penny, though a couple of francs might satisfy him. What he is saying is 'Bene' (short and lazy for 'Benedicti')." So, we were blessed at Notre Dame; and felt none the worse for it.

Napoleon's Tomb is in the great asylum where France cares for her aged and indigent soldiers. How like the French, who always think of exactly the right thing to do, to bury the great Corsican in that very place, among the broken men who had followed his turbulent ambitions with such dog-like fidelity. If our Americans had had it to do, some enterprising businessman would have donated a large field, ten miles from town, for the site of the tomb; and we would have built thereon, by popular subscription, something huge, high, and hideous. Presently it would come out that the great tomb was neighbor to a new real-estate allotment promoted by the man who had donated the holy field of valor. One cannot say much that is good of Napoleon; but he was a genius in his own line and the French adore his memory; and he is buried in the right place.

We visited a celebrated old cemetery where only the snoots are planted. Crowded with them. Crowded with little mausoleums, *crowded* with them. Acres and miles of them, as close together as the trees in a forest.

While we were there, a funeral came in. All horse-drawn hacks, driven by men in the livery of ancient days. The hearse was an open affair that looked like a pickle-dish on wheels—big high wheels with steel tires—a canopy over the top—and the coffin of yellow oak—out in the open. Several stiff, black, high-wheeled cabs followed—drivers all in old-fashioned livery. Then followed a flock of people on foot—some wearing three-cornered hats and tight silk knickers (the men).

Last night we went to the Folies Bergères. It was said to be a naughty show, and the saying was true and righteous, altogether. Eve parading about in a fig-leaf had nothing on those chorus girls, and the girls had nothing on anybody else.

Everybody in the audience smoked and talked out loud all through the show—which didn't bother *us* very much, for we couldn't understand what was being said on the stage, anyway.

It's surprising, though, how well we can make our wants known. If we were to stay here for a month, we would be talking French with the best of them. Mother gets along very well with her French—and when they say they can't understand *me*, I say, "Bessie, *you* tell 'em." Tonight I tried to tell the chambermaid that we wanted a bottle of iced water. I would talk awhile in my choicest combination French-English, and she would query me in her excellent English-French. But we weren't getting along very fast until Bessie came to the rescue.

Today we drove out to Versailles—where the Louises spent so many millions building palaces, parks, etc., that they brought their Empire tumbling down about their ears. Gorgeous place, though! It cost their regency and their heads, but it was almost worth the price—it is that beautiful. Our party included another couple—some New Yorkers who were almost totally innocent of any knowledge concerning the historical background of these old places; and the questions they asked the guide were a constant source of amusement.

On the way to Versailles, we stopped at Malmaison which was delightful. There, in a glass case, we saw Napoleon's hat—the famous hat that one sees in the pictures. I got quite a decided kick out of it—as you girls would say. Later, we saw another of Napoleon's hats in a glass case at Versailles, another in the Louvre, and others wherever we go. I have become quite used to them. They should have only one.

There are palaces everywhere all over Paris—now used for State offices, etc.

We visited the Louvre this afternoon and tonight had dinner out on the sidewalk at a restaurant down at the Luxembourg Gardens—gorgeous place. Then we climbed into a horse-drawn victoria and rode for an hour for a dollar, on Champs Elysées and the Bois de Boulogne.

Tomorrow we drive to Chartres, Sèvres, and some other towns —to be gone all day.

Sunday night

Well, we went to Chartres. It is a hundred miles from here. We were scheduled to leave from the Raymond & Whitcomb office—7 blocks away—at 9 A.M. We woke at 8:20. Gad, but there was excitement! But we got there. The drive was lovely! Through quaint little towns where every man's home, however humble, was his castle—and surrounded by a stone wall ten feet high and two feet thick, and covered with ivy. He lived with his pigs in the room to the left, and his cow in the room to the right, and a big, fine valuable manure-pile flanking the dining room window.

Chartres is a town of 25,000, quaint beyond description. The cathedral there is said to be the finest in all France. The building was begun in 1025 A.D. Formerly the Druids had a temple there and the present crypt of the church is an old Druid affair, dating from 600 B.C.

We were there about two hours and had lunch at a first class restaurant. All the way back was interesting. Bessie got sleepy in the wind, and put her pretty little bobbed head on my shoulder and snoozed for about 30 Kilometres. I woke her up when there was something shriekingly interesting on the road, such as a dimunitive jackass about the size of a big collie, drawing a little cart containing a whole family.

We learned a new formula for the disease that often attacks

our family on a long motor trip. (Low bridge!) We saw frequent parties of French tourists who had become possessed of the wish to do Le piddie. They hopped right out of the car and went to it in full view of the 5000 cars that passed in the meantime.

The French are very simple and childlike in all their ways.

In the men's W.C.T.U., a girl of about 20 came in to offer us towels, etc. I wasn't quite used to having a woman officiate at this rite, but she seemed to think it was all in the day's work; and it was, of course. The French are right. *We* are silly.

Dinner tonight at Paquetes' on the Champs Elysées, and out in front, on the sidewalk. Called for hors d'oeuvres and they brought *16* little dishes, by actual count, containing everything that could be pickled, from fish to celery, including beans and every sort of vegetable; also some strange bugs which Bessie dared me to eat but I wasn't quite able because the damn things had long whiskers and orky feelers.

Then after a good dinner, we sat on a bench on the curb of Champs Elysées and watched the pleasure traffic go by, for awhile. When it was time to go back to the hotel, we hailed a taxi (accent on the ultimate)—and here we are. Bessie is in bed reading about Fontainebleau, where we go tomorrow. It is a busy life!

Will write more from Dijon. Paris is a-glitter with flags and stuff, getting ready for their July 14th (Revolution date).

Avignon, France
July 15, 1925

Dearest Babies,

This old town is within an hour's ride of the Mediterranean Sea. We got here this evening at eight. We walked about awhile in the narrow little cobbled-stoned streets; and sat for half an hour on the Plaza, at an open-air café, watching a rather tattered and slatternly lot of natives (mostly women) go flapping by. Tomorrrow we see the Papal Palace where a string of Popes

ruled in the first half of the 14th Century, while another string
of Popes were still doing business at the old stand (Rome).
Youse pays your money and youse takes your choice of which
string of Popes suits you best in the solemn continuity of the
so-called Apostolic Succession.

We spent a wonderful day in Dijon. I would gladly have
stayed a week. We ran into an old guide, yesterday, who drove
a silly little open victoria (horse-drawn) and he took us to all the
old, old places—dating from the Duke of Burgundy period.
Some of it from away back in the 12th Century. And one old
church is built over a crypt where Christians were martyred
in 343!

Well, we'll try to tell you more about *that* when we are all
together again. Incidentally you two little chaps seem quite
far off tonight. For it is midnight, and you haven't had your
supper yet. We are just that far away. We are closer to *India*
at this moment, than we are to *you*. But we will all have a happy
fambly reunion, one of these days, and will tell you all the
history we have learned.

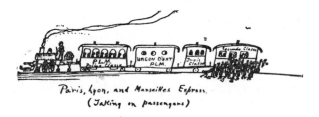

Paris, Lyon, and Marseilles Express.
(Taking on passengers)

Last night (it was Bastille Day) we followed the swelling
crowd, on down the street toward a big park. We walked a
mile or more. Thousands of people—30,000, easily, were there
to see the fireworks. I believe, confidentially, that we were the
sole representatives of the U.S.A. We put back after awhile and
went to bed. This morning we took another long ride and at
12:46 we took the train for Avignon.

It was a long, dusty, uncomfortable trip. Mother bore up

like a good sport, but I got very tired of it. Some French women ate their dinners out of a hamper. They were almost on top of us. I love the French. But they are just animals. I love animals. I love the French. Same passion.

Tomorrow we ride out to see the old Roman ruins in the neighborhood—Nîmes, Arles and Pont-du-Gard (an old bridge). Next day we go to Nice; and Saturday into Italy.

Mother will add a line to this in the morning. She is coming along nicely, just recovering from a couple of *very* sore legs she acquired while climbing to the top of the Cathedral of Chartres. (People at the hotel at Dijon thought her a permanent cripple, and lifted her around—much to my amusement and her disgust.) We are learning lots of French. I can parley-vous quite nobly. Mother bought some mustard pots at Dijon. They have been making mustard there for 700 years, and mustard is still their main industry. Enough for tonight. We will go to bed, and you can eat your supper.

Rome, Italy
July 21, 1925

Dear Little Girls,

We were quite disappointed on not finding any mail from you here. There was a letter from Grandma Porch, reporting your visit to her on July 4th, etc., also that you were both well. But we have had no direct mail from either of you yet.

Well, no news is considered good news, especially at long range, when mail is tardy.

You probably wrote, but got your letters off too late to catch us at Paris. True that was a week ago; but forwarding facilities are not good. Nobody on this continent is reliable. Everybody shirks. Everybody over here feels that to go through the motions of doing a thing—and getting it done badly, or the wrong way, or not at all—is exactly as good as doing it properly. But I guess that will be enough on the virtues of Go-Getterism.

From Avignon we went to Nice. Nice is a sort of "Atlantic

City" on the Mediterranean; and we were sorry to leave it. One day we took a long drive to the Italian border over the most scenic road I have ever travelled. We stopped for a half hour at Monte Carlo, where a lot of tired old men and frumpy old ladies were seriously betting small change on the roulette wheels. I found Monte Carlo a very dull place and would not walk across the street to see it again. I had pictured it as a most lavish and spectacular institution. I think it has been vastly over-rated.

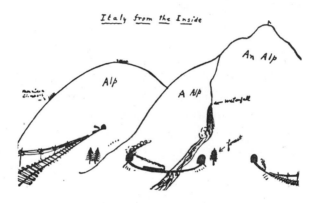

And so we left Nice, on another indescribably hot and dirty train for Genoa, where we spent only a few hours.

Too tired to look about. We saw the statue of Columbus, but paid it only a listless attention. We were now headed toward Rome and nothing else mattered much.

Bessie and I got to Rome last evening at 7 after the hottest, nastiest, dirtiest, most uncomfortable trip I ever took in my life. We left Genoa at 9 and were at it for ten hours. We went through 120 *tunnels,* by official count; and were therefore about 1/3 the distance milling along in the darkness with the soft coal smoke pouring in at the windows; and not a breath of air to breathe. I am glad we are here. I wouldn't have missed seeing Rome. But I wouldn't do that trip again—not for the whole Holy Roman Empire, ancient and contemporary.

It was some compensation to find a well-equipped bathroom, plenty of towels, etc. So we are cleaned up. Had our dinner. Took a silly little one-horse carriage, and rode down to the Colosseum; and a guide with a torch showed us through the ruins—where the Christian martyrs were brought into the arena—rusty iron gates still there, where the beasts were let in. Where the Emperor sat and did his thumbs up, thumbs down trick which signalled the victorious gladiator whether he was to polish off his antagonist with a final death-thrust—or let him die later at his leisure, with his boots off.

It was very impressive. I got quite a decided kick out of it. The stars shone brightly over head—and we peeked into the prisons and caverns where so many people waited their brutal finish to please some moronic Emperor.

Then we drove to the Forum, but couldn't get in through the locked gates. Then over to St. Peter's and looked at it from the Plaza in front. We were back at the hotel about midnight.

This morning, we started with a guide and a carriage to see the sights systematically.

I can't tell you of all the famous churches and shrines we visited. It is too long a story. But our trip included St. Peter's, which is, as you know, the largest church in the world—by a very great deal.

All the reproductions of the most famous ecclesiastical saints are done in mosaic. Strange priests, in all manner of curious garb—barefoot, shaven crowns, ropes about their waists, long cassocks.

Devout pilgrims kissing away what is left of St. Peter's copper toe. In some places we visited they have metal shields over the marble feet of images to protect them from the inroads of pious lips. Saw a virgin statue especially good for women anticipating children. (Low bridge.) Scores of women were about, kissing the feet of the virgin; all of them looking as if they had come to the right place.

St. Peter's is the most garish, the most magnificent thing of its kind in the world—so it is said—and I am willing to believe it.

This afternoon we go at 3 to see the Appian Way and the Catacombs.

One of the big sights this morning was *The Pantheon*. I shall not try to tell you about it until we are home.

We are both well. The weather is hot. I washed Bessie's head last night. Oh, but it was dirty! And now her hair is straight; and she is thinking of having a marcel. We haven't had one since we left the Majestic.

7 PM

We spent this afternoon at the Catacombs and Colosseum. I have tired feet. Mother is in her shorts writing to the goodole papa and mama. I have just had a good bottle of beer to cut the dust out of me throat. Also I have properly smelled myself up—so Bessie says—to go out to dinner with some parishioners whom we met this morning.

Tomorrow we feed some more Christians to the lions and hear some more paeans about the Popes. Feet tired, especially heels thereof. Rome is sure some nifty little village. Quite a thriving town, for some time past. Our room is on a noisy street. Have to yell at each other.

Rome, Italy
July 22, 1925

Dear Girls,

We are tired after an all day trip among the old churches and galleries. Saw a skull of St. Peter, the chains which bound St. Paul, part of Jesus' cradle; and watched scores of people kissing the blood stains of Jesus on the Holy Stairs which they ascend on their knees. Saw all the famous things in the Vatican galleries —Raphaels, Michelangelos, etc. Also saw the mummified *body* of Pope Sixtus V in a glass case. It was opened for a pilgrimage of priests and we just happened along. There is also a great missionary exhibition on at the Vatican, showing the Catholics' labors all over the world, to convert the heathen from their vain superstitions.

We have too many sacred relics at Rome. They become so taxing to one's credulity that one is apt to lose faith in the whole outfit of them.

I am sending a few rotten pictures. I can't figure out myself what they are. At all events, you will recognize Mother. Mama has some pretties for angel childs. No, I can't tell. It's a secret.

Naples, Italy
July 26, 1925

Dear Girls,

This is the filthiest city on earth. We have not been in all of them but I am ready to give Napoli the medal without looking any further into the case of other contestants for the dirt prize.

Bessie and I had a very comfortable trip down here from Rome. It gets very hot in midday; and people lie up until late afternoon; so about 4:30 we took a taxi to the center of town and walked about for awhile. This hotel is on a high spot, quite a mile or more from the heat of the city, and overlooks the celebrated Bay of Naples. We have a beautiful front room, on the top floor. I think the best room in the house. Our big double windows open on to a balcony, where we stood for a long time completely lost in admiration, when we first arrived. Smoking Vesuvius in plain sight, on the left of the picture; the Island of Capri dimly outlined, directly south; and the whole Bay the most gorgeous blue—the bluest blue that ever was seen.

We looked at it a long time; and then we took our baths and cleaned up. It's all a great mistake about the difficulty of getting a bath in Europe. Our hotel rooms have always been beautiful and roomy and airy, with large bathrooms, exquisitely appointed and plenty of the biggest, finest towels on record. We also had a nice large cold bottle of beer; for the water in Europe is said to be unhealthy. I haven't had any yet; but they say it isn't good for you.

Then we took a nice little nap; and dressed and drove down town. The city seems to be made up of main thoroughfares, filled with beautiful, fashionable stores—such as one sees in Paris, Chicago, Cleveland or New York—and these thoroughfares are as the tire of a wheel whose spokes are narrow—streets filled with the dirtiest, filthiest, and smelliest hovels ever known to the uplifted nose of mortal man. In these narrow streets are swarms of naked, filthy children, goats, cows, donkeys, markets, cats, shops, manure piles, open restaurants, washing on the line, wheel-barrows full of unwrapped bread and filthy women nursing unwrapped babies; and over all and around all the combined fragrance of stale fish, attar of goat, cow, donkey, etc., held together in a solution of just plain dirt.

I dared Bessie to have a nice little stroll up one of these streets and she came along. She is a nice travelling companion—and will do *anything* once. Occasionally we would run into a church tucked away in the riot of grime. I wondered why goodole Mother Church hadn't done something to clean up this horrible plague-spot. Now and then we saw filthy old women cleaning combs, with a critical eye. This is a profound research which belongs more in the field of entomology than simple hygiene.

Last night we turned in early to watch the changing colors in the Bay from our window balcony. Twilight was settling as a group of Italians gathered across the street with guitars and mandolins to accompany a brown Neapolitan girl who sang, very beautifully, some snatches from popular old Italian operas, including "O Sole Mio." I shall not again hear that tune without reconstructing the whole picture. It was most *romantic*.

We slept like a top last night. It was a relief from Rome where we were over a hot and noisy street. There are no fleas here but

plenty of flies. I don't know why the flies should come clear up
here to the top floor of Parker's when there is such fine hunting-
ground down town in the Via Smelliferious.

A NEAPOLITAN DAIRY

This morning we took a long ride with a guide and visited
the Cathedral (800 years old) where they have the blood of
San Gennaro. The blood is hard and dry, but three times a
year it liquefies, and performs a miracle on the sick—so they say.

Visited also the Naples Museum full of things fetched in from
Pompeii and Herculaneum, viewed simply from an artistic
standpoint, these marbles and bronzes are exquisite. But they
also tell the story of early Italian and Greek civilizations. This
afternoon at 3:30 we go out again for a ride—this time on the
boulevards overlooking the Bay. Tomorrow morning early we
go to Pompeii, Sorrento, and the Island of Capri. We take a bag
along and spend the night at Sorrento in an old Capuchin
Monastery. It will be very nice. We talk about our girls, and so
often wish you were here with us when some delightful interest
comes to hand. Imagine a city where within the distance of *50
yards*, you have seen a donkey-cart, a Rolls Royce, a naked child
of four, a victoria bearing an exquisitely gowned matron of

Naples, an old woman paddling along in her bare-feet; a prancing team with silver trimmed harness drawing a carriage full of swell Neapolitans, and an old hag milking into pint bottles for customers while they wait. Meanwhile the holy friars chant to the old bones, Vesuvius still smokes, the Bay is ultramarine blue, and Capri rises out of the mist like a marble island set in a turquoise sea.

Naples, Italy
July 28, 1925

Dear Girls,

Your Mother and I are very weary tonight. We have been going it pretty hard. Yesterday morning we went through the ruins of Pompeii—a great sight. Then a 100-mile drive via Amalfi to Sorrento over a road that hung precariously to the edge of very high mountains. Lunch at an old Capuchin Monastery, so high up that we had to be carried in chairs by men who had the chairs on long poles. You should have seen Mother going up— a damned good sport. Last night we spent at Sorrento in a room with an alcove and balcony looking out upon the sea—with old Vesuvius, so close we could watch every puff of smoke drifting in long plumes—away off to the south. We were, in fact, about 15 miles from Vesuvius, over there in Sorrento. Mother shopped a little. We were very tired and got up tired this morning. An all day boat trip from Sorrento to the Island of Capri. We had to go out in little boats to board the steamer. Mother never batted an eye at all this, climbing in and out of little boats today, and scrambling up the soupy little steps of the steamers. We were taken off in some more little boats to visit the Blue Grotto. We had to lie down in the bottom of the boat to go through the narrow passage into the Grotto. Big jam of boats in there; water very blue; but when you come over here don't bother to do it or the Isle of Capri, either.

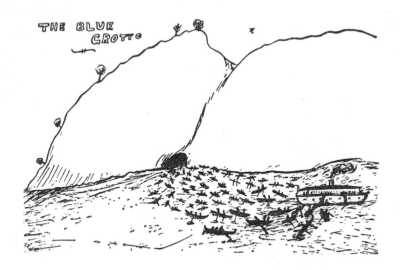

We went to the top of the Island (the little town is on top of a high mountain) on a funicular railroad. Lots of goats, donkeys, trinket shops, and dirty, toothless natives in their bare-feet.

Lucerne, Switzerland
August 6, 1925

Dear Girls,

We were not quite ready to leave Lugano yesterday afternoon at two; for it was very beautiful over there. And for awhile it looked as if we might stay longer; for the bus (which usually dumps us out at the R.R. station an hour before train departure) forgot to call for us; and we had a merry trip to get the train. The bus just hit a few of the high spots on the road, and went around all corners on one wheel. We scrambled on to the train after the exalted Cyclops at the station had rung the old cowbell signal for departure. And for four hours we travelled swiftly (by electric train) through the very thick of the Alps. One hears people saying that our American mountains are as picturesque and magnificent as the Alps. That is mere nonsense. I have seen all the important mountain ranges in America and none of them are in any way comparable to the Alps. We have a large front room at this hotel—Carlton-Tivoli, with a large balcony and double doors opening on to it. From where I sit I can see Rigi—one of the most noted Alpine peaks. I can see vast masses of ice and snow and clouds clustering about the mountains halfway up. Before me, in the foreground, lies the beautiful Lake Lucerne. And while I gaze in wonder on this impressive spectacle, I hear the sound of scrubbing in the bathroom; for little Bessie has decided to do a three weeks' washing. We are to be here for five days. We have unpacked all our dunnage, and have dug ourselves in for a nice long stay. You can't realize just what that sensation is until you have knocked about at the rate of a town a day for some time. The time comes, after you have packed, and unpacked, and re-packed your dunnage everyday; and stood guard over it; and chucked it through windows and jammed it through station-wickets—that you wish somebody would take it and make off with it to the northwest mountains of Hepsidarn. The packing and unpacking—and catching trains—and spending eight and ten hours, at a clip, in a dirty, hot and cramped car, on one of these toy railroads, gets to be very irksome.

We have no definite program mapped out for our activities while in Lucerne. We will take some strolls; and I think we will take at least one motor-coach trip up into the high mountains, though we can't afford to do much of it. Everything in Switzerland is high as their Alps. Their franc which is worth 20 cents of our money has a purchasing value about the same as the franc in France, which is worth five cents, or the lire in Italy which is worth four cents. The porter who wrestled with our baggage in Italy was quite content with a dirty little 5-lire note or 20 cents, for he is cordial and only beats you out of a few lire at a time. Here he growls over two francs, or 40 cents. Mother is now through with her washing, and is sitting on the floor cleaning her ring with a taper of tissue paper. She is having a regular debauch of cleaning. She even thinks of having her head washed, some day. She did have it washed down in Rome, and it hasn't had a chance to get very dirty since, for we have only travelled through 4,000 tunnels since Rome. She is now dressing, and says she is going out to do some shopping. I am loafing today. I don't want to go anywhere or see anything.

It is pretty chilly here. Last night I wore heavy clothes and my overcoat. It makes me feel rather badly to know that my babies are hot. But keep up your courage; we will be back, too, in the heat in a few more days.

We have picked up several little trinkets for you over here. Not anything really important; but some little things that mᵃy interest you because they are different. Labor is very cheap over here, and people are interested in all sorts of art-forms. They do skillful things in wood and stone. And the trinkets they make are beautiful and practically imperishable. They also do nice things in glass—many kinds of beads; we bought some. But you can go through the litter of stuff, when we get home; and see if you would like any of it.

We will be here until Monday, when we leave for Munich via Zurich and across Lake Constance by boat. We will see Bud Dieterle and his bride in Munich.

Hope this finds you both well and having a better time than you had on Cape Cod.

Nuremberg
August 13, 1925

Dear Ginger,

(We always say "Nuremberg," but these people write it "Nürnberg," with a little telleithyuh over the "u" which I think is a short way for making an "e."

To make a short story long, we had a really remarkable day yesterday. The Robert R. Dieterles—man and wife—were slated to spend the day with us; and that they did—from 10 AM of August 12 to 1 AM of August 13. 'Twas a wild day and a bad night for poor sailors. But you shall know the truth.

Early morning of August 12, and a pouring rain, Hindenburg the mighty, erstwhile of the "Hindenburg Line"—war lord, brute, beast and devil; more recently President of the so-called German Republic, (which isn't a Republic at all, but only an Empire waiting for a good chance to promote something with a fierce moustache, a hob-nailed conscience, and a lofty family tree)—said Hindenburg was due to arrive in Munich at 8 AM and would show himself at the Rathaus—(the City Building) about 11:30.

So, we get up at 8:30, eat a leisurely breakfast, and wait for the Dieterles—man and wife. The man you know. The wife is a charming girl about 26 or 27—a brunette of pleasing presence and good manners. We like her from the first moment. They came and the weather cleared. We wandered about the streets for a couple of hours. Under Bud's guidance I bought a case of nice little surgical instruments to take home to Dr. Parks (who has never billed me for any of the attention he gave us last winter). At eleven we went to the Rathouse and stood out front to see the famous clock strike. The Germans are fond of toys, and the clock-tower at the Rathouse is full of funny bronze figures who do things when the clock strikes eleven.

The clock strikes eleven, and the figures, probably mounted on a circular thing like a merry-go-round, move jerkily around: saints, hunters, horsemen, soldiers, priests, a king or two, and a few fat angels.

The crowd was getting pretty dense. There must have been upward of 10,000 people there watching the silly clock, but really there to see Hindenburg. The crowd grew denser, and the pushing (the Germans are great pushers) grew tighter.

Carriages came and went, depositing fat hulks of prominent Germans in brilliant uniforms. Mounted police rode through the crowd in true teutonic fashion. One horse was trained to kick people who failed to move promptly enough, and another horse stepped on a woman's foot. She squealed. The excitement was mounting higher every moment. Presently a big limousine came tearing through the lane the soldiers had ridden in the crowd, and everybody knew that Saint Hindenburg had arrived!

After awhile flunkeys appeared at a balcony, just below the clock-tower, and began removing the flower boxes from the ledge. And then a mighty shout of "Hoch!" went up from the crowd—and there stood old von Hindenburg, the fine old patriot, chopper-off of children's hands, revealed in all his majestic splendor, surrounded by a group of large and impressive states- men and big-wigs of the city. He uttered a sentence or two, and the crowd sang all five verses of "Deutschland Uber Alles." Everybody took off his hat, and sang with great gusto. Bud Dieterle did not take off his hat, and had it promptly knocked off by some patriot to the rear of him. I left mine on, and nobody knocked it off, but there were many dark looks in our direction. We thought for awhile that we might be starting another war.

Well, that's about all there was of that; so we went back to the hotel, and Mother took Ruth Dieterle up to our room and put her into dry shoes and stockings—for she had been knocking about all morning with wet feet.

Then we had a long and tasty luncheon. Some more shops, and tramping about. And then it was time to go to a tea given by members of the British Embassy for the Dieterles—and we were invited. Several German artists, musicians, etc., were there; and a full crop of British.

A very queer party. Bud sang some songs. We looked at a lot of paintings. We didn't get away until 7:30. So we taxied to the Dieterles' apartment to clean them up, and all taxied from there to our hotel to clean us up. And then we all went to a cabaret for dinner. It was held to be a very wild and wicked place. There was a sort of bull-pen in the middle of the room with a fence around it, and the tables circled it. A few youths, who looked like they had just come in from a Ku Klux parade in Barberton, danced with some kitchen mechanics who looked like they had just been dragged away from the wash-tub. Presently the lights turned low and it was announced that little Flossie would dance. Flossie was a peach.

Flossie was rather stiff legged, due to a spavin she had contracted while drawing a load of corn to market.

Then little Maisie danced. Maisie had a very fine figure. We didn't care much for the wickedness of the show but the food was fairly good.

Hoch den Republic ! ?

Later we thought it might be wickeder downstairs. (We had come upstairs, thinking that was the worst they had.) But downstairs they only had large mobs of jabbering Chermans, and an orchestra that played Liza Crossing The Ice music.

Then we took the Dieterles home and went back to our hotel. It was late; and we rolled into bed with a fine record. We had (a) seen the famous clock, (b) old man Hindenburg, (c) tea with Ow, fawncy thats, (d) we had seen the wickedness of Babylon (and had almost gone to sleep over it).

This morning we riz late and let a train go by. We took another at 10:50. Two German women played hog (the customary German game) by closing the windows tight. Germans never need any air. They live only on beer. They acted as if it was their train—as usual—and were grouchily permitting us to ride on it.

We got here at 2. Lunched, and took a one-horse carriage about the city—a really remarkable old place. We visited an old museum, strolling idly through without looking very intently at *anything;* for we are rather jaded on the subject of museums, having seen 2,674 of them, in various places. There were some hideous old sculptures of saints and angels,—long and slim saints like the following: and an occasional well-fed angel as per illustration:

We saw several nice little instruments that they used to torture prisoners with, back in the 12th Century. We wished so for you when we saw the "Iron Maiden"—Mother said, "How Ginger would love this."

We are here all day and night. Tomorrow we go to Heidelberg. We will see the Earl Moores in London. It will soon be time to start home; and we will be glad to see our babies.

Friday morning:

We are at breakfast waiting for the food to come. At 10 the old man with the horse and victoria will come for us, and haul us about some more.

It is a fine day; the goose hangs high and the bird's on the thorne, etc.

Cologne
August 20, 1925

Dear Bettina,

We had dirty weather all day yesterday—the first we have had since coming to Yurrup; for you know we are in Yurrup now. You may remember that we talked about it for some little time

before we came. Well, we *came,* and we are now in Yurrup.
We have seen it all.

We rode all over town yesterday in a rubber wagon in the
rain. The guide would point out a building and say, "Das iss der
Ratholenwhackerdamfinepifflebacken," and we would peek out
through the soggy curtains, look at the thing glassily, and reply
with a yawn, "Oh, yah, yah; das iss blosh!" Mother often stands
by and grins when I, with a straight face, talk pigeon Deutsch
to the porters and sich. Their language sounds like they had their
mouths full of half-chewed rotten bananas. A porter will inquire,
"Der handegepochtening goloshes splish der milash?" and I reply
solemnly, "Yash, splosh der squash und plish der mush!" Then
they shake their heads, and rub their chins, and we all jes howl.

The Cologne cathedral is immense. You will see it someday.
It is the best one we have seen. And we have seen all of them.
The bones of the three wise men (The Magi) are buried in this
cathedral. They were found by Helena, the mother of Constan-
tine. She was sure some fine little bone-finder. Everywhere we
have been we have seen some important bones that Helena dug
up. Skulls of Adam and Eve. The ax Cain used to rebuke Abel,
the hubcaps and carburetor off of Pharrah's chariot, the tail of
Balaam's ass, the wristwatch of Potiphar's wife, and Moses'
monocle. Among the discoverers, Helena has Columbus and the
rest of the boys knocked for a row of set-'em-up-in-the-other-
alleys.

But the Cologne cathedral is very great and beautiful (for
that sake).

Prices here are high. Night before last we ate our dinner at
this hotel (Monopol-Metropole) and found, after eating our
way through soup and fish, that we had already disposed of
$5.00 worth of food, so we went no further. I think if we had
gone into the matter seriously, adding a meat course, salad, and
dessert, we would have gone to the debtor's prison to rot until
Helena or somebody found us.

We were to have left at 7:40 this AM, but it looked a bit early, so we decided to leave at noon. We are all packed up, and ready to go. They sell Cologne perfume here. We went in a store and inquired for some, and the clerk got out a perfume gun and squirted a lot of it all over us. Mother emitted a loud shriek when she saw them coming at her; but she was too late, and all day she smelled like somebody's colored cook on her way to a ball given by the "Sons and Daughters of I Will Arise."

Mother speaks the language fluently. She goes into a store to inquire for a certain kind of fancy work pattern, and after she has exhausted her vocabulary, she entertains the clerks by making funny motions to indicate what she wants. She usually gathers up quite a crowd.

And now, beloved, it being an hour later—we are on the train. It has not yet already started, but it will, after awhile. We have a large compartment all to ourselves except for a small woman who has a dog with her. *She* is not much to look at, but he is a nice dog. Mother turns up her nose and says the dog does not smell good. Neither does *she*, since she got the cologne.

I think I spoke of our baggage being quite voluminous. When we got to a train, our retinue of porters and stevedores looks somewhat as follows: (Note how fat papa iss. It's der Chermany vot did dot!)

Our lady has got out a lunch kit, spread a tablecloth and she and the dog are sharing a bite. He looks rather bored, and I fancy he would rather go out to the diner.

The train has started now. A boy just came through the corridor ringing a bell, and I stepped out and asked him to reserve me 2 places in the dining car for the "second service" which occurs at 2:30 when everything is decidedly sloppy.

Mother is reading one of Shaw's plays, and she isn't very agreeable. She always gets mad when she reads them. Last night she took the book away from me, leaving me nothing to read myself to sleep on but the Cologne telephone directory; and she read "The Devil's Disciple" till she got so mad she wouldn't kiss me goodnight. One would have thought I had written it. Just now I showed her a picture of us and our baggage, and she hissed something that sounded like damphool, and kept right on reading. She is working on "Caesar and Cleopatra," today, and probably thinks Cleo got the dirty end of it. Ah well, the woman pays—even innocent little daffodils like Cleo. We have seen several photos of Cleo, here and there. I hold that she was too fat. Old Caesar could with great difficulty reach around her.

It is now raining, a large, cold November rain. We cross the border into Belgium presently; and I dare say that, according to custom, a lot of official ruffians and burglars will come in and spill our dirty clothes all over the compartment and make us feel like pikers. *We* don't know what they are looking for, and neither do *they*.

The dog has been fed, kissed, and wrapped in a shawl, presumably to take his afternoon nap; but he isn't going to take it

because he just heard me rattle a paper and thinks there is more food at hand. All his affection is worth is for food. He would kiss me for a bone just as cheerfully and fervently as he kisses his mama. This may be a cynical view to take of the matter of a dog's love; but I can prove it by Ginger who shares my sentiments on that subject.

Mother looks very stern. I think Caesar must have given Cleo another sock on the jaw. I showed my pictures to Mother just now; and she said, "You should have stayed in Paris!" How's that for a dirty crack?

The lady has just taken the dog to a door marked, *DAMEN ABORT*. I wanted to steal a sign in the train a few days ago. It meant do not spit in this car. It read:

NICHT IN DER WAGON PUCKEN

Or, more freely and disgustingly translated: DO NOT PUKE IN THE WAGON.

Later:
Ickle Children,

Well, here we are in Brussels. Mother and I became so absorbed in our books this afternoon that we didn't know when we had arrived in Brussels. I thought the train didn't arrive in Brussels until seven, and it was only five; so we sat tight and read our books while everybody got off. Presently the sweepers and roustabouts came in, and asked us if we were getting out at Brussels; so we got out, and found that the train was completely empty and everybody gone—including the hotel bus.

But that only made us smile, said the Jolly Rover Boys, skillfully extracting from their pockets the price of a taxi, and hunting up porters to lug their 102 bags a mile or so up the platform.

So we were in Brussels; and we came to the hotel and washed the cinders out of our ears, and took a nice long walk looking into windows.

Mother bought a bagful of hard candy, and we had dinner. She is now sitting opposite me in our room at a big table, reading the Paris Edition of The New York Herald.

Tomorrow afternoon we take a train to the Hook of Holland and cross the Channel to England. I hope there is not a sign in the cabin saying: Nicht in der wagon pucken. For we may be slightly disturbed. They say that only an occasional amphibian crosses the Channel without whooping up his socks.

That is all Betty and I found in the little packet of European letters. The ones from England are lost. It is hard to read Daddy's hasty scrawls written on trains or in bed after a long day sightseeing. He must have had fun drawing the pictures.

In a letter from Mother written from Nuremberg she says:

Daddy has written a letter to Ginger because he felt artistically inclined and has laughed so much over his pictures that it has been hard for me to keep my mind on the notes I am writing to church folks.

They came home at last after ten weeks abroad. Paris was Mother's love; Daddy said, "London is my town."

9

Time To Move

THE NEXT YEAR in Akron was our last. The season started off at top pitch. More and more people seemed to want to be connected with the First Congregational Church. The method for attracting them is described in this letter from LCD to a fellow minister:

A full dozen years ago I left off inviting people to attend my church. I decided it was as unprofessional and undignified for me to ask a man to come to our church as it would be for a lawyer to ask a casual acquaintance to come to his office for legal counsel and for a doctor to invite strangers to come to him for their pills.

I think I am generally known among my colleagues to be something of a Martinet in the management of my church's affairs. I do not permit people to make a playhouse out of my church and refuse to countenance anything which undignifies it. It has been a long time since I have had anything to do with a church which hocks egg beaters, chocolate bars and soap in an effort to pay expenses.

I have shrieked my disgust against rummage sales and other undignified traffic under the auspices of the church, until that nuisance is no longer an issue with me.

The typical Protestant minister has no more notion of psychology than he has of banking. His attitude is usually one of

obsequiousness and sycophancy. He romps about spreading the
glad smile and greeting his customers with a dulcet coo. He
plunges from the pulpit Sunday morning and gallops down the
aisle to the front lobby to paw over the customers in a spirit of
almost pathetic gratitude that they have conferred upon the
church of Jesus Christ so large a blessing by contriving to leave
their important affairs long enough to attend divine service. The
psychology of this, to my mind, is rotten.

Daddy had woven himself deeply into the life of Akron and
his days were full of town and church affairs.

It was Betty's second winter away from home and in the
following letter to her at Oberlin College he gives a description
typical of his life during that year of 1925–26.

Yesterday was a red letter day for us in the church. I am doing
a series of Sunday morning sermons on "Miracles" and the public
seems attracted to the idea. At least if one may judge by the
crowd we had yesterday, the subject is a live issue. In the afternoon I shared Burton's musicale to the extent of telling a story,
for a half hour—my goodole story of Fan Bascom, the old maid
who was an infidel, got converted, and seeing how nobody paid
any attention to her anymore, relapsed into her former state of
infidelity. It was a nice little story and I am persuading myself
I should do it for a magazine. Incidentally we had a fine crowd
in the afternoon too—probably six hundred souls on board. Good
for an afternoon musicale. The music was good too. We will
run this afternoon affair as long as there seems to be an active
market for it, and it doesn't begin to chew holes in the morning
congregation.

Mother got your corsage this afternoon the which she has put
in the ice-box, against the day of a party, or something demanding a high state of ornamentation.

I had a heavy trip last week. Five lectures in three days. Rained
cats and dogs in Boston. In New York I saw my new book in the
making. It is going to be a nice little volume and Scribners think
it will have a good sale.

Tonight I am making a dinner speech in Canton. Mother and Ginger are riding down with me and will eat in a restaurant and go to a movie while I make the Grand address.

Home all this week, attending to the piffling affairs which make my life more or less hideous. Friday night I make a speech in Cleveland. Wedding Saturday afternoon. Thursday night the Masons give a dinner to the deacons. Wednesday night we are to dine at the Dales'. And thus the time goes whizzing by, with no large amount of real excitement, but a certain quantity of labors—social and otherwise—required of us.

My office has been running at loose ends. My secretary has had the flu for about ten days and is now beginning to totter about feebly. We are doing over the billiard room in the Parish House for the church office—may relieve the congestion slightly.

I sometimes wish I had a little more time to myself for reading and writing. Somebody always wants something. I have to make scads of calls which take an enormous amount of time. I am on a lot of silly little committees which tie me up, and my correspondence these days always takes as much as two hours.

I see no way of remedying these conditions. The longer a man in my business stays in a given locality the more he becomes involved in such things—the only way to cure it is to move. Someday—when you and Ginger are through college, I shall cast my eye about for some soft job where I can have more time at my own disposal for writing and research. My sermons are hand-to-mouth affairs, hastily dished up after a Saturday brewing, and served half raw and cruelly hot to the long suffering sheep.

Write to us often. I miss you quite terribly. I have always so enjoyed you when you got some big bee in your bonnet and pumped yourself so full of enthusiasm you were ready to burst. Your mama says you are just like me. C'est ne pas?

In 1926 Lloyd Douglas was forty-nine years old. We have figured that out carefully and it must be so, but it hardly seems possible. In reflection we remember him then as a young man with young ideas. Later he confessed to us that it was at about this time he woke up to the fact that he was what other people would call well into middle age.

"I had always thought of myself as the Boy Wonder," he said. "I began to realize I was no longer a boy and not much of a wonder."

But he had been remarkably successful in his chosen profession. His rise to the top had been steady without setbacks. He had written several religious books which had been well received by the clergy. His lecture dates had climbed from small-town opera houses to the auditoriums of famous universities across the land. In each town where we had lived he had become a prominent citizen, an active leader in civic affairs. He could stay on in Akron and live out a full and useful career among friends who loved and appreciated him.

But, as always, he was not content to sit and bask in his laurels. The need to start fresh and conquer new places burned in him as brightly as in a young man. He had told the people in that town everything he knew and they no longer contradicted him. It was time to move.

We saw the restlessness begin; it's there in the letter to Betty—wishing for things. But this time we were not so ready to listen to talk of pulling up and starting over. Betty was happy at her college, near enough to come home for week-ends. My high school circle was a world I could not imagine giving up. Mother was particularly contented with her little group of charming, rather thoughtful-minded women friends.

Daddy teased her about the long hard books they read in their reading club—Russian novels, history and current social problems. At night she would sit beside him in bed reading, the little lamp casting its glow just short of his long body under the covers. She would feed him such selected paragraphs as she thought would stimulate his interest. Although he seemed half asleep these digested ideas would register. Sometimes he assembled all the bits she had spoon-fed him and she would catch him holding forth cleverly in company on his opinion of the author and his work. But she never gave him away or even laughed at him.

"Bessie, did I see you smiling tonight when I was telling them what I thought of that new Wells book you're reading?" Daddy would ask when they were undressing for bed after a party.

"No, dear, I was very interested."

"I know you were, my faithful little wife; you wouldn't laugh at your husband no matter what he did."

Mother saw everything, but she rarely commented. Everything went in and stayed. Years later when the press of Daddy's fame and the buzz and fuss around them got too much she would withdraw into that well-stocked inner house of hers and quiet herself. She could be in two places at once more successfully than anyone I've ever known.

In the late spring of 1926 the First Congregational Church of Los Angeles wrote Daddy and asked if he would be interested in coming out to look them over with a view to accepting a call to their pulpit. In July Betty and I were again parked with our Aunt Glen and Mother and Daddy went out to Los Angeles. To the James Van Vechtens of Akron Daddy wrote this letter during that visit:

July 26, 1926

We have had an exciting ten days here—with every hour full of dinners, picnics, drives, and all manner of entertainment.

Yesterday morning I preached to 200 more people than I preached to last Easter morning and this is an "off season."

It is a great city, with beautiful parks, metropolitan buildings, a $2,000,000 library, Art Galleries, museums, clubs, great auditoriums, the mountains in sight and the sea just around the corner.

It is a great church, packed and crammed with people from all over; plenty of help on the staff which means practically no "pastorial" on detail duties for the minister.

They have offered me all and more than I had in mind as their share of the responsibility.

I have made no definite commitments and am reserving my decision until later; but—you see how it is, don't you?

It isn't that I am dissatisfied in Akron but the difference between what I have in opportunity and advantages *there* and *here* is pretty noticeable.

If we come we will miss our friends. That is the only thing that holds us up and makes us sorry—that we can't have everything and everybody at the same time.

I have promised to let these people know in a couple of weeks. Meanwhile I sit tight, say nothing, and think fast.

In the fall of 1926 Daddy announced his resignation to the Akron church, warning them that this time he could let nothing interfere with his decision. "My relations here have been very happy and I am going only because I have been summoned by a greater opportunity," he said.

After this announcement which is pasted in the Akron scrapbook there are a few pages of editorial farewells from papers and city publications.

The town will seem lonesome after Lloyd Douglas steps down from the First Congregational Church pulpit and moves to California to a larger pastorate. Somehow Douglas has been a tonic to this sleepy town. He has started folks to thinking. . . . Some of his remarks have hurt like the hurt of iodine on a wound, but like iodine they have been needed.

Another paper writes:

Occasionally his opinions have laid the community by the ears. Once his declaration before a noon day club that Akron is a "hick" town induced a controversy that did not die until there had been reams of discussion in the papers. His reference to the "rabble mind" that sometimes invades the forums of newspapers caused another tumult. Likewise his rating of quacks and mountebanks. Not all such antagonists, of course, are swallowed up as Dathan, but whatever the event of these disputations the community was given to know that Dr. Douglas was in town, and that he was a censor in whose presence dullness, smugness, convention or pretense should watch their step.

The farewell sermon was preached to the congregation on October 31, 1926. It reviewed the events of the five years in Akron and finished with a statement of the beliefs that their minister had presented to them.

I have asked you to believe in Jesus as a son of God and to remember that you are another; that Jesus was in constant contact with the divine spirit—and that we might be too if we would.

You will remember it of me that I was always pleading for tolerance; that my right to have an opinion reached only to the point of denying some other man the right to a different opinion.

I have talked considerably about the value of Christian sportsmanship. I saw no good in churches that quarrel—either within their own ranks or with others outside their gates. I proclaimed that whatsoever spirit it was that made people mean and critical and captious, fault-finding and petulant—you could be sure it was not the Holy Spirit.

I have taught that religion and science must be at one—if God is God.

I have taught that humanity is on the way up, by the Grace of God, toward some exalted destiny.

You have been encouraged by me to believe in evolution, a theory of evolution which describes a vast physical, mental, moral and spiritual pilgrimage through the ages—increasingly marking man's rise on the stepping stones of his dead self to higher things; a hope and quest he still pursues without much more certainty of his ultimate goal than John conceived, when, out of the mystical faith that distinguished his radiant soul, he wrote: "Beloved, we are children of God. It doth not yet appear what we shall become, but we know that when we shall see Him, and know Him as He is, we shall be found to be like Him."

I have told you that we can add length to our earthly days through altruistic service; that whatever may be the nature of our future life, we know enough about this life to be assured that men do not quickly die and leave no trace; who in the quest of the Christian ideal have contributed something of their hope, faith and work to the generation in which they have lived.

I have taught you that belief in a life beyond this world is consistent with orderly thought on the present values, and duties of our earthly day; that it is inconceivable God would endow us with this eternal hope, and disappoint us in the end with death.

These things have summarized my creed. I go away with deep affection for you too strong to be woven into the flimsy fabric of mere words.

I pray that God's blessing may be with you, every one, through all the coming years.

In November the Douglases packed up their household belongings once more and set out for the land of sun and blossom —California.

Land of Golden Sunshine

LOOK AT the sunshine, girls, and the palm trees, and the flowers—they're all real." Mother and Daddy watched our faces and delighted in our cries of amazement as we stared at Los Angeles for the first time. Nothing looked real. The bright stiff flowers seemed stuck into the earth and one wanted to finger the air to see what made it so glittering. (It was before the days of the smog.)

"How do you like our weather?" everbody asked us. It was their weather and they all felt personally responsible for it. When we said "glorious," they would accept that as adequate if repeated often enough; the word had not been invented that would truly satisfy the people who were selling Los Angeles, and everybody was.

During the first few days we spent much time driving about in our car. It was hard for Daddy to keep both hands on the wheel when there was so much to point out. "Look there; did you ever see anything like it?"

Never. We saw the mountains and the sea and the beautiful homes clinging to the hills around the city. Betty insists that I record here how she and I sat on the back seat and examined sharply every passing car for movie stars. I dislike to recall that we were such nuts, but she says: "Don't you remember the day we pulled up beside a long low touring car and saw Wallace

Beery driving?" Yes, I remember, and how we stilled our excitement and whispered to Mother and Daddy to look.

"Wallace Beery? Who's he?" they asked; but they looked.

The brilliant colors and the lavish displays of nature—everything we saw made us gasp in amazement. It wasn't hard to match Daddy's enthusiasm, even Mother could rave on endlessly about California. The sun went down every afternoon in a stupendous blaze of glory. Was that the same old sun that went down behind Ohio? It all seemed fantastic, painted up for a holiday. We awoke each morning and rushed to the windows to see if it was still there. It was.

But people lived and worked in this town. They took their eyes from the scenery and got down to ordinary matters. Already Daddy was becoming absorbed in his ministerial duties at the big rambling wooden church on Hope Street. He plunged into his work with a zeal stimulated by the spanking newness of everything.

At first we lived in a furnished apartment and then, when our furniture arrived and a house had been found, we settled in our own place. It was too late in the semester for Betty and me to enter college and the days, warm and sunny, ticked by like an endless vacation.

The First Congregational Church was our only point of contact and there were enough meetings and social gatherings at that place to keep anyone busy for seven days of the week. The church was highly organized. They continually had suppers for this group or that. It was necessary for Mother and Daddy to go to everything and we, lacking any other occupation, tagged along.

On Sundays our church was packed, but all the churches in Los Angeles were packed. The city had a preponderance of old people who had moved out to California to retire. They filled the churches, seeking companionship as much as religion. To many it was their whole social life, and they loved to have the preacher talk about heaven. "It's their next stop, poor things," said Daddy.

Not many weeks had passed before he learned exactly what he was up against. The things he should have seen and pondered before accepting the new pulpit came into focus as his eyes grew accustomed to the glittering sunshine and picture-postcard scenery. The working theology of his congregation as a whole was about twenty years behind the times. It soon became clear that the church wanted the old-fashioned kind of minister—the kind who spends his afternoons calling on old ladies and giving them little private prayer meetings, steps in for a few minutes to every gathering of the ladies' societies and tells a few watery jokes to which they titter obligingly, makes himself a dear good man always at their service and amenable to every suggestion. "Oh, Doctor, old Mrs. Gotrocks was quite annoyed at what you said last Sunday about wealthy people. She thinks you meant her. You must go and smooth her down."

There was nothing very unique about the situation; every church has its little group of fussy people who expect the minister to toddle about soothing and placating, stepping warily over sensitive toes, but here there were too many of them. They held the important positions, they had the money.

Daddy expected a certain amount of pastoral duties, wanted his people to turn to him for spiritual comfort and counsel but over everything he wished to render a larger kind of service. He had always felt it his mission to reach deeply into people's everyday lives and teach them a fuller realization of the possibilities of Christian living. He saw spread before him in the Los Angeles church an enormous job of reconstruction. But with so many old people in the congregation the task appeared too hard. The challenge was there, but it was not a bold and virile one.

At this date we cannot explain or understand why Daddy allowed himself to be overwhelmed. There were many people in the church who were enthusiastic about the work he was trying to do. As time went on their numbers increased rapidly and the tone of the Sunday audience changed to an alert and stimulating response. But on weekdays that vigorous body was absent. While the pastor trod the dark carpets of the church parlors the carping ones tiptoed into his study and laid suggestions on his desk.

The first year in any new town is hard. People are friendly but not friends, faults appear glaring when unsoftened by familiarity. One remembers the old place, the good times and affection. Los Angeles was a far bigger city than any we had ever known. Daddy realized that it would take years to make a place for himself in the civic life of the town. But one large fact smothered him and could not be overcome: he did not like the deep-down flavor of the place. The combination of Western breeziness and Hollywood vulgarity he had no desire to touch or be touched by. "This is not a real city," he wrote to friends in the East. "It seems to have almost no metropolitan spirit. I don't think it's destined to have any—at least not in my lifetime."

On Sundays he was happy. He devoted himself to the preparation of thought-provoking sermons and in the pulpit flung off his depression and his voice rang out with conviction. Behind him was a magnificent choir whose conductor, Mr. Smallman, was sympathetic to the moods of the service. But quietly underneath the burrowing criticism went on: "The preacher is too highbrow; the music is too classical; why can't we have announcements made from the pulpit in the good old way? The minister's wife doesn't want to take any offices in the ladies' organizations; his daughters don't attend Sunday School."

One morning Daddy was shaving in the bathroom and called Betty and me in. "Sit down on the tub, children, I want to talk to you."

We sat down side by side, sobered by his tone.

"Now don't tell Mother about this," he said, "but we're getting lots of criticism in the church. Our family's being criticized.

I know I told you girls you didn't have to go to Sunday School after you were eighteen, but we're new here and these people seem to think you ought to go. I don't like to go back on my promise. All I can do is offer you an alternative. It's either Sunday School or sing in the choir."

The choir was very large and well trained. Many of them sang professionally in other groups. Their specialty was singing *a cappella* and they could string along endlessly on the key without a squeak from the organ. Betty and I could sing *a cappella* too, and did so often loudly and confidently at home, but our vocal limitations would not have been overcome even if we had learned how to read music. We had taken music lessons in Ann Arbor, but musical talent often skips a generation, they say, and in our case it was true. However, we offered our services to the choir conductor.

Betty was more successful in her tryout. Mr. Smallman looked at her dark hair and eyes and played a hymn in an ordinary range and she sang it through quite prettily. When it came my turn he must have decided I was the flighty type for he began to tinkle away up in the high notes and nodded for me to begin. I opened my mouth and stretched my neck. I did my very best to get up there. Mr. Smallman looked up rather startled. He didn't play the whole hymn through. "You have fine teeth, Miss Douglas," he said, dropping his hands from the keys.

I don't know why he accepted us. "We'll have to go to Sunday School," we told him, "if we don't get in the choir." Betty was assigned to the contralto side and I was put with the sopranos. I suppose Mr. Smallman thought it didn't really matter.

The choir rehearsals were affairs of great importance. It was mating season all the year around with them. Some were already married and formed the outer circle of interested spectators, many were engaged and they held hands and smiled at each other; in the center ring the real show went on: the stags wooing the shy maidens. The air was heated with young love.

Singers seem full of the biological urge. Even on Sunday the
vibrations went back and forth. There was one particular
anthem which was especially adapted to that choir and it was
often on our program. "How Lovely Is Thy Dwelling Place,
O Lord." The tenors and basses would look across the choir pit
to the altos and sopranos and their eyes would speak mellowly
to the one they chose. "How luuv-ly, how luuv-ly," they would
chant meaningfully.

The difficult year crawled on. Betty and I began the second
semester at the University of Southern California. We joined
a sorority and began to make friends. Mother and Daddy didn't
seem able to find themselves. They clung together in their loneliness and talked of getting old—a new thought for them. They
took long drives on the ocean roads. Daddy spent much time
writing. Since he was not being asked to make speeches all
over the countryside, his creative energies were turned almost
wholly upon the composition of his sermons and they were
never better. In a letter to Eastern friends he wrote:

> We have had bigger crowds this spring than I ever hoped to
> command Sunday after Sunday. Bigger, they tell me, than ever
> in the history of the church. Moreover I get a steady stream of
> favorable comment from many quarters commending me on the
> changes I have made in the general technique of the church, and
> hoping I will see my way clear to make more of the same type.
>
> But I have to pull the load of an enormous number of old
> people whose views are settled and who resent any new methods,
> ideas or aims. They feed on me and to so little purpose. After
> sixty, not many people are capable of new ideas. They can't even
> rephrase their old ones. They can't even pick over the apples of
> their fancy and pitch out the rotten ones for the salvation of the
> good.

He did not tailor his sermons to accommodate his elderly
parishioners. They were as modern and provocative as ever. One
series which caused a good deal of interest he assembled into a

book called *Those Disturbing Miracles* which was brought out
by Harper and Brothers later in 1927.

The weather and beauties of California continued to be a
wonderful novelty to us all, but even Betty and I felt the shal-
lowness of all our relations with people. We came together with
them for an hour or two, then separated, each to his unknown
life in the far corners of the vast city. Essentially we were small-
town people. We had prized our solitude when we had to
fight for it, but when it lay there all around for the taking we
were lonely. But it had happened before on a smaller scale.
Daddy had always had to struggle in each new place to make
himself known. Again I say I cannot explain it; something about
Los Angeles defeated him before he began. He wrote in a letter:

> The organization of the church is in good shape but there are
> no people with whom I have any hand-to-hand dealings. To
> them I am "our pastor" and they apparently intend to keep me in
> that role. I have no real companionship at all. However I have
> lots of things to fall back upon. Our family is very congenial
> and I have a chance to work at things which may prove
> rewarding.

"Some day I'm going to try my hand at a novel," Daddy often
said. In fact he said it so often that Betty told him she was going
to have it engraved on his tombstone. He had an idea for a plot.
The germ of it he had found in a newspaper item in a Detroit
paper long ago when we lived in Ann Arbor. The little scrap of
print had been carried around in his wallet ever since. It reported
the death of a doctor who had drowned from a heart attack
while his pulmotor, which he always kept ready in the boathouse
for such an emergency, was being used to revive a young man
across the lake. The idea never failed to intrigue Daddy. What
had the young man thought when he realized his life had been
saved at the cost of another's? Had he been stricken beyond
natural remorse by the fact that an experienced, valuable doctor

had died, and he—young, but of small use to society—lived? Had he been conscious of a duty to replace the older man?

"I have thoughts of tackling a novel this summer," he wrote to friends. "I shall want to do something to amuse myself during my vacation. The girls will be through with college in a week. I hope they won't want to go someplace hard by a jazz foundry. Oh well, they will only be young once while I am going to be very very old from now on."

We rented a small cottage at Carmel, California, for July and August. It was near the place on the beach where Aimee Semple McPherson had appeared from the sea in such a spectacular manner not many weeks before, but in no other respects did Carmel echo the craziness of Los Angeles. We even welcomed the change from sunshine to the gray mist which hung over the little artists' colony—quiet in those days and undiscovered by the cults.

We were within sight and sound of the beach and rarely met people when we walked along the sand. The water was bitterly cold and swirled around the barnacled rocks. Sometimes far out we would see the black head of a seal bobbing on the waves. Daddy and I oftentimes got up early in the morning and ran on the hard sand in our bare feet. We pretended we were pirates and went looking in the caves and jagged inlets for spots to hide our loot.

He found it difficult to work in the small cottage with his family about him and rented himself a room over a garage nearby. There he went every day for several hours to commune with his typewriter. In July he wrote to Jim and Betty Van Vechten of Akron:

Now and again I scribble for an hour or two. I still have a novel fermenting in my system and I take spells of fussing with it. I find it so completely off my beat that I hardly know how to approach it. Some of the stuff I do doesn't sound too bad, but many of the situations I am trying to deal with are larger and more complicated than I have the capacity to handle. It's a queer employment and my respect for novelists has gone up considerably.

The coast in this region resembles the Gloucester shore, but has very high mountains added to the scene. Very lovely. The sun does not shine brightly except for an hour or two in the middle of the day. Otherwise cloudy—a sort of grayish-blue haze reminiscent of Cape Cod. This little town is full of artists and writers. We don't see any of them. I guess they keep pretty close to their kennels. We take long walks on the beach. At night the four of us sit around the fire and read.

The cottage is well stocked with literature, including a complete set of Henry James. The other night we resolved to begin with "The Europeans." It was decided that the head of the house had a right to initiate the movement. We settled cosily to our improving task. A pine log glowed in the grate. The surf swished sedatively. We constituted an ideal picture of domestic felicity. Besse tranquilly stitched on a bit of tapestry. Betty was knitting. Ginger, on the floor before the hearth, was manicuring the dog. For, when a book has been undertaken communally among us, they who serve as auditors are permitted to amuse themselves with minor diversions—any light employment being allowed except the investigation of another book, which is frowned upon as too distracting.

By the time Father had read for an hour in the close-packed pages of "The Europeans," whose interminable sentences interspersed with incidental remarks in far-flung brackets frequently start at the top of one page and finish at the bottom of another, the family scene had changed somewhat. Bessie had completed the tapestry, at least for the time being, and was comfortably coiled on the day-bed in the corner, shielding her eyes from the light with a limp forearm. Our first-born was sprawled at full length on the chaise longue in a state of harmony with the universe. The younger, having completed the dog's toilet, was at ease with him on a row of pillows in front of the grate, their rhythmic breathing indicating that they were attending "The Europeans" with about the same degree of concern.

At the end of Chapter Three—for these chapters do, at long last come to an end—I roused the elder daughter, pointed to the place with a patriarchal thumb, and sank back to enjoy the tale second-hand.

It happens that there is a soothingly soporific quality to Betty's contralto register—especially when toiling through the deep sand of uneventful narrative, landscaped with complicated syntax. Presently I found myself yielding to tired Nature. I was told the next morning that Betty, having dutifully completed Chapter Five, prodded her sister awake with a toe applied to the short rib. The younger (I do not vouch for this, having it from one whose integrity is too vast to take cognizance of insignificant details) is said to have roused her Mother at 1:45 saying, "Here, darling. Call me if you come to any people you don't know." I don't know if the dog had his innings. I am told there is a dog watch.

That summer Betty and I had many long talks with Daddy in our rambles along the coast. He seemed inclined to be philosophical and to view life as if his work had passed its peak and he must now see his ambitions come true in the lives of his children. He questioned us with a pretense at casualness which failed to disguise his serious interest. What did we want out of life? Were we happy at college?

"Not particularly," we said. "It seems an awful waste of money—what with the sorority and all—for the actual good we got out of it."

"How would you like to go to Europe for a year?" he asked us. "I doubt if it would cost any more than what you spend for tuition and extras in college."

We beamed and said we'd love to go, thinking of all the wonderful schemes Daddy had proposed in the past which were just part of his conversation. But he seemed unusually intense about this.

"Go to college for one year more," he said. "Learn all you can of French and history and art. I promise you a year from

now you will be setting off for Europe." His eyes burned on us
when he said that.

I don't remember that we had ever ached to go to Europe. We
supposed we'd go sometime, but meanwhile we could wait.
Nor did we think he would expect us to hold him to that promise. But now I realize it was to himself he made that solemn
pledge: we were to go, we were to enjoy in our youth all the
experiences and advantages he had never had. In Europe was the
real culture; it was bound to fall upon you like a cloak as soon as
you stepped upon the cultivated soil. We were to have it, even if
he were forced to borrow on his life insurance to send us. And
that is what he did, as we learned many years later.

He continued to go to the little rented studio and putter with
the episodes of his novel. "I can't write a novel," he would tell
us when he came back. "My characters perch on my typewriter
and defy me to make them say anything that sounds realistic."
Then an idea came to him for an article which he thought might
interest the *Atlantic Monthly*. It was in his own field of religious
theory and he worked on it night and day until it was finished.
It was called "Non-Conformity" and he sent it off with high
hopes. The *Atlantic* promptly and enthusiastically accepted it.
They wired for his photograph for publicity purposes. It was the
first time he had ever been accepted by that magazine to appear
under his own name in a serious piece of work. It was a triumph
he had tried for often. Now everything was changed. His outlook was confident again. When we drove back to Los Angeles
at the end of August Daddy was whistling and singing the
whole way, talking of the church and his problems with optimism as though he meant to cut through the difficulties there
and succeed.

Naturally we found everything just about the same; Los
Angeles was still an overgrown bughouse and in the church the
members who opposed Daddy had not become any more
resigned to his ideas. A little of his summer joy slipped away,

but he was refreshed and more vigorous in his plans. In late
September he wrote to the Van Vechtens:

> We were glad—not hilarious, but simply and plainly glad to
> get back to the city. I am very busy trying to keep up with my
> church schedule, but the whole business is more pleasant than
> last year and I have hopes of sometime being approximately happy
> here. This fall I am not a new-comer trying to please everybody.
> I don't think I could go through another year like the last one.
> Every church has a group of sour old men and women to drain
> off their poison around the church. I have made some endeavor
> to conciliate with mine. I have petted, cajoled, endured and lov-
> ingly grinned at them for long enough. This year whoever of
> the saints can't stand my style can go someplace else. I have been
> religiously pursuing this policy since my return and feel much
> improved.

He continued to put the best he had into his sermons, for he
felt that in them lay his only hope to prove himself and draw
in the type of people who could help him in the church. Their
numbers grew: one by one they left the floating body attracted
only by the Sunday sermons and became active members, interested and loyal. But time was required and patience. Patience
was not one of Lloyd Douglas' more obvious virtues.

That fall Daddy bought Betty and me an antique Chevrolet
to take us to our classes, for the university we attended was far
across the city from our home. Lena was so old and battered
that it seemed unkind to force her another mile, but for us she
clattered along uncomplaining, dropping bits of tin and super-
fluous nuts and bolts, but always getting us to our destination
without serious mishap. She wasn't quite so obliging for Daddy
when he borrowed her. Not that he actually borrowed her,
but when we borrowed his Buick he had Lena.

Most of the girls in our sorority had cars, but theirs were
natty roadsters which made a glittering effect when parked in a

row in front of the sorority house. Ordinarily they kindly
tolerated Lena, but when rushing time came and handsome rugs
and furniture from their parents' homes were hustled in the back
way to beautify the rather bare interior of the House during the
brief period when the rushees were being entertained, they
complained to us that our car, heaped up out front, simply
ruined everything.

We explained the situation to Daddy and he generously offered his car for the few days of the emergency. The first thing
that happened to him in Lena was that she ran out of gas at
Figueroa and Seventh, a very busy intersection. Daddy said we
should have told him that she was getting low. "I had to walk
three blocks and carry a heavy can of gasoline back for that
old rat-trap of yours."

"But, Daddy," we said, "Lena never runs out of gas for us.
We hardly ever buy any."

The next day he had two blowouts. He was driving a visiting
minister to our house for dinner when the first tire went. They
got out to inspect the remains and decided it was too far gone
to repair and might as well be ridden in to the nearest service
station. As they flapped and bumped along another tire went
with a bang on the other side. "This is just like those funny cars
in the circus," said the visitor, wondering what was going to
happen next. "It belongs to my daughters," said Daddy rather
grimly.

Mother, so democratic in most things, regarded Lena with
suspicion from the first. When we offered to drive her to some
afternoon tea she would look pathetically at Daddy, hoping he
could rearrange his plans to take her himself. When it appeared
it was Lena or the streetcar she would consent unhappily to go
with us. Dressed in her finery she would come out of the house
with papers under her arm and carefully spread them on the
seat to protect herself from vile contact with the upholstery.
"What was that?" she would cry in alarm as we leaped forward

in the take-off. When we approached her destination she would say, "Just leave me at the corner. I can walk to the house from here."

Daddy often complained that we planned an exchange of cars just before we expected Lena to have a collapse. This was quite untrue. We were always sincerely horrified when he described the casualties he suffered in our car in the space of a few miles. It seemed that Lena would behave only for us. After Betty and I left for Europe Daddy sold her to a young boy for ten dollars. The boy phoned an hour after the transaction to say he wanted his money back. Lena had caught fire, he said, before he got her home and there wasn't enough left to haul off to the junk heap. Poor Lena.

In midwinter of that year Daddy preached a series of sermons which he called "The Secrets of Exultant Living." He had long been trying to convince people of the very real power of religion as a working energy in their lives if they would only experiment with it. He wanted them to think of it as a positive force—the "dynamics of Christian faith," he called it. The clues to this energy lay in the New Testament. Taking for example the words of Jesus—"Take heed that ye do not your alms before men, to be seen of them"—he explained what power could be stored in the personality of anyone who heeded that advice, the power of secret altruism known only to one's God. A magnificent relationship was there only waiting to be recognized. "Behold," says the Master, "I stand at the door and knock. If any man will hear my voice and open the door I will come in to him."

The sermons were particularly vivid and clearly illustrated. I remember during the third and last Sunday of the series the huge crowd strained in their attention as though they were hearing some wonderful secret of living and feared to miss a word of it. Even I was impressed, and moving out with the thoughtfully departing throng said to myself, "I shall try that," and wondered how to begin.

Our lunch was late that Sunday because so many people had crowded up to the front of the church after the service, waiting to shake Daddy's hand and thank him. He came home tired but exhilarated.

"Well," he said, "no matter what the old guard think of me, there seem to be many people who are grateful and yearning for that kind of talk."

We were having cold ham that day. I remember all the details of the table, for it was a meal which registered a milestone in our lives. Mother sat down at her place and said, "I was helped by your sermon today, Lloyd. I think for the first time I understand exactly what was meant by the idea of secret altruism."

Betty and I murmured that we too had felt a personal tug and had been inspired by the sermon. It was unusual for us to make such intimate revelations and Daddy was touched.

He took up the carving things and started to serve the ham. "The idea has been there in the Bible a long time," he said, "but its simplicity disguises its power. Once you try it, you realize you have laid hold of something. I wish I could get the meaning across to more people. If I have a message it's probably that."

"Why don't you put it into your novel," said Betty, calmly buttering a piece of bread.

Daddy seemed transfixed with the carving knife and fork in his hands. Seconds passed and we three looked at him, waiting. Then Mother said excitedly, "Is that it, Lloyd?"

He nodded but his face forbade us to say more. It occurs to me now that perhaps he was gratefully acknowledging the power of some of his own secret altruisms. We ate our meal almost in silence. Daddy was far away.

He began to work on the idea at once, but progress was slow and his duties at the church took up much time. He shut himself up in his study at night and we would hear him pacing the floor. At last he seemed to get the thing going and at mealtimes we talked the story over. The blending of the theme with the original incident concerning the doctor who drowned and the young man who was saved came as a natural and opened the whole plot to the end, shaping every step of it. Daddy loved to write about doctors. This one was to be a great philanthropist as well as a brilliant surgeon. The young man was to be a wealthy playboy who could have been drowned without much loss to the world. We asked Daddy questions about his story and often he was not able to answer them. "If the doctor's philanthropies were all secret how is the young man ever to learn about them?"

"Perhaps he kept a diary?" Daddy suggested. "In code," he added seeing our doubtful faces.

In June he wrote to the Van Vechtens:

> The novel moves along most amazingly well. Of late I have stolen considerable time for it and the results please me. I have some 24,000 words of finished copy and expect to have that much more by the end of this month. Writing a novel is a large order. Just the mechanical drudgery is an item. Just the physical effort of putting down that many words on paper is hard work— to say nothing of the vast amount of scheming one must do to make the story fit together and the characters stay put.
>
> The girls are getting ready for their trip. They plan to go to Paris and establish themselves there until such time as they feel the urge to move on. They'll live with a French family and saturate themselves in the language. Besse is not too enthusiastic about the idea yet, but agrees that it will be a wonderful experience for them.

We stayed in town that summer. Daddy was at his typewriter night and day. Betty and I continued our French lessons. We had both taken a course at the University on the history of art, but Betty had done much better than I. It was not in my nature to apply myself very seriously to anything. However she was determined that before we left for Europe I should know the titles and artists of all the masterpieces of the great galleries where she expected to take me. Forcibly detained, I submitted to her tutoring. She would hold up a reproduction of a famous picture covering the words at the bottom with a blotter.

"Who painted it?"

"Ohhhhhh . . . that's . . ." Silence while I racked my vacant brain.

"Can't you remember?" She would give me a hint, and point to her ear.

Light dawned. "Tin Ears!" I would shout happily.

"Teniers," she would correct. "What school?"

"Flemish. Seventeenth century," smugly I recited.

On and on it went. My sister was not going to let me fritter away Daddy's money and expectations. I had visions (quite realized later) of myself being dragged by the wrist through miles and miles of art galleries.

By September we were all ready to set forth on our travels. The four of us were going to Akron, Ohio, to visit old friends, then Mother and Daddy would spend time with their parents and Betty and I would continue on alone to New York where we would sail on the *De Grasse* for France. It all seemed very much a dream. I would not have been in the least surprised any morning to hear that something had turned up and the whole project was off.

But we packed our suitcases and the big day came nearer and nearer. All the time Daddy was in his study pounding away, trying to finish his novel. On September 6 he wrote two letters. The first was to the James Van Vechtens, his loyal and interested friends.

Well, at last, the famous novel which has taken me by the ears and robbed me of my sleep, the Old Man O' The Sea who has ridden astride my shoulders for so long, that perched on my bedpost and raised hell with my dreams and got me up at five in the morning—is done. Laus Deo! And Allelulia! I finished up at four yesterday afternoon. The completed job has a mileage of 80,642 words, and if I do say it as oughtn't, it's a good book, as I have already been assured by my literary landlords, Mr. Harper and his Bros. About four weeks ago I sent them 45,000 words and they were good enough to say—"You have hit upon a most interesting theme." The final chapters start down to them tomorrow and then we shall see what we shall see.

The second letter is to the publishers.

Harper and Brothers
49 East 33rd Street
New York, New York

Dear Mr. Exman:

I finished the novel "Salvage" yesterday afternoon. The final chapters are going forward to you tomorrow and ought to be in your office by the tenth of September.

On Sunday night I am going on a hurried trip to visit relatives in Indiana and Ohio. In case you wish to communicate with me my address will be simply Monroeville, Indiana, until September 25th. After that I shall be difficult to reach for about five weeks, due to the fact that I am going to San Francisco where I sail on October 3rd for Hawaii to deliver some lectures. I shall not return to the States until about the first of November.

If there are substantial alterations to be advised, I should be greatly accommodated if I might know your mind on that subject in time to carry with me your wishes on my voyage, where I shall have considerable leisure.

It would please me greatly if I might have a line from you or a wire telling me what your decision in this matter is before I leave on my Pacific voyage.

Thanking you again for your continued courtesy [etc.]

When Daddy returned from his series of lectures in Honolulu

he discovered that the unpleasant little group of people in the church who had been opposing him, had organized themselves and appointed a spokesman. This man came to call the first evening of Daddy's return. After polite and smiling preliminaries he delivered his message. "I'm afraid we are going to have trouble raising our budget this year, Dr. Douglas."

"And I am the reason?" queried Daddy.

The man did not say no.

"Then I shall resign," said Daddy; and he did so the next Sunday after his sermon, in these words:

I have a brief announcement to make which will come in the nature of a surprise to a great many people, friends and members of this church, who may have been scarcely aware that throughout my two years here there has been developing a left wing, increasingly out of sympathy with my administration.

From the first I have been aware of this opposition; but hoping it might be placated, I continued, happy in such service as I was enabled to render the church, believing the stress might soon be relieved.

Upon my return from abroad, I learned that the minority has become quite aggressive and outspoken. Were there any principles involved, I might be persuaded to contend for them. There are no principles at issue. What storm there is, centers about myself. The natural solution is that I eliminate myself, and the confusion will be abated.

I have never been a party to a church quarrel. It does not seem to me that the church is the place for them. Anybody who, seeing a church row in the offing, can think of a good way to head it off, should be called blessed, I think, by both factions, if he suggests his remedy. I now crave that blessing. Rather regretfully, grateful to the very considerable majority who have been loyal and cooperative, and without any bitterness toward those who have not seen eye to eye with me, I offer my resignation to take effect on the last day of January.

We now have three months left to us to demonstrate what sort of people we are. The persons in the church who wish for other leadership will presently have it. As for my friends, I trust they will realize how important it is that the church should carry on with a minimum of friction. I want my friends to be identifiable by the well-bred calmness with which they accept my decision, and the resoluteness of their refusal to discuss it.

What we have had here is just one of those little predicaments which are apt to arise when there has been a maladjustment. Nobody in particular to blame; most of it arising out of temperamental incompatability.

Let us spend these next three months working together like Christians, and give the Los Angeles public a pleasant and perhaps unusual illustration of what the Lord was talking about in the Sermon on the Mount.

I am glad I was not in the audience that Sunday when Daddy made his dramatic resignation. How Mother must have suffered sitting through the sermon, knowing what was coming when the last calm words of it were spoken. But Daddy would never betray by a quiver of a nerve what he had planned for the unsuspecting congregation.

Betty and I were barely settled in Paris when his letter came telling the whole story.

Don't worry about us. You girls go on with your plans exactly as though nothing had happened. We may not know where we are going, but we have a notion that the Lord will provide.

There isn't anything happening now that could possibly alter our relationship to the church except to make it more pleasant. When I announced my resignation it looked as if the whole auditorium was moving to the front to take my hand and protest my action. We have discovered friends we did not know we had. My mail is gorged with letters from local fans in and out of the church urging me to stay, to take another church, to fight it out with the reactionaries, to hire a hall, to start a new denomination (Heaven knows they have enough out here now. A couple of blocks away some wild man has started "The Temple of the Magic Flame"). Just at present I feel as if I never wanted to hear of or be in another church again. I dare say I'll get over it.

Don't worry. I feel I am breathing the first free air I have had since I came to this land of golden sunshine. The prospects of the new novel keep me up.

Daddy's wonderful optimism, although characteristic of him, had its roots, no doubt, in that last sentence. The publishers had returned the manuscript of "Salvage" for extensive revisions. During the last weeks of 1928 he worked enthusiastically on it, realizing the story was being greatly strengthened. He had no fears concerning the final decision. One turns away in pain from the thought of his sensations when on January 8, he received the following letter from the publishers:

At last I can make a final report on your manuscript. I am sorry that we have been delayed so long in giving you our final answer . . . therefore it is with a sense of deep regret that I write this letter telling you that it will be impossible for us to publish your novel. I really believe that it should be published, although this may seem a paradoxical statement; I am sorry that the imprint of our house will not appear on your book when it does come out.

I am holding the manuscript here for direction from you. You may want to have me send it to some other New York publisher for consideration. It also occurs to me that Willett, Clark and Colby of Chicago might be interested in seeing the manuscript.

I can only imagine what he did. He must have dropped his head to his hands and let sweep over him the exact details of his predicament. A man must have his moments of despair when alone he faces a future that seems totally black. Then fear must rush in and overwhelm him for a few moments no matter how he struggles to retain his grasp upon the strong hand of his Faith. There with that letter before him Daddy must have had to look squarely at his future, without benefit of retouching. He had given up his job and was stranded in the West when all his connections were in the East; he was fifty-one years old, past the height of his career, many would say; his daughters were in Europe, requiring money to keep them there or bring them home; the novel upon which all his hopes and prospects were centered had been refused.

There was no keeping it from Mother, but he certainly did not show her that letter until he had received enough strength to convince her he was not afraid. I have no doubt they spent many hours cheerfully recounting to each other what blessings remained. Many months later when we questioned her about those fearful days, she said, "Daddy didn't seem to be worried. The only thing I noticed was that he stopped whistling."

They stored their furniture and moved into a three-room apartment. Daddy did his work at the table in the little kitchenette. "There is an electric plug here by my elbow," he wrote, "which provides all our current:

7 a.m.	Electric Typewriter
8 a.m.	Toaster
9 a.m.	Typewriter
2 p.m.	Waffle Iron
3 p.m.	Ironing-iron
4 p.m.	Sewing Machine
5 p.m.	Curling-iron
8 p.m.	Typewriter."

In February he wrote to the Van Vechtens:

No, all this has not got my goat. I'm as full of vinegar as ever. However, we're getting out of this longitude. I'm not temperamentally geared to this locality. It's a screeching bedlam of circus methods and vulgar propaganda paced by the lurid blather of Hollywood.

I am working very hard these days on my novel, revising it again. I intend to send it out once more. This time it will be called "Magnificent Obsession."

II

Land of the Frozen North

IN MARCH of 1929 Lloyd Douglas was asked to be a guest preacher at St. James United Church of Montreal, Canada. He and Mother left all their goods stored in Los Angeles, except the car, and crossed the country again. Daddy was to preach in Montreal for six Sundays. There was a tacit understanding that if, at the end of that time, the arrangements were satisfactory to all parties, a call would be extended and the pulpit offered to him on a permanent basis. Such an offer would have struck the Lloyd Douglas of 1926 as rather beneath his dignity, but water had gone over the dam since then.

Betty and I were still in Europe. Cheerful, amusing letters came to us from our parents and our monthly cheques arrived each month on the dot. It was cheaper for them to keep us where we were, and if Daddy spent sleepless nights wondering how he would finance our trip home, no inkling of it came through to us.

March can be a horrid month in Montreal. The snow is piled in high mounds along the streets, but is no longer of a freshly fallen, dazzling whiteness—the soot of the city coats it. On the days when the sun shines there is the soft crushing sound of a vast thaw, and on those evenings when the cold returns, the melting snow becomes a glare of ice to threaten all but the most agile. The people are tired of winter and drag about sallowly in their dark, heavy clothes. Spring is yet far away.

Later, when it was a time to look back upon, Mother and Daddy told us about their first six weeks in Montreal, how they had tried to keep up each other's spirits. They had a gloomy little furnished apartment and, Mother said, the lady who owned it must have spent her life collecting sofa cushions—because there were at least a thousand in the tiny living room. They jammed them all tightly into a closet and pressed the door shut, not daring to open it again lest the cushions spring out like wild animals from a cage.

April came and the real thaw began. Days of strong sun honeycombed the untidy snow and cold rains washed at it. The holes in the streets thrown up by the long frost collected muddy water which passing cars sprayed on pedestrians. On their wedding anniversary Daddy sent Mother a bouquet of bright flowers with a card saying, "Besse, Spring is Coming, Lloyd." Mother tucked it in the corner of his picture on her dresser and there it stayed all the rest of her life.

The novel *Magnificent Obsession* was going the rounds of the publishing houses. Daddy had apparently resigned himself to the fact that it was just another of those disappointments that make up life. Perhaps his hopes had been a little higher for this story, but it was an old sensation.

His letters describing the city and the church were as full of rosy enthusiasm as in the old days. When he liked a thing he liked it at once, and thereafter it would require a great blow to shake his opinion.

April 1, 1929

Montreal is everything we had hoped it would be. We were met at the train by cordial people, shown to an apartment owned by a lady now en tour around the world. Living room, bedroom, bathette, kitchenette, hallette. She had moved the contents of a ten-room house into this place before she left. To the clutter we added seven pieces of hand-baggage and two hefty wardrobe trunks.

Yesterday was a red-letter day at the church. Fully two thousand were there in the morning and at night hundreds stood around the walls after the place was packed. Large chorus choir of excellent voices led by superb soloists accompanied by organ, piano and orchestra. It was quite lifting.

A most intelligent audience. I couldn't flatter myself they came to hear me.

We are delighted with everything as far as we have gone. Weather yesterday delightful, today pretty terrible; sleet, etc. The city is beautiful: massive buildings, weathered gray stone. Our kind of a place. We will have to learn French if we stay. Very Frenchy.

The church is huge. When I looked out over the sea of faces in that big tank I wondered what my voice would sound like when I uttered my first yip. It's a very queer feeling when you get up to make a noise in a place that seats so many people.

I guess my sermon went all right. Everybody stayed through and I heard no complaints. I was tired when it was all over last night.

April 12, 1929 [to the James Van Vechtens]

Sunday was a good day with us. We had thought that Easter would be the record breaker, but last night the big pack was there again. I am still not sure that they came to hear me. There had been announced some special numbers of a touring Welsh Choir and after the evening service was over the crowd stayed to hear them do some more. But whether I pulled the crowd or the Welsh they were there—some 2700 of them, and I, myself, had a whale of a good time.

I have learned from friends that they didn't think my Easter night sermon was as good as I thought. They said it was too heavy for the evening crowd. One man, whom I have known for a long time, called on us yesterday and said that if I should continue to preach sermons as heavy as that, I would empty the church in five nights. He is quite British and outspoken, but not offensive. He seemed much pleased with what I did last Sunday night and predicted it was the mental gait which that crowd could follow.

I think they underestimate their mental value. They all looked pretty intelligent to me from where I stood. Of course, I can't see very well. And I'm a stranger here.

Anyway, it's a lot of fun and I'm glad we came. I have made no attempt to delete the occasional drollery that I like to indulge in and the British seem to like it.

The only trouble will be the Old Guard who are horrifically sober—just as old folks are in every country—just as I shall be when I am munching my gums and wearing bella-donna plasters on the small of me back. To my surprise they haven't let out any shrill yelps of distress yet, but I am all braced for a riot at any time.

Last Sunday an old friend who has more political power than any four men in the Congregational outfit in the States was in town and ran out to see us at our apartment. He wants us to come back and look over a place in the east which will be open in a few months. I shall be interested if the church here does not measure up to full expectations; or if, to put the matter more bluntly, the Canadians should decide they can jolly well do without my interpretations of the Gospel.

But—let the heathen rage and the people imagine a vain thing—; the fact is I like this place. It's quite a tremendous tug that big crowd makes on me. If I learned I had to stay here for a long time I think I could bear up.

Besse—she thinks she'd rather live in the goodole USA.

Write to us often, won't you? We're perishing of loneliness up here. I haven't much pastoral work to do and am pounding away on a few religious articles for The Christian Century. Doubleday reports of my novel, "It has many fine points and some publishing possibilities, but it is not for us." I am sending it out for the last time to a little religious publishing house in Chicago. If they don't want it—t'ell wid it.

Well, anyway, my Sunday night mob here, as compared intellectually with some I've seen, are a lot of Platos, Aristotles and Einsteins. The church is massive and beautiful, and it has as bad ventilation as any holy temple I ever preached in. So that's that, no matter what Bessie says.

May 12, 1929 [to Betty and Virginia in France]

Well, little children, your sweet mama and I have been here in this city of the frozen north for about six weeks. The powers that be are having a meeting tonight or tomorrow to decide whether to extend us an official call. We aren't worried because there are several other supply jobs we can step into until we make up our minds about a permanent place, but we rather like the people here and would like to get our plans settled.

I am anxious to get a report of this meeting for, however blessed we have been,

> What we shall be eating next May
> Depends on this meeting today.
> We are not very thrifty
> And the age of past fifty
> Does not apprehension allay.
>
> A fellow who works by the day
> For $three-fifty or $four let us say
> He may never be rich
> The poor son of a b——
> But he knows what he gets for his pay.

This poem comes to you by the courtesy of an anxious parson, and is copyrighted in all langwidges, including Scandinavian and the dialect spoken by persons living in Ohio who have spent a few days in N'Owleans.

March 14, 1929 [letter to the Van Vechtens]

We feel securely anchored again. The negotiations when we finally got around to making them proved easy and brief. Not only have these people made me the most generous proposal, but they have gone out of their way to be considerate. They had previously engaged a London preacher to supply here during July and August and I am to have the two months on full pay. Isn't that quite sporting of them?

We cabled the girls (they have been horribly worried about us for fear we might not get a good job) and had a reply in a few hours. Two words only, for they have been living very frugally and cables are costly. They wired "Hot stuff." Sounds like them, doesn't it?

I haven't taken to wearing a monocle yet, but I've been looking at them. I must get a cane. If I don't stop taking on weight I'll have to get crutches.

Besse is having a good time here. She is quite content about my decision to stay. The people are rather shy and reserved on first acquaintance and that is to her advantage for she is that way herself. I can see from the fuss they are making over her she is going to be taken in as a kindred spirit. I am glad. She was wretched in Los Angeles. In the racket of all that strident ballyhoo she was as helpless as the fellow at the party who ordered ginger ale and was soon drowned out of the conversation.

When Betty and I received the cable we were in London. We were very homesick by that time. The anxiety of the long winter had been felt by us too, and when the steamship tickets from Daddy arrived and our sailing date on the *Duchess of Athol* was set for June, we thought it called for a celebration. Our one idea of a celebration was to eat, and to eat in a place that had a real tablecloth and napkins. Our economies had led us through some strange experiences during those months.

We had grown up considerably in our year away from home and were a little worried as to how our new sophistication was going to affect our innocent parents. The question of smoking, for instance: we had smoked mildly in Los Angeles, but never in their presence. We knew they more than suspected it, but the matter had never been discussed.

A lady in the Los Angeles church had reported to Mother that her daughters smoked, but she was never one to give tattletales any satisfaction. She would have smiled pleasantly and said,

"Yes, I know," if she had been told we were in the habit of taking opium in some underworld joss house.

On the boat on the way home Betty and I discussed this smoking problem. We had passed the experimental stage and now enjoyed our morning coffee with a cigarette much better than without. We came to no decision.

Daddy and Mother drove to Quebec to meet us. The boat was to dock sometime during the morning. They arrived the night before and had a room at the Château Frontenac overlooking the river. Later they described to us how, after tossing all night, Mother had got up very early and gone to the window. "There's a big boat down there," she called back to Daddy who was still in bed.

He got up and fetched the binoculars they had brought along. They stood together at the window, Daddy adjusting the lenses while Mother waited anxiously. "Why, Besse, it's the *Duchess of Athol*. They're here!"

They threw themselves into their clothes and tore down to the dock to greet their long-lost children. It was a wonderful home-coming, made a little poignant by the fact that we were all happy after months of uncertainty.

When the landing formalities had been seen to we went back with them to the hotel for breakfast. It was a clamor of four voices. I noticed that when Betty or I spoke our parents listened with a new respect, as though we were adults now and what we said important. I only half liked this new attitude. In a way I would have preferred to sink back into the child role. I wasn't sure that I liked the responsibility of being treated as a grownup, and felt a sadness that my parents had so willingly stepped down from their pedestals. Loudly as I clamored against authority in my teens, its removal was not what I wanted.

When the waiter had taken away the dishes and we settled over our second cups of coffee, Daddy calmly took out a package of cigarettes and held it out to Betty, and then to me. Unsmilingly, a little awkwardly, we each plucked one in silence, and then, to our utter amazement, he passed them to Mother and she—with such nonchalance—also helped herself and allowed him to hold the flame for her.

We stared so dumbfoundedly that they began to laugh. "Well, girls," Daddy said, "Your little mother's been a good sport this winter. We've been lonely and worried once or twice and she's done everything she could to be a companion to me. If I smoked a pipe she'd be lighting up hers right this minute."

Mother's smoking petered out after she had made her big effect and shown her traveled daughters that they weren't the only ones who had learned a few new tricks. Just as she could never bait her own hook she never learned to light a cigarette to stay lit and the habit did not take with her seriously.

We all went back to Montreal and for a few days crammed ourselves into the tiny apartment where Daddy and Mother had lived since March. As usual, Daddy was full of enthusiasm for his new town and drove us about pointing out the wonders, calling for admiration.

By June, Montreal had at last broken from the long embrace of winter and was a lush green of grass and trees. We drove up a narrow, winding street in a residential part of the town. "Here," said Daddy, pointing to a house behind a stone wall, "is where one of the pillars of our church lives. He has a big family."

"Any sons?" I asked languidly from the back seat.

"One. But he's a very serious doctor," Daddy said rather sternly. "Not at all your type." (Two years later I married the man.)

Betty, Mother and I went down to Gloucester, Massachusetts, and found a little cottage at the tip end of Cape Ann. Daddy joined us there the first of July. The novel *Magnificent*

Obsession, having been rejected by several New York publishing houses, was now being favorably considered by the small Chicago firm. Daddy wrote the Van Vechtens in August:

> Well, Colby, of Willett, Clark and Colby, came through after five weeks with a long letter in which he said everybody had liked the story, but it needed a lot of revision. He made many suggestions—all of which I thought extremely good. So I had the copy back and went at it again. You've no idea what a terrific job a novel is! It's entirely different from a short story; entirely different from a discursive book of essays. I doubt if I could ever get up the courage to tackle another. A dog's job.
>
> I spent days working nearly all the time, trying to get the things done Colby had asked for; and sent it back. Came another letter from them saying wouldn't I like to have it back again for the month of July to check over stray bits that were still ragged and lacked continuity. I wired I would try to do it.
>
> Of course, I would have pitched the whole thing overboard long ago but for the fact that I *know* I have something there. So I am plugging along, but am wearying of the job and wish it done with.

In late August we were back in Montreal to find an apartment big enough to hold all our household goods. We had always lived in houses before, but the idea of snow-shoveling and furnace-tending, in a climate where those jobs could be a full-time career, did not appeal to Daddy. "You'd only be out in a garden for a few weeks of the summer," he told Mother.

We found an apartment on the seventh floor of an imposing looking building. In the afternoon the janitor put on a plum-colored uniform, inserted a front pivot tooth, and became a very grand doorman. There was a self-service elevator. In spite of our convictions that some day one of us was sure to come to grief in it, we realized it was either that or the seven flights of stairs. Not long after we were installed Daddy pressed a wrong

button that let him out on a lower floor, and he walked inno-
cently into a strange apartment. "I knew it was too quiet for
our place," he said.

"Didn't you notice the furniture was different?" asked Mother.

"Oh, I did after I had a good look around." His eyes rested
thoughtfully on the arrangement of our living room. "Besse,
let's move our piano nearer the window, I think it gives more
balance to the room that way."

Mother loved to tell that story.

We made our plans for the winter. Betty was to attend New
York University and learn to be a department-store executive.
I was to stay at home and go to McGill where a very fine
course in Creative Writing was offered. Our family was established again. "It is pleasant," Daddy wrote, "to sleep in our own
beds and handle our own books. It's a pretty long haul from
January to September without the things you count on to make
you comfortable."

After the final revision *Magnificent Obsession* had been accepted by Willett, Clark and Colby, and Daddy had settled to
await its publication with as much patience as he could. He wrote
to the Van Vechtens:

> The release date will be October 22nd. Proofs are to come now
> almost any day. Mr. Colby is quite keen on my getting to work
> on another book at once, but I'm not really fit for anything until
> I know how my novel is going to get on. I'm a bit goofy on that
> subject.
>
> Besse is still toting things about the apartment looking for a
> better place to put them. I have a snug little study with good air
> and a reasonable amount of seclusion. I am looking forward to my
> work in the church this winter with alertness. Everybody seems
> eager to give me a chance to do my best.
>
> Write me a long letter when you get my book and tell me
> exactly what you think of it.

At long last *Magnificent Obsession* was published in October of 1929. The first printing was for three thousand copies—a cautious beginning for a book which eventually passed the two-million mark.

Betty was in New York when the package of advance copies arrived, but Daddy called Mother and me in to share in the grand opening. There they were in their bright orange jackets. "A novel of strong color and varied interests," it said, "dealing with strange transforming life forces." I remember opening the book with considerable awe. For so long it had been a matter of hope and doubt in our lives that now it seemed hard to realize it was an accomplished fact between hard covers. I turned a few pages and saw Mother and Daddy watching me in a queer, smiling way. Then I came upon the dedication—To Betty and Virginia. My tears were mostly because I felt I so little deserved the tribute. Betty, yes; she had sat untwitching in her chair while Daddy read the pages of a day's work. But I remembered my inward groans when I would see him coming toward me with a sheaf of papers in his hand and an excited smile on his face. "Tell me what you think of this."

Daddy was thoroughly pleased by the way the book took hold. He was kept informed of the weekly sales by the publishers. The first three thousand were sold at once and a second printing was brought out. For a few weeks it looked as though this had been a rash move, but gradually the sales began again; forty one week, seventy-seven the next, and the week before Christmas a wonderful sale of two hundred and ten. "Why, Besse," Daddy said, "our book may even go into a third printing if this keeps up."

It was aggravating to be out of the United States where the books were on sale. A few people in Montreal had read it and there was a complimentary review in the *Gazette*, but it's no fun to be an author if nobody in town knows it. However, Daddy did not think much about that. It was a religious book and it appeared the general public was not going to be attracted any more than they had to his earlier things. Besides, his real job was at the St. James United Church and there most of his interests must be concentrated, as this letter to the Van Vechtens reveals.

I have a feeling we owe you a letter and that no one has written to you for some time which is a dirty trick and only to be accounted for on the ground that my church takes so much of my time these days that when I'm not actually there I'm putting on my spats and long-tailed coat preparing to go, or taking them off at late hours of the night after having been there.

Word comes from round about ways that the Akron Times Press is printing my book as a serial. We heard there was a nice review of it in the press. Was there one in the Beacon Journal? We are as thoroughly cut off up here as if we were encamped on the waters of the Zambesi. If you think of it and it isn't any bother would you cut out an instalment of the story from the Times Press and let's have a look at it.

Had a letter from Burton Garlinghouse yesterday warmly felicitating me on my novel and telling me he presumed I know what points of it are weak. I'm not sure that I do, or I would have fixed them.

I find I can have a few preaching engagements in London if I want them in August. It is quite possible that Besse and I may run over there if we get enough to pay our shipping.

Already I find myself tinkering with the blueprint of another story, but the thing is too nebulous to bear even the most sketchy resume on paper. I don't know when I shall actually settle to work on this. The pulpit I now have is quite exacting. We are having amazing crowds. A good deal of money is spent on the music and there has been a feeling in the musical end of things that the crowd comes largely on that account. Wanting to discover how much of this is true I have deliberately closed down on special music and advertising of music three times lately and the crowds were the same as ever. I enjoy it hugely and am working like the devil on my sermons.

After a man has turned out ten thousand words of that sort

of stuff per week—demanding somewhat of research and a little ingenuity—he hasn't much time or mental pep left for outside writing. I hope that when I do get this next story boosted over the first stile, I shall find myself sufficiently engrossed in it to do both things.

February 17, 1930

It was cold enough up here yesterday to freeze the hinges of hell. Some said eighteen degrees below. Notwithstanding the weather large quantities of the saints assembled at divine service to hear the Word. Unknown to them their minister was wearing a new suit of woollen underwear into which had been knit every manner of thistles and burrs. Ordinarily I am a man of few gestures, but yesterday I flung myself about in an abandoned fashion whenever there was the least excuse for it.

Besse and I have steamship tickets on the Duchess of Richmond for July 23rd. We will stay all of August in London where I will be preaching every Sunday. First of September I shall sail for Montreal. Besse will go on to her beloved France for a month.

She is down in New York now looking after Betty who turned up with an emergency appendix about a week ago. We knew nothing about it until the doctor phoned us a few minutes before the operation. Besse flung her things together and rushed off in a high state of agitation. They are both recovering, she writes.

Ginger is my cook and dish-washer, my bed-maker and match-scratcher, my joy and delight. She is very ambitious with her cooking. We even had a roast chicken, we still have some of it. How she can run the house smoothly and efficiently, attend the University all forenoon, study all afternoon, dance all night and still have time to entertain me is a mystery.

Daddy and I kept house alone for about three weeks. I wanted to indulge him in all his particular food-fancies and very soon the air in the apartment became almost visible with the reek of garlic sausage, smoked kippers and cheeses of strong character. I did not have time to shop for these articles, when I might have discovered the prices, but blithely ordered them by phone. We were both very fond of shad roe, then briefly in season, and we had it for breakfast with bacon nearly every morning. The charge slips were hastily slammed on their pin and neither of us thought of looking at them. When Mother finally came home and saw her bills she uttered shrieks of horror.

Daddy and I accumulated a great deal of sour cream. "What shall I do with all these little bottles half full of sour cream?" I asked him.

"Let's make cottage cheese," he suggested.

"Do you know how?" I asked.

"Why, yes; it's very simple. You just pour all the old cream into a pillow case and hang it up to drip like a jelly bag."

He held the bag while I poured in the cream which was in various stages of decomposition. Then we tied it to a cupboard door and let it drip over a pan in the warm kitchen. It hung there for several days, during which we would prod it speculatively but doubtful of just when to turn it out. It got a bit strong.

On the fourth morning when we opened the kitchen door Daddy said at once: "Ginger, I think the cottage cheese is ready—or something."

We emptied it into a bowl and each tried a sample. He looked at me and I looked at him, both of us nibbling uncertainly at the ends of our tongues. "What do you think?" he asked me.

"It might be better with a little sugar," I said.

"I think it's perfectly terrible," Daddy said. "Let's throw it out."

It had always been his habit to get a cold snack late at night before going to bed. Mother tried to keep appetizing bits for him on hand, but his tastes were moody. One night the only thing in the refrigerator which appealed to him was a bowl of cold broccoli. He was in his bare feet and wearing the green silk suit Mother had made for him so long ago in Akron. It had shrunk a good bit, especially in the legs, and retained almost none of its original shape. He wandered into the living room munching thoughtfully at his paltry feast. The hum of the elevator did not disturb him, nor the sound of the front door opening. His daughter was coming home, but she invariably parted with her young men at the door. He merely stepped into the corner of the room out of view from the hall and started on another branch of broccoli.

But that evening I asked my escort in. While I went to my room to get a book I had offered to lend him, the young man stepped into the living room. The apparition he met lurking in the corner was enough to startle even one older and more prepared for social emergencies. I don't know what they said by way of greeting. When I returned they were standing in about the same positions as when they had first confronted each other.

"Daddy, this is Colin MacLeod," I said.

"How do you do," they murmured, bowing to each other with the utmost ceremony.

"I will now bid you goodnight," my father said. He walked away from us with great dignity, putting his thin bare feet down carefully as though intent upon making the distance down the long narrow hall to his bedroom in as orderly and unhurried a manner as possible.

Often Daddy would come into my room when I was studying and ask me if I had anything fit for him to read. I bought my books in the wonderful secondhand bookshops of Montreal and, at that stage, my taste leaned to the mystical and symbolic. He would say: "Now choose something for me I can understand; remember I'm just a simple country boy and haven't had all your advantages. I don't care for stories about satyrs or people who turn into animals. I like to know when I come to the end of a story too; some of your books read as if they forget to put in the last chapter."

I would hunt around until I found something I considered he

ought to like, even though I knew he probably wouldn't. I was very serious about my father's education and annoyed that he thought my efforts so marvelously funny.

But that winter I was more impressed than ever by his sermons. When he stood up in the pulpit in his long black gown I would be swept with the old admiration and awe. "Is that my own father?" Cynical as I considered myself I was unfailingly uplifted at the end of the service. For the first time I listened to the actual words of the Bible as he read them and was overcome by their loveliness. He read simply and in conversational tones, but by his pauses and slight emphasis the significance of the words came through to me and I realized the beauty and truth of passages I had heard all my life.

In Montreal Daddy made no attempt to impose on the church his strict ideas of Sunday Service such as he had developed in Ann Arbor and Akron. He seemed entirely content to relax and enjoy the old hubbub of people being ushered in, whispering, testing their earphones, rustling through the hymnbooks. He loved to hear the huge congregations of St. James sing—as Canadians love to do. A few favorite hymns he would call for again and again. "Lead, Kindly Light" was one of them, and the tremendous swell of voices, he said, was one of the most impressive things he had ever heard.

The novel *Magnificent Obsession* continued to interest him, but in the spring of 1930 there was no reason to think otherwise than that it had spent its force and would now gradually taper off into obscurity. He wrote to the Van Vechtens:

> I am trying to think up something to write another story about. Can't seem to get much further than that with my ideas. I would like to have another go at a novel. It takes a lot of hard work, but it's worth doing.
>
> I have been asked to do a good many articles for religious magazines this winter and have been turning them out quite regularly. If you do enough the sum is fairly respectable. But I get no par-

ticular wallop out of it when they are sold. The thing that gives you the big kick is when you send off something that has not been solicited and you wait and see what happens—like tossing a worm into the river and hoping you'll get a nibble.

Had a note from Ellery Sedgwick, editor of the Atlantic Monthly, asking me when I was going to send them an article, which set me up to the extent of sitting down at once to draft something for them.

Preaching takes up a good deal of my time these days. I fear I have lost interest in the main enterprise of the churches—missions, boards, committees and all the fussing of organization, and I know I shall never recover that lost interest.

That summer Daddy and Mother went to England. He came home in September alone, having cheerfully urged her to stay and enjoy the fall in Paris. However he no sooner got back to the empty apartment than he began to miss her to the extent of fancying himself coming down with fatal diseases. Betty and I had found jobs for ourselves in New York in spite of the depression and lived in a wretched little walk-up in Greenwich Village hard by the Third Avenue Elevated.

Daddy wrote: "I have a persistent cough which is alarming me, but I am looking after myself as well as I can." The next letter was even more pathetic. "My eyesight is going," he wrote. "I hope I will not find it necessary to ask one of you girls to come home and look after me."

Betty and I were on the point of giving up everything and going back when Mother returned and his health did likewise. Then they began to worry about us. They were not amused by our descriptions of the inconveniences of our miserable apartment or the eccentricities of our neighbors. Our friends sounded very horrible to them and they were shocked by our accounts of the parties we went to.

Especially were they worried about me from my letters telling of the work I was doing. I was acting as secretary to an author who was a decidedly unusual character. Robert, as I will call him, lived in attic rooooms stuffed with fantastic objects and furniture. I used my own typewriter because Robert had pawned his, and I brought my own paper too, as I had a good supply of it. "He doesn't pay me anything now," I wrote to my parents, "but he will when his book comes out." Robert was poor to the point of slow starvation. However, he seemed to have accommodated himself to the condition, although at times he would interrupt our work and moodily ask me if I would mind his leaping out of the window. He had an occasional fit too, which frightened me far more than the suicide threats.

Of course, I carefully toned down most of this in my letters home, but I said enough to bring Daddy down to New York for a surprise visit. He was very polite in his comments about our living quarters. After all, we were in Greenwich Village, a place he had always read about longingly, and the artistic atmosphere was undoubtedly there. Betty and I took him to cellar eating-places where candles stuck into bottles glowed dimly in the gloom. We introduced him to our friends—most of whom were out of work and talked scathingly of the ones who had given up their art and gone home to help Father in the store.

"Oh, if I could only think of some novelty to catch the public fancy," they would groan. "Look at the chap who invented the Eskimo Pie: simply ice cream with chocolate around it. He's made millions."

After absently acknowledging an introduction to our parent, they ignored him. He was just an old parson from the Sticks who sat listening, elderly and faded, no one at all.

I did not arrange for Daddy to meet Robert; I was afraid he would not understand his peculiarities. "When am I going to meet your employer?" Daddy asked, and it later appeared that was the main reason for his visit.

On Daddy's last day in New York I told Robert I could not come to work. I was spending the whole day with my father and I mentioned the place where we planned to have our lunch—our favorite Italian restaurant on Forty-Second Street. Daddy and I spent the morning down at the docks looking at the big ships, and by noon were starved. We went to our restaurant and found ourselves a table next to the big front window. There we were busily talking and winding spaghetti on our forks when Daddy sudddenly said, "Who is that peculiar-looking individual staring in at us so intently?"

I turned my head and was horrified to see Robert standing outside watching us lift our food to our mouths with an abject expression of hunger. There was no use pretending I did not know him. He was smiling and bowing in the courtly, old-world manner he affected.

"It's Robert," came painfully from me.

"Well!" Daddy said. "But the man looks half starved." He tapped on the glass and beckoned, pointing to our extra chair.

Robert bounded in with only a small show of dignity, although he was an aristocratic-looking man who always dressed neatly in his threadbare clothes and carried a handsome gold-headed cane. I introduced him to Daddy and he sat down explaining that he had just been passing by and happened to look in and see us, that he had wanted so much to meet Virginia's father, etc., etc.

"Well now that we've met in this fortunate manner," Daddy said, "you must join us in a plate of spaghetti."

"Oh no," said Robert, holding up a pale slender hand in polite refusal, "I couldn't think of it." He eyed our food wolfishly.

Daddy insisted. "Please just to oblige me," he said, "I find it very hard to eat unless everyone at the table is eating. You can just play with yours, but do keep us company."

Robert consented and the waitress soon brought him a heaping plate of spaghetti covered with a hearty sauce. While she ladled this out his fingers hovered tremblingly over the silver.

He spent the rest of the afternoon with us and was very charming. We went to Central Park to see the animals and he and Daddy strolled about from cage to cage exchanging witty and profound comments on animal life. I tagged along carrying the peanuts.

"Ginger and I will take the bus back from here," Daddy said, when we came out of the park.

Robert said "goodbye," but when the bus came he got on too and bowed most graciously when Daddy paid his fare. I was quite pleased the way everything had turned out. They seemed to have taken a great liking to each other. Daddy was quiet for a while after Robert left us. Then he said, "Is your typewriter still at that man's place?"

I nodded.

"I'll go with you tonight to get it. After that keep away from him. I've nothing against the man, but he's unhealthy."

As soon as Daddy got home to Montreal he wrote us what he really thought about our apartment and acqaintances.

It worries me to know you are in cold quarters. I know how much the little luxuries mean to you. You hate to be cold, don't you?

Well, if anybody likes attics with the plastering off in big hunks and pale people sitting about wishing they had the price of a couple of ounces of carbolic acid I suppose your present connections in New York should please you immeasurably.

There is a well-established theory that real art is produced in such kennels. I don't know enough about Art to be in a position to pass on that. What little scribbling I have done has amounted to nothing—or next to nothing. I make no pretense of understanding how people ought to feel, how cold and miserable they ought to be, how empty of gut, how full of ideals, how frowsy of hair, how out at the seat of the pants they should be in order to make the Great Contribution to Reality.

Perhaps Ginger thinks she can do some writing in that environment, but if I had to consort with hungry eccentrics blobbering fine nothings about the Upper Ether of Art I should lose my taste for literature and get me a peanut stand—one with a horse in front and a whistle on top.

In November I found myself another job—with pay this time. I wrote trying to describe my new work to my parents, but again without much success. They seemed to have no worries at all about Betty. She had a good position in the personnel department of a big Brooklyn store. But in spite of the fact that I was now employed on a respectable newspaper they still failed to understand what I was doing. My work was in a temporary department which collected money for "The Hundred Neediest Cases"—a Christmas project. I tried to explain what I did, but it was difficult since I had no clear idea myself and went to work each morning fearful of how I was to get through the next eight hours without giving away how utterly little I knew about secretarial work. I have often wondered since if any of the papers I filed away were ever found again.

Daddy wrote to me:

> I can't quite understand what you are doing, dear. I daresay this bewilderment of mine is one of the advance portents of a dizzy and dull old age—I regret to report that I don't understand your job, because that is exactly what every dotard has said to his son and daughter since the world began. Even old Adam must have said to Cain: "Little one—I suppose I am falling into decay, and getting out of touch with the times, but will you tell me why the devil you killed your brother?"
>
> The letter you enclose—as a sample of your work you are doing —reports the sad case of somebody out of a job and needing help. This is not a unique condition. Indeed, I am obliged to listen to such misfortunes every day of my life—and have been doing so since our old dog Tray was a very small and unpromising pup. . . . But why you should be also writing letters to Mary Pickford, Louis Bromfield, Sinclair Lewis, and Bernard Shaw, in the course of your ministry to this unfortunate Mrs. McMahon—whose letter I herewith return to your files—is not so clear.
>
> Do tell me all the ups and downs and ins and outs and through and throughs of your new vocation. I long to know what you might be doing. It is so hard to visualize you doing anything at all.

I note that you got your job on bluff. That may all be. I fancy
it is true. But you can't hold your job on *bluff;* and, much as you
protest that you don't know anything, I fancy you must be
making a stagger at it or they wouldn't be keeping you there—
regardless of the fact that you are ornamental, and would add
a certain fine distinction to any office, even if you didn't do anything but look out of the window, and polish the nails of your left
hand in the palm of your right.

I want you to come home with me on the 26th of December
and settle down to the job of writing stories. The money you are
making barely keeps you in food and raiment (I mean food not
raiment). I am quite capable of taking care of you until you win
your spurs. You may consider this as an offer or a command. But
I intend that you shall do it; so no back talk is in order. Selah.
Amen.

I did go back to Montreal on the date Daddy had suggested,
but my employers were more responsible for that than my father.
By then the depression was being deeply felt in every business.
New York was a hopeless place even for those with years of
experience. People were being let out of their jobs or were in
constant fear of being the next one. Some turned to bathtub
gin, while others fumbled searchingly for spiritual security.
This widespread need had its effect upon the novel *Magnificent
Obsession.* Daddy wrote: "My publishers tell me they are
bringing out another printing of my book. It's rather odd.
I had thought the thing had about run its course."

During its first year the book's sales had been mainly to friends
and parishioners of past churches. Ministers reviewed it in their
sermons. Most of the advertising was done in religious papers.
Then people began to tell each other about this rather strange
story. The word gradually got about. In the third six-month
period the book sold more copies than in the entire first year.
But this was as nothing compared to the sudden, surprising
demand that leapt up almost overnight at the beginning of 1931.

Daddy's scrapbook records that in the following spring new printings were made every other month by the astonished publishers who were constantly required to replenish their supplies.

I can't remember that Daddy seemed very impressed by this. It was all so far away and unconnected with us. Being in Montreal we heard little of what was going on in the States. The only reviews kept in the scrapbook are those which were sent to Daddy by ministers who had spoken of his book in their sermons. Things were a little easier for us financially, but Daddy had a good many debts to pay off and we didn't notice much difference for a long time.

Rather than delighting in his success he became worried that he had no second book coming along. The bubble would burst any minute, he thought, and people would forget him. In May he wrote to the Van Vechtens:

> Recent reports on Magnificent Obsession make me want to do another book. I have spells of tinkering with a story but it doesn't go very fast. It has big possibilities, but somehow I can't seem to get going. However—it was exactly the same way with the other one. Again and again I utterly despaired of getting it under momentum. I may not be able to do more than start it this summer. I'm really not a novelist. It's awfully hard work for me.
>
> I've been having a great time in the church here this year. Big crowds. Big enthusiasm.

That summer of 1931 Daddy and Mother went alone to the little rented cottage on Cape Ann. Betty had married a young architect in New York and was living in Bohemian quarters not far from our old Greenwich Village address. I had been sent back to Paris (Daddy's idea) with my typewriter and advice to learn to write by writing. "Paris is the place for the real artistic atmosphere," he said. "Greenwich Village is just a sham. Over there on the Left Bank you'll meet people who are really doing things—not just talking. You'll have all the opportunities in the world to see life and write about it."

My poor father, deprived of such opportunities, stayed home and practised what he urged upon his unaspiring daughter. His letters to me that summer rarely mentioned his own work; they were full of encouragement and advice concerning the few fragments I sent home as proof that I was not spending all my time gallivanting and getting myself engaged.

To Betty he poured out the details of his own labors:

June 20, 1931

The new novel* has laid hold upon my imagination, mightily. It will be a bigger job than the other one, in many respects, because I am dealing with a much more difficult group of people than in Magnificent Obsession. It will be a somewhat easier job; I learned two or three things while writing the other one, and can spare myself a lot of unnecessary toil. I do so hope that I am not just kidding myself, but I am possessed of the fool idea that this is to be big-time stuff. It fits my mood so well. It rolls off so easily. I know my people. I can smell them; and count the wrinkles in their scrawny old necks. I know all about my sullen youngster. I was through it. I have always despised the drab tragedy of my own youth. If I can capitalize on it now I shall forgive all the circumstances that made me a little old man at a time when I should have been a care-free little boy.

July 3, 1931

Last week I gave almost every waking moment to my new book. I think you would be much pleased to see the decided improvement on the early part of it. You may recall—(you ought to: I devilled the life out of you by reading it to you a dozen times)— that the first chapter included all of Julia from the time we met her to the day we buried her. The chapter was too long. I have made two of it, and omitted large chunks of irrelevant narrative and a few barge-loads of dumb conversation.

* *Forgive Us Our Trespasses.*

August 27, 1913 [to Betty]

What a lovely box of cookies you have sent me for my birthday. When I was a pale, scrawny-necked little boy I used to go with my parents to country dinners on Sunday where they had cakes covered with red and blue and green sugar. I often wished that somebody in my connection could make such beautiful things to eat. And now at long last I have a daughter who not only deals in all manner of flamboyant sugar, but stars an occasional cookie with silver drops that you want to be careful of or they will knock hell out of your false bi-cuspids and play the devil with your third molar (the one south of the remaining wisdom tooth).

Your poppa was fifty-four today. I am old. I've aged terribly in the past few years. I can tell it by various signs. I'm all off detective stories. They are the bunk, and I haven't read an interesting love story in a donkey's age. Of course I know that beautiful love stories and adventure stories are being published and read as of yore, but to me they are nothing but bilge water. I am getting to be an old man. I tell you I am 109 years old and all is Vanity.

If you coax me a little I will tell you some more about Julia in my new novel. She doesn't stay in the story very long. I just want her to have an interesting baby and die. You know I am never satisfied with the first crop of actors I bring on the stage. I kill 'em off, and start fresh in the second chapter with some nice new ones.

I have just read my horoscope and it says that people born in the sign of Taurus the Bull should endeavor to spend their energies in that field.

I am sending you a little money to give to Ginger when you meet her boat tomorrow. I expect she will be pretty well broke. Half of it is for my other daughter—the one who makes the beautiful cookies for her poppa's birthday.

October 29, 1931 [to the Van Vechtens]

I haven't done another line on my new novel since I came home from Cape Ann. Magnificent Obsession is steadily mounting in sales. It was in the list of the first twelve best sellers in September and October according to the Bookman's monthly score. My publishers are bringing out new editions every four weeks. They tell me they are hard pressed to keep up with the demand. This is all very amazing but gratifying to us.

Montreal looked pretty good when we came back this fall. It's really a very lovable old city. It would not surprise me much if we were to be here for some time. Ginger will return to England to marry her doctor but they will eventually settle here and this town will always be more than a temporary post in our lives.

My church pleases me. I am quite dreadfully spoiled for any blown-in-the-bottle kind of a job. If I've got to preach (and it seems that I must for a while yet) I'd rather do it here. It means a good deal to me to be assured of a steady crowd rain or shine, not to be responsible for the administration of a lot of church activities, not to care one limpid damn about the raising of budgets. I have told you that I have days when I feel I have amply done my bit in this whole enterprise and would gladly sneak off in a corner and pretend, at least, to retire. But I can't do it yet. So here we go for another long 10 months haul. I must begin thinking tomorrow what I am to preach about next Sunday. And every Tuesday morning from now until the middle of next July the same dilemma will face me.

But my Gosh! shouldn't I be reasonably satisfied with things as is. How infinitely worse if I had no job.

Bessie and Ginger toil steadily on in the dressmaking business of getting the child ready to be married. I haven't seen my wife without her mouth full of needles and basting threads for ten days. I've a notion to retire and let her keep me with her needle.

January 7, 1932 [to Betty]

I had a few strong words to say about the Pope last Sunday night, apropos of his proposal to the Protestants. We had a bumper house, and the Gazette gave me two and a half columns next morning. I am now getting mail from local fans and critics, plus a lot of boobs who fail to sign their names. These last, however, I am not required to reply to; so that helps relieve my bill for stamps. All in all, the thing has been pretty well accepted and I do not expect assassination, expulsion or any calamity. I had an anonymous letter of a single line—"You talk too much."

I agree with the fellow, and if he had signed his name I would write him and tell him that he is smarter than his bad penmanship gives him credit for. I do talk too much, and I'm so tired of talking that I could lie right down in the big mud-puddle out in front of our apartment and cry aloud.

A. O. Dawson and I had lunch today and attempted to figure out what relationship we are now that he is my daughter's father-in-law. We came to no conclusions but that the arrangement is entirely satisfactory. I grow increasingly fond of him. Today I half expected him to suggest that I tone down some of my pulpit statements, but there was nary a hint from him. The old boy is a good sport.

Your pretty mama, the lazy little loafer, stayed home from Divine Service last Sunday night so she could be all set with a delicious T-bone steak and f.f. potatoes when I returned from warning Israel against images and gluttony.

I presume she has told you she is renewing her French with much ardor. She has a tooter now, a handsome, dapper Swiss gentleman with a cute little goatee. I am thinking of raising one myself in the event he seems to be too popular.

January 8, 1932 [to the Van Vechtens]

This A. O. Dawson who is the sire of the Dawson who has lately entered my fambly, receives, every Christmas, a large Stilton Cheese from England.

This year, as a tribute of his love for me, he sent over a large wedge of it—probably containing four pounds. I wrapped it up in waxed paper, several layers, and put it in a cool place. We first tried the refrigerator, but found that its influence there was subversive to the mortality of the butter, and made the milk taste as if it had been procured from the cow about the time of the great Chicago fire—There is a little bathroom off the maid's room. The maid's room is a mere affectation. We have no maid. But we have that little bathroom. So—I put the Stilton out there. And ev'ry night, for these two weeks, after the day's hard work is done, and all is quiet, I have brought Bessie a nice red McIntosh apple to keep her amused and distracted, while I ate another slug of Stilton, washed down with a bottle of Black Horse ale.

For the first few days—nights, I should say, for it isn't the sort of thing one does in the course of the business day—I loved the cheese and smacked my lips, hoping to excite the envy and covetousness on the part of the champion apple-eater who believes that if you eat one apple a day, you keep the doctor away; two apples, two doctors; three apples, three doctors; etc., ad lib.

Of course, I realized that on each successive night the Stilton was taking on maturity; but I managed to keep up with it, and hoped for the best—Last night, I got out the reading glass and studied my slice of Stilton a long time to see if there was any excitement going on that couldn't be discerned by the naked eye; but all was calm. I ate it manfully; wrapped up the remainder; and put it back in the open window of the little bathroom. This morning—if you will believe it—The Stilton was *gone!* That is—*I* can't find it—and Bessie swears by the beard of her French tooter that she knows nothing as to its present whereabouts.

Houghton Mifflin Company want my new book and are writing pretty warm letters for a concern located in Boston.

January 30, 1932 [to the Van Vechtens]
My new story moves very slowly, but I think it has the making of a readable book. It is clearing up a little, in my mind, and I almost see the end of it from where I sit. Magnificent Obsession had the largest sales in December that have been registered in any one month since publication.

March 17, 1932 [to the Van Vechtens]
I have been strongly counselled by book-sellers not to be in any rush about bringing out a new novel while M.O. is still going so well. They tell me that when a new book comes out, it throws the latest one in the shade, and nothing remains to do with it but bring it out in a cheap edition and mop up whatever sales may come through that process. M.O. sold as many books in February as it did in December, which, due to the holiday business, is

counted on as the best month of the year. Perhaps I would be foolish to project another book just now. However—I am going to keep plugging steadily along on the new one so that when the time is exactly right for publication, I shall have it ready.

Easter will be along presently (comes much too early!) and when the crowded season around Easter is over I hope to settle down to some heavy boning on the book-mss.

September 28, 1932 [to the Van Vechtens]

I finished the novel yesterday. It was a long job, and I am glad to be set free of it. I have been sending the finished work on to Houghton Mifflin, and they have been having it set; so that more than half the galley-proof has already been revised. I go down to Boston Monday and Tuesday to read the rest of it, and discuss a few little details of publication.

I think you will like the new novel. In many ways it is a more important book than the other one. It will not meet the occasional criticism the M.O. had . . . "that nobody could do these things unless he had a pot full of money." Money does not get into this story very much.

The thesis of M.O. was, briefly: how to get what you want and be what you would like to be through a practice of a Galilean principle of secret philanthropy.

The thesis of the present work is: how to get free of the encumbrances which block the way to the expansion of personality. The most common of these encumbrances are hatred, prejudice, toxic frustrations, cancerous might-have-beens, bottled-up injustices. The solution is based on the only comment the Lord offered on "The Lord's Prayer"—If ye forgive men their trespasses, your Heavenly Father will forgive yours.

Virginia went home from the hospital yesterday and is contented and unscratched. The baby is healthy, noisy, and possessed of a full complement of arms and legs, ears, eyes, noses, etc. As to pulchritude, manners, genius, and savoir faire, we will have to wait a few weeks to estimate his gifts.

November 2, 1932 [to the Van Vechtens]

We see Ginger nearly every day. Her son has said nothing important yet, but has learned to get what he wants by means of a vast racket. Ginger has accepted him philosophically, alternating between the attitudes one takes toward a new fox terrier and a boil on the neck.

The new book was published today, and we are quite a-flutter to know how it will be accepted. The advance sale, according to Houghton Mifflin, was very gratifying. In fact, there were more copies of Forgive Us in the hands of book-dealers on the day of publication than were sold of Magnificent Obsession in the first eighteen months.

I have definitely contracted with a booking agency of NY for a lecture tour next fall, winter, and early spring. I shall wind up my church business here at the end of May. I have not let them know yet; will do so at the annual meeting in latter January or early February. They will not mind: they are accustomed to very brief pastorates. They would probably begin to be very restless if I stayed much longer than this year. Anyhow—I have told them everything I know, and have already repeated some of it several times.

November 2, 1932 [to Betty]

This is the big day for the new book! The book-stores downtown are full and running over with them.

I am glad that you liked it. I am anxious to talk with you about it. We are quite on tip-toe now to see how the critics and reviewers will receive it. No doubt it will have good attention. It may be roundly damned by the reviewers, but I think we can depend on its being well noticed and freely commented on.

It was kind of Mr. Kent to ask you for a close-up of your poppa. You might write him the kind of a little sketch that could come with good grace from a loving daughter. Please don't say anything that might make your poppa look like a monkey, for not everyone has our sense of humor.

You are well acquainted with my traits. I am impetuous, and

would prefer to do a thing badly today than to wait until tomorrow even if I stand a chance of doing it better . . . I am very easily imposed on, and a good salesman can sell me a dead mouse to hang on my watch-chain. . . . When I work at all I work like hell, and when I loaf I am patriarch and patron saint of all the Indolent. . . . I eat kippers for breakfast and smoke entirely too many cigarettes.

December 27, 1932 [to Mr. Ira Rich Kent of Houghton Mifflin Company]

The reviews of *Forgive Us* continue to come in and I am having better treatment at the hands of the critics than I deserved or expected. It pleases me to see the book rated so well in the lists of best sellers. *Magnificent Obsession* felt the effects of the publicity. Willett writes me it had an excellent sale during December—quite the best ever, in fact.

Warm, unseasonal weather up here. Most people have swapped their galoshes and red mittens for bad colds.

January 29, 1933 [to the Van Vechtens]

My resignation has been put through the usual machinery for such matters. We finish here the last Sunday in May, thence at once to Cape Ann where I do a little spot of magazine writing and loaf a great deal until fall when (unless the country is absolutely broke) I am to deliver some lectures.

After October 1st we will live in Boston—perhaps buy a house in that neighborhood.

As you know the new book is doing very well and has given Magnificent Obsession a shot in the arm. The best seller report for December rates Forgive Us third and M.O. eleventh. "Maggie" certainly has a lot of vitality. We have had a bona fide offer for the movie rights. My mail is very heavy just now, mostly arising out of the books.

It is Saturday night and I must go to bed. Tomorrow is a hard day as usual. I am tired of preaching. I have enjoyed my church here as much as any I have ever had, but I yearn to get away from the everlasting toil of turning out two sermons each week, year after year.

Besse is airing our dog. For Christmas I presented her with a Sealyham pup to divert her now that she has no children. Zocco is growing rapidly, but in an apartment is a larger pest than I had anticipated. Spends a good deal of his time shut up in the bathroom chewing reams of toilet paper and scratching at the door. He has finished the laundry basket. Besse threw out the hull this morning.

April 3, 1933 [to Betty]

This is a drab, bleak, muddy morning, but if we sit tight spring will come. I have only eight more Sundays left to preach. I am lashing myself to do my work in the pulpit. There haint no bottom to my hallelujah anymo'. My attention has been so thoroughly diverted from the church business that I find it difficult to carry on with anything like interest. I need to move.

We Douglases are a bunch of vagabonds. We have what is known as the Elsewhere Complex. I don't know where I got it, but I know where you got it. Bessie must have got hers by infection. Neither her ancestors nor mine seem to have gadded about very much. I fancy the whole responsibility rests with me.

May 12, 1933 [to Betty]

Nothing very important has happened lately, but something important is going to happen in nineteen days.

We are beginning to gather up our dunnage. If you want your bedroom slippers you will find them either in the kitchen wastebasket or that large brass umbrella stand in the hall. Moreover arrangements have been made with the Moving, Breaking, Over-Charging and Losing Company Ltd. to convey our household effects to the good old USA.

Ginger is having a tee-hee this afternoon. Besse is there with the maid and most of our spoons. I was left to entertain the dog and get out a sermon for Sunday. The former grows mightily and has learned to bark loudly at strangers. He had previously learned how to shed white hairs all over the furniture, and so earnestly has he devoted himself to this vocation that we ourselves look like polar bears and fastidious friends pick at us when we draw near.

The days are slipping along, a few at a time, and our freedom is just around the corner. Ye Gods! but I am fired with zeal to accomplish this great boon.

May 15, 1933 [to Betty]

Things went very nicely at church yesterday. I took in forty new members in the morning, more than half of whom were youngsters in their teens. Besse appreciated your wire for Mother's day.

Bowker's report for April reports Forgive Us No. 2 on the best seller list and Magnificent Obsession No. 6. This is very pleasant. The June American will be along presently with a story of mine and maybe a little picture of Poppa. Zocco is also in the picture. It is a remarkable likeness of him, so sincere and natural. I wonder what you will think of mine. He is beginning to cool off and is half-decent at times. Tomorrow we are sending the velvet carpet to the cleaners.

This week I make a speech before the Rotary Club. It will be Ladies Day and Bessie will be a-settin right by me at the head table all dressed up in her new checker-board dress. She is busy packing every spare minute. Gosh! I am all on the grand qui vive now about getting off.

Lots of dinners and other things to do from now on. And—as the wife of the Texas Senator wrote home—"we have hardly had our knives out of our mouths for the last two weeks."

I enclose my last week's sermon.

May 24, 1933 [to Betty]

This is Empire day and we celebrated it by spending hours on our heads in closets rooting for stuff we didn't want. For, you see we are in the throes of moving. We love to move. We've become quite nonchalant on the subject. Do you remember the time we moved and forgot the date and were sitting around the breakfast table about half-past nine when the strong men came to carry us out? We told them to keep their panson for a little while until we had finished what we were talking about. But we got moved allesame.

This morning I went to my study and tore hundreds and thousands of wonderful sermons into small bits and threw them into a large basket. I also tore up gallons of fan mail and a lot of rubbish that we have been carting about with us since you were ten years old. And earlier—long before you were thought of.

Sunday is the glad and big and joyful day. We are just hysterical to have it over and be off. I never was so pippy with joy and delight and anticipation in my life.

It was in May 1903 I went to North Manchester to take my first church—thirty years ago to the month.

12

A Little Place To Retire

DADDY AND MOTHER spent the summer of 1933 in the little rented cottage on Cape Ann. Grandmother and Grandfather Porch were with them, and for a while Grandmother Douglas. The three were getting very old and that summer the two old ladies managed to patch up their long-standing feud. The correct date of my birth had been the declared point upon which they disagreed, but they had never seen eye to eye on a wide range of subjects. For years they had been neighbors in Columbia City, Indiana. Grandfather Porch was pastor of the Lutheran Church where once Grandfather Douglas had preached.

"Why!" Grandmother Douglas used to tell us, "I get up and have my housework all done, and when I'm coming home from market I pass the Porches' house. Blinds all down. Still asleep in there."

But that summer the two grandmothers sat together long hours in lawn chairs overlooking the sea, murmuring happily about who had been buried where back in the old family graveyards. "We moved the baby into the Cassel lot when we buried Papa. The casket was crumbling but everything inside was as nice as could be. Her little shoe buttons were as shiny as the day I laid her away."

Daddy worked on his story "Precious Jeopardy." It was the

old story about Mr. Parker who had stepped on a needle and only recovered half of it. The idea of the mean old man living in daily fear of death and hastily making up for past sins Daddy had preached and lectured on, sold as a story to *Cosmopolitan*, and now was expanding to a little novelette for Christmas sale.

"That ought to be about the end of that," said Mother.

In their spare time they went house-hunting in the small towns around Boston. They were going to buy a house. It would be the first inch of property they had ever owned. Mother wanted a nice garden, Daddy wanted a big study: other than that their requirements were limited only by the amount of money they were prepared to spend.

One day they went to examine a house in Wellesley Hills. The lady who met them at the door listened as they introduced themselves, then opened her mouth in astonishment. "Why Lloyd Douglas, I know you. You pulled me out of the river when I broke through the ice, skating. I went to Wittenberg College."

Naturally they had to buy that house. A few defects were discovered later such as a leaky cellar which had not been noticed in the friendliness of the first viewing; but on the whole, it was a charming, simple place in a neighborhood which reminded them of Cambridge Road in Ann Arbor. The garden behind the house had great possibilities. The study wasn't very good, but Daddy planned to improve that later.

The last weeks of summer they spent at Pigeon Cove making arrangements for the next move. Daddy wrote to me in Montreal:

September 14, 1933

It is raining cats and dogs here. Most of the summer people have gone back to town and the point seems desolate. The weather has been rotten; rains every day; thunder and lightning all night, and gray soupy fog every morning. Everything is damp and mildewed. The closets smell like chicken coops, the postage stamps are all stuck together, the plaster is falling off, and, taking the situation by and large, it could be nicely described as DAMP.

Yesterday Bessie and I drove to Boston where we went through the formalities necessary to legal acquirement of our new house. Also went out with a landscape gardener to look at three trees which we hope to have transplanted into our yard. They looked to me like pretty big numbers to be rooted up and set down again in a new hole, but the man assured us it was being done every day and we are taking his word for it. Mother is all a-pip over what she plans to do in the garden.

We move in on Saturday, the sixteenth. Early morning Saturday we leave here with our baggage, the dog, the bird, the flowers in pots, Georgette (the maid) and a broom. The rest of the stuff will go down that morning on a truck. Grandpa and Grandma Porch will remain here for a couple of weeks while we get settled.

I leave on my lecture trip October 7th, the first date is in Lexington, Kentucky. The agent says there will be more than forty lectures in the season. He has me booked solid until Nov. 15th. "Without a break," quoth he. There will be scattered engagements to follow.

What this amounts to is that your bald-headed old Father will be obliged to turn out—in his advanced age—and live in a couple of suitcases all winter which will be hard on him. How much more becoming for an old thing like me that I should sit by the fire with my mittens on and let the pestiferous world go by.

Thanks for your letter. You are welcome to the gift I sent your son. I miss him very much. Please make him a snoot for me. Give Howard our love. He is a good egg.

It was late in September when Daddy started out on his long lecture trip. He had prepared four speeches of graduating degrees of profundity. The topics were: "Muddled Maturity" (a rather light and whimsical treatment of the perplexities of middle age); "How To Be Interesting Though Decent" (also light treatment of the difficulties of writing interestingly about decent people); "The Golden Bowl" (serious suggestions to

people in quest of an adequate code for purposeful living);
"The Flight to Freedom" (serious thoughts on where we are
going and why).

The dates were set up; the topic selected long in advance by
the group putting on the lecture. But the subject matter of his
talks was elastic enough for Daddy to switch from one to
another if he felt the response of his audience to be sluggish. He
told us about one engagement where the lady president was determined the speech should be elevating and intellectual. "We're
a very thoughtful, serious-minded group of women," she told
him as they stood in the wings of the auditorium. "We always
have addresses on a high cultural level."

Daddy followed her out on the platform and looked over his
audience while she was introducing him. It was Husbands'
Night, and beside every lady, bright-eyed and eager for her
dose of Higher Thought, sat a poor man sunk in his seat and
glowering with resentment.

Daddy always had a very strong sense of loyalty to his own
sex. That evening he felt he must do something to make the
occasion a little more entertaining than the men seemed to expect.
When it was his turn to step up and begin his address he launched
at once into a string of stories which had only a remote connection with the elevating topic announced. The husbands sat
up, their faces brightened and they began to enjoy themselves.
Most of the ladies enjoyed the speech too, but afterwards the
president thanked him in rather cold and disapproving tones.

He always had fun while he was speaking. No matter how
tired he might be, the stimulation of an audience lifted him and
he exerted himself to the utmost. "I had a corking good time
with the crowd," he would write us in hurried notes on hotel
stationery. But after weeks of banging around from town to
town he became very weary. In late October he wrote his friend
Shirley Smith of Ann Arbor:

I am making about four towns a week now, my son, and the novelty of packing and unpacking my long-tailed coat, standing about waiting in draughty theatre corridors for ladies to line themselves up pending an effective entrance, too-hot trains, stuffy hotel lobbies, etc., is about worn off. I started out September twenty-sixth; am not at home until Thanksgiving (which will be celebrated by me with a full measure of gratitude).

In a letter to the Van Vechtens in January he wrote:

No—don't say a word. Let me begin first. I hereby acknowledge that as a friendly correspondent I am the winner of the world's all time record as javelin thrower. All last summer I was writing, what time we weren't house hunting. And then I went on the road lecturing.

I have lectured in Buffalo, Indianapolis, Altoona, Nashville, Memphis, Des Moines, Toledo, Columbus, New York, and intermediate places. Middle of March it will all be over and I shall come in off the road to stay. Then I hope to begin my next long piece which is already taking on some semblance of form in my mind.

As you probably surmise the whole set-up of my life has been vastly changed. As a "free-lance" I am enjoying myself tremendously. Just the fact that I am not obliged to be responsible for the raising of funds (or at least the fretting about funds in times when funds are scarce) is worthy of note. I hope that the missionary money is all promptly collected, but I don't brood over it much in the stilly watches of the night. It is also rather nice not to have to write sermons any more.

Besse has had Betty with her nearly all winter. She, Betty, has now gone out to Las Vegas to get herself a divorce. This seems to be the best arrangement all around for all parties concerned. We've tried to stay strictly out of her troubles, but we'll be glad when it's all over.

Besse carries on with her habitually calm acceptance of the Universe no matter what capers it cuts; best balanced person I ever knew in my life. I never could understand how she contrives to stay that way in the midst of a family as impetuous as ours.

In the spring Daddy went back, weary and spent from his hectic winter. Mother had completely settled the house and all the old furniture, which had been hauled back and forth across the country, crated and knocked about, seemed placed now in what she fondly expected to be her own and final home. A large beautiful carpet had been bought for the living room and a big oil painting of Gloucester fishing boats by Anthony Thieme hung over the fireplace.

When I went down from Montreal to visit I admired the new additions, but I was very glad to see the old furniture and knick-knacks. The pictures I had criticized in my teens as being old-fashioned, I looked for now in their new places and stood remembering how they had puzzled me in my childhood. I was delighted to see on the piano the ugly brown metal lamp with the dreadful colored-glass shade which Betty and I had many times threatened to throw in the ash can. "Why! we got that for a wedding present," Mother always said, aghast at our suggestion.

Daddy found the garden just beginning to come alive. It was a lovely garden that curved gracefully in and out around a wide lawn under a few old trees, and fell gently away to the neighbor's hedge of flowering bush. Mother had put in a rock garden under a giant oak and all day she puttered happily with her plants.

Zocco, the Sealyham who had lived through one of the most tempestuous puppyhoods ever suffered by man, was now a respectable citizen, not averse to chasing the odd squirrel, perhaps, but generally reliable and comforting. He trotted at his master's heels as he sauntered, hands in pockets, around the place—commenting and approving. Daddy was a man of property at last. Of course, he was utterly useless when it came to getting down and putting his hands in the dirt, but he had many directions to give the part-time gardener.

"I tell you, you won't get no berries offen them bushes this year, Mr. Douglas," the man said, when Daddy questioned him.

"You just put 'em in last fall." He went off grumbling, "No use talkin' about pies all the time."

Daddy refused to be so pessimistic. "Surely, Besse, there will be enough berries for one pie."

Mother had become acquainted with some of the neighbors during the winter and she wanted Daddy to meet them too. He protested that he was tired of people and didn't care if he never saw another human as long as he lived. However, one Sunday afternoon she led him down the road to a house where they had been invited for tea.

When they arrived they found the ladies all in the living room chatting over their teacups; the hostess led Daddy downstairs to the playroom where the men were gathered in a genial haze of smoke with glasses in their hands. They were playing darts. Daddy was introduced and left alone to face the suddenly quieted, uneasy group of strangers who wondered what to say to this man who was supposed to be a writer—or something—and hadn't someone said he used to be a minister. Then the host, in a burst of inspiration, handed Daddy a dart. "Here, Mr. Douglas, you take a turn; we're just starting a new game."

The situation was very awkward. Seriously left-handed, but schooled to use his right, Daddy had never been able to throw anything in the direction he aimed. It had been a long time since it mattered terribly, but now, here he was facing an old dilemma. He looked at the board at the other end of the room. It was not on the wall but set up on a highly polished mahogany table. These men, apparently, never missed their mark. He reached out slowly, took the offered dart, and threw. There was an appalled silence.

"I opened my eyes," said Daddy later, "and looked. No one was hurt, but the dart was firmly imbedded a good inch into my host's fine mahogany table."

Before they left that evening Daddy was able to dispel the impression of his unfortunate introduction by great feats of storytelling. He came to be appreciated by the neighbors for his entertaining prowess. The dart story was told as a great joke, but he was never offered another to throw.

April passed and the garden became a delight of early bloom. Mother and Daddy took long drives into the country and for a few weeks it seemed that he was going to be content in the quiet of retirement. But he was not constitutionally constructed to sit about long without an occupation. His few youthful hobbies had been abandoned long ago and even reading for entertainment was losing its old appeal. He wrote to me:

> Seems to me that most of the novels I read, these days, have an unfortunate habit of petering out in the last few chapters; finally coming to an end because the author has run out of ink. It would be a nice arrangement if the author could run out of ink and ideas about the same time. I hear it said that persons who write stories lose their appetite for fiction. Perhaps this may be true in my own case. I don't think it is because I am such a ruthless critic for I am really as artless as a little boy when I read another person's story. In any event many times these past weeks I have settled myself comfortably to enjoy a new novel, begun with brave zeal almost never to get beyond the first three or four chapters.
>
> I have an idea for a story of my own, but can't seem to find a jumping off place.

This period of restless wandering about, picking up books and looking dull-eyed at the words, staring into space, was familiar to Mother. The only thing to do was to wait patiently until he passed the first stage and got to making outlines in longhand, prettily decorated, and tapping out first paragraphs on the typewriter.

The idea* he was mulling over that spring was one he had worked up in his lecture "Flight to Freedom." The thesis he wished to embody in a story was of civilization's long climb from the jungle to Paradise—the long parade, he called it. It was

* *Green Light.*

full of setbacks and interminable stretches of flat country, but ultimately upward, upward. A man's spiritual life follows the same course, but if he can free himself from the burdens of frustrations and old bitternesses he will get the "Green Light" to proceed. "Whatsoever things are just, lovely and of good report; if there is anything virtuous, anything praiseworthy; let us think on these things."

By the end of May the story which was to be the vehicle for this thesis began to take form in his mind and he was able to get to work. He planned to start off with a promising young doctor who received in the early stages of his career a severe professional setback. Daddy thought the best thing was to have him make a fatal mistake in an operation. To deepen the young man's bitterness the real fault was to lie with the senior doctor he was assisting. In order to find an operation where such a calamity could occur and where the blame could possibly be shifted from the older doctor to his assistant, Daddy went to the Harvard Medical School Library and pored over old journals. My husband, a surgeon, had given him the idea of a kidney operation where the quantities of blood would make it difficult to see exactly what had happened if something went wrong.

Daddy spent an entire afternoon wallowing in the description of one operation after another. He looked up articles on surgical mistakes and read of dreadful complications that could arise. From time to time he would be forced to stagger out for air and to compose himself; then back he would go to read more gory details. At last he found all the material he needed for a kidney operation in which the important blood vessel was accidentally cut and the patient ruined.

From then on the story moved quickly. The prowling period was over. In late June he wrote to the Van Vechtens:

I have been working on my new story for several weeks. It is not easy to start a novel. The first five thousand words cost more in hair-pulling, floor-pacing, waste-basket-filling, and insomnia, than the next ninety-five thousand. I have the thing going now, with about fifteen thousand words to show for what I have done. It is likely that The Cosmopolitan Magazine will use it as a serial probably beginning with the November issue, released on the fifteenth of October. I am expected to hand them the first thirty thousand words on the fifteenth of August, and I presume I shall be able to do it.

The book will come out in March, published by Houghton Mifflin. Its title is Green Light. It has just a little of the flavor of Magnificent Obsession, though with a quite different thesis. I am pleased with the general movement of the piece and believe the people who like Magnificent Obsession will like it as much as the earlier book.

In July Betty drove Mother up to Montreal to be with me while my second baby was born. Mother went through agonies at such times and we all did what we could to alleviate her suffering. When at last she had the child in her arms great relief was felt by all. Daddy stayed in Wellesley Hills but wrote to me:

> I am earnestly thinking about my little girl through these days when you are waiting for your baby. Mother wires me you are in fine fettle and I am not worried about you, but we will all be as glad as you when you are at liberty again and the baby too.
>
> I am rattling around here in the house with only Zocco to keep me company. The novel is making good progress and at this rate I am a little ahead of the schedule I had planned for the summer's work. I have done about 29,000 words. It was my hope to have 30,000 finished by early August so, you see, I ought to have 45,000 done by that time, if the ideas hold out.
>
> The plot is pretty clear in my mind for the next three chapters, at least, and I daresay I shall be able to see the road ahead when I have passed the point of my present visibility.
>
> I shall be sitting here on the door-sill waiting for the good news about you and the baby. Tell Howard I am thinking about him too. Being a Father at a time like this is no picnic.

July 12, 1934

How happy you must be! I suppose a mere man has no conception of the sense of freedom and joy that rewards a woman for her long period of discomfort. I am getting just a little carom shot off your happiness and am in a rollicking mood myself because of your getting out of your confinement and back to normal. I am very anxious to see you and the new boy.

The house here does not resound to the clamor of mirth. Zocco is getting to be a staid old dog; as for me I am a bit lonesome. However all things work for good and I am making steady progress on "Green Light." I have about 30,000 words ready for Mr. Kent to show Cosmopolitan and a synopsis of chapters yet to come. He may ask them for an initial payment on it, though they may not consent until they begin to set it up. I am rather hopeful there may be some money coming in on it pretty soon, for I would like to buy a new car. I have had three second-hand cars in succession and the one we have now has 40,000 miles on it. I am half-minded to blow myself to a very good car this time.

I am eagerly looking for a letter from Bessie giving me full particulars about the baby. I should like to be up there when Arthur makes the new boy's acquaintance.

In August he wrote to his cousin Edith Kirkwood:

Bessie the Incomparable toils in her garden assisted by the gardener, and Zocco the dog. She was in Montreal for three weeks assisting her daughter to give birth to the child, and it seemed to me she was gone for three years. I am a fool about that woman. Nobody has any business getting himself in such a state about a mere woman.

My book is proving to be an easier job of composition than any of the other things I have done. One nice feature of my plot is that it moves forward by direct chronological sequence without any cut-backs or other devices for keeping the people approximately abreast. It is a straight-away chronicle. "That was on Thursday, and on Friday Mary stubbed her toe and on Saturday Claude came down with the mumps." No ruminating on what Claude was thinking at the age of two, or attempts to recover a sad incident in the life of Mary's grandmother when she was a little girl back in Singapore.

I shall keep you posted about the book. It is fun to do it, but oh dear—a novel is, at best, such a hell of a long job.

And just to give myself a little pat on the back, I bought a nice roadster for Bessie and me to ramble about in. It came yesterday and we are delighted with it. It is one of Mr. Ford's products. It has a 145 inch wheelbase, black body, silver stripes. We are crazy about it. It is quite the nicest toy I ever owned. We think we will have a lot of fun in it this winter, loafing up and down the road between San Francisco and San Diego.

Tomorrow is the Lord's Day and I don't have to preach. It is a comforting reflection to take along to bed.

In the October issue of *Cosmopolitan* the first instalment of "Green Light" appeared. It was very exciting to see the big full-page magazine illustrations, the only drawback being that Daddy was still hammering away like mad—five chapters to go until the end. "I'm getting tired of sitting humped over my typewriter seven days per week," he wrote. "Here's hoping I don't fall down the stairs and break my neck before I get this thing done. Somebody would be in a pretty pickle then."

The strain and pressure under which he worked those last few weeks brought about several discrepancies which were corrected in the book when it finally came out between hard covers, but which brought howls of protest from all over the country at the time. When the last instalment in the magazine appeared, letters poured in pointing out the fact that the blue-eyed heroine was described in the final embrace as having eyes of brown. So many people wrote about this that a form letter was made up thanking the readers for their interest and helpfulness, but stating blandly: "It is not generally known, but the eyes of blue-eyed women are often seen to become brown under the stress of strong emotion."

In October Betty married a mining engineer, Weary Wilson,

whom she had met during her stay in Las Vegas. At the time she came home from getting her divorce she was wearing his ring on a chain around her neck, hidden, but she planned to tell her parents at once her wonderful news. There were guests for dinner that first night and they stayed until late. Daddy went upstairs to bed as soon as they left and Betty was relieved to be able to make her announcement to Mother alone.

"Oh, oh," wailed Mother, "you will have to tell Daddy at once."

"I will first thing tomorrow," Betty promised.

"No, you must tell him tonight. You must go upstairs now. I am afraid he will be very upset."

Daddy was asleep. Betty turned on the light and he sat up blinking at her. "I've something to tell you," she said, "which will probably make you very cross. I've met a man. I'm going to marry him."

Daddy leaped out of bed as though the sheets had suddenly become scalding. He had much to say as he paced back and forth in his bare feet, lighting one cigarette after another. "Out of the frying pan into the fire," was the general trend of his remarks.

However, as he heard more about his prospective son-in-law he became reconciled and when Weary came East for the wedding he and Daddy took to each other at once as kindred spirits. Very soon Daddy had him closeted in his study and was reading him his novel as far as he had gone. "Now this is my terrible problem," he confided, "the *Cosmopolitan* has published the first instalment, the next will soon be out, and I can't for the life of me think how to end the story. I need some kind of a spectacular scientific discovery for my final climax."

Weary thought as hard as he could. "How about Rocky Mountain Spotted Fever?" he suggested. "They're working on a new serum for that."

Daddy looked at him intently. "Tell me about it."

Weary, as a prospector and rugged outdoor man, was able to give a great deal of colorful information on the subject. A few hours before the wedding the groom rushed out and bought Paul de Kruif's book *Men Against Death*.

"This is exactly it," said Daddy. "It all fits in perfectly."

They had the wedding that afternoon and Daddy managed to perform the ceremony, but his mind was only half on what he was doing. As soon as he decently could he excused himself and rushed back to his study to plan the new turn in his story which his remarkable son-in-law had suggested.

Betty and Weary went back to Las Vegas and Daddy sent them a copy of each chapter as he finished it. An Irish setter named Sylvia, belonging to the young doctor in the story, had become a very lovable character in it. The dreaded spotted fever attacked her. Betty, foreseeing that Sylvia was going to come to a tragic end, wired Daddy to spare her, but to no avail.

November 14, 1934

I was sorry too that our poor Sylvia had to die to serve the savage needs of the plot, but she had done her stuff very competently and deserved a nice little tragedy, with all her friends a-weep, which is ever so much better than for her to have died of sore-eyed boredom in her pot-bellied old age, unwept and unsung. As the matter stands, a million people will blow their noses for Sylvia which is a damned-sight more nose-blowing than the average human collects on the occasion of his demise: so Sylvia has no kickacummon.

When the novel was finished in November—101,000 words—Daddy and Mother gave themselves a little vacation, going by sea and canal to California. They spent Christmas in Nevada with Betty and Weary. When they arrived by car Betty rushed out to greet them. "What's that in the back seat?" she asked at once.

They hauled out a gangling, wriggling red setter puppy.

"Christmas present," Daddy said, handing Betty the leash. "Don't you recognize her?"

"Oh, she's Sylvia!" Betty cried.

Green Light was published in book form in March and hit the top of the best-seller list seven weeks later, where it remained until the end of August.

March 16, 1934 [to Shirley Smith]

The book has got off to a very nice start, the advance sales, according to wired advice from the Houghton Mifflin Company on the day of its release, totalling 50,393 copies, which is very good for these times; or any times, for that matter. The HMCo tells me it is the largest advance sale in the history of their house.

Of course the commercial value of the novel is not to be sneezed at, but I think the very considerable amount of mail that is coming to me now is of more significance. Ever since the story began running in the Cosmopolitan I have been getting more mail than I have ever had concerning any of the previous stories. Some of the letters are quite interesting; some rather touching.

May 21, 1935 [to Betty]

Clippings from the length and breadth of the land testify that the Light is still Green. The critics rave and moan and invite High Heaven to explain this monstrous infraction of justice in the appraisal of literary works, but Green Light calmly glows on every turnpike. And Houghton Miff continues to wrap and ship comforting re-orders to all points. So—let the heathen rage and the peepul imagine a vain thing: oursels, we are a-settin' on top o' the world.

These letters are a decided change from the surprised, amateur comments he made during the run of *Magnificent Obsession*. Now he was a professional writer quickly learning the tricks of the trade. He kept a close watch on the best-seller charts, subscribed to a clipping bureau which sent every press notice from the important reviews in big city papers to one-line mentions from Podunkville. He tortured himself by reading every word of the scathing comments of the more sophisticated critics.

"But look at all these nice ones, dear," Mother would insist. She would hand him a fresh batch of fan letters posted from all over the country. "Now read these; they'll make you feel better."

To realize he was giving spiritual aid to so many more people than he had ever reached before made up for a good many scorching phrases applied to his books by the critics who were merely exasperated by the preachiness and appalled that a novel so full of stretched coincidences and undisguised sentiment could appeal to such a wide public.

In *Green Light* a character had appeared named Dean Harcourt. It was he who voiced the spiritual message of the story and advised the troubled souls who came to him. This counsel which shone like a gleam of hope through the story appealed to many readers who probably would never have written the author otherwise. "Your book has helped me," they wrote. And they then described their own personal problems and asked for advice. Daddy answered most of the letters himself. It was almost a full-time job. "I'm getting to be a regular Dorothy Dix," he sometimes complained.

The name Lloyd C. Douglas was becoming famous. Mother and Daddy ran up against the fact more and more frequently and never failed to be astonished. They were invited to literary gatherings where they were feted as celebrities. They balanced teacups and smiled politely at ladies who twittered and gathered around them. Mother tried to think up intelligent answers for the ones who, pushed aside from the crowd surrounding the lion of the occasion, turned to her and gushed, "How does it feel to be the wife of a best-selling author?"

How did it feel? At home it didn't feel very much different than before. Daddy still roamed about the house in his terrible old green silk suit. He still went to the refrigerator in the middle of the night and left the kitchen a mess. Sometimes the novelty of being famous came over them and they would exclaim to each other, "How did it all happen?"

They continued to live in the same simple way, but from time to time they would indulge in bursts of extravagance, enjoying the sensation of being wild and irresponsible. They had bought a Lincoln roadster with red leather seats and they drove about through the Massachusetts countryside with the top down, the wind buffeting their pince-nez glasses. Daddy wrote, "We tend to suffer from lame joints and assorted charley-horses," but they persisted in this sporty demonstration of their freedom from the restraints of decorum.

Betty wrote to me: "The parents say they have bought themselves little black berets and are driving around in an open car and those things clamped to their heads, 'at a jaunty angle,' as Mother says. What shall we do?"

We could do nothing, of course. They came to visit in Montreal to see their grandsons and were so high-spirited that I felt like the parent, and an old stuffy one at that. Daddy wrote to me on their return to Wellesley Hills:

> We had a wonderful drive home through the mountains. The three days we spent at Crawford House were restful and luxurious. Not a soul there knew who we were and we did not exchange a word with anyone except the help. So—if you ever get famous you can expect the thing to pip out on you occasionally and leave you a-settin' there, all dressed up and no place to go.

During the summer of 1935 Daddy began work on his novel *White Banners*. At first he planned to call it by the name of the chief character, the maid upon whom the family of the story depended for every sort of service from menial kitchen tasks to encouragement in times of despair. He wrote to Betty:

I have spent the morning tinkering with a character sketch of my leading lady. I thought a couple of weeks ago her name was Annie, but Annie suggests to me a perpetual bad cold, a weak back and a tendency to sneak off and weep a dishragful of self pity. So I have changed her name to Hannah. This alteration is about all I have accomplished so far, which leaves quite a good deal of the book still uncompleted. But remembering similar experiences in the past, I am undaunted. In due season we shall reap if we faint not.

The story progressed easily and he worked in pleasure. It was a simple, homey plot not calling for any spectacular situations, but demonstrating the theme of service and kindness as it would be possible for ordinary mortals in everyday life. The novel was to appear in serial form in *Cosmopolitan,* but in the first months its author worked under no pressure of a deadline date. Then in August he wrote to Betty:

I have been asked to interrupt my novel to do a little Christmas story for Cosmo. I discovered it isn't quite as simple as it seemed when I first began it. I used up more than half my space and hadn't got to the real business of telling the story. So today I began at scratch and threw marvelous wisecracks into the waste-basket—all in the interest of economy of words. I'm calling this little piece "Home For Christmas" and I think you'll like it. It's got food—much food in it. I think a Christmas story should involve a great deal of belly-stuffing.

I wired to my cousin (my age) who lives on a farm in Northern Indiana and told him to wire me collect the full details on how to make country sausage. As a kid I had seen pigs butchered, but I've forgotten everything about the process except that it didn't smell very good.

I think this was probably the first telegram my cousin ever received and he didn't know how to organize his reply with economy in view. His telegram to me read as follows: YOU GO OUT

TO THE HOG PEN AND KNOCK AN OLD SOW ON THE HEAD THEN YOU
HEAT A BIG BARREL FULL OF WATER AND DOUSE THE HOG UNTIL THE
BRISTLES CAN BE SCRAPED OFF.

After that Watts got scared for fear he was running up too
much of a bill on me, and by the time he got the hog disjointed
he quit the job—and I've never found out how to make the
sausage.

Your mama has been doing well in her new Ford. It's a snappy
coupe with white tires. Her teacher graduated her last week and
now she drives alone to the grocery store in Wellesley. She's
mapped out a route for herself which involves no left hand turns
although she has to go about two miles out of her way to achieve
this.

She threatens from time to time to have our bedroom repapered,
but I know my Bessie. She has some samples pinned to the window
curtains upstairs where they will hang until Gabriel toots his horn.

I am mildly dieting—no potatoes, no bread, no fat of any kind.
Naturally I have lost all interest in my meals and attend them
only for old time's sake. I shall lose ten pounds or so; also my
gaiety, my optimism, my general interest in the human race. But
when I am fifteen pounds lighter I shall be pleased with myself,
I think. I shall no longer be a puffing, panting old fellow, but a
sombre spectre with a flabby neck and loose folds of criss-cross
wrinkled skin draped over my collar.

"Home for Christmas" was a good story and Daddy enjoyed
working on it, but it had put him back four weeks on his
schedule for *White Banners*. He had lost the mood for Hannah
and the characters who revolved around her. Before he had a
chance to recover that atmosphere, fall came and it was time to
set out upon a lecture trip to which he had previously committed
himself.

The dates of this trip had not been arranged by the agency
with any thought for the comfort of the lecturer. They followed
one another thick and fast, required long hops on bad trains,
changes and waits in small stations. Often last-minute plans were
wired necessitating wild taxi rides across country to fulfill en-

gagements. Daddy started out with his usual enthusiasm. "Your poppa is lifting the darkness in the wastelands," he wrote. "I am riding the trains furiously and making frequent stops to dispense sweetness and light." Then later, "Travel last week more than usually irksome; long jumps, zigzagging back and forth as in picture I now draw. Tomorrow I double back to Sioux City to get a good start toward Sioux Falls."

In November Mother went to Detroit to meet him and give him a little break in the rigors of his schedule. He wrote:

Arrived here from Cleveland in a carnival mood to meet my Bessie. She sailed in bright and smiling to the Book-Cadillac late Friday night, after I had been out to Dearborn consorting with Henry Ford and swapping stories with the brittle old boy. Then we had a day to ourselves and went over to Belle Isle to look at the flars, and the animals and saw the same little ponies that you and Ginger rode when you were small, and we both laughed and cried a little and damned our tears and laughed again and held hands for Bessie is very hand-holdable. (She really gets sweeter and lovelier every day of her life; nobody can touch her for charm.)

Then we were off to Syracuse and then to Rochester where in the evening Dr. Beavens threw a wonderful party full of wit and sparkle. Then we put Bessie on a train by a very split second and I boarded another for Chicago and all night long we were rushing away from each other as fast as we could go—a dreadful situation if there ever was one. I was terribly fagged with hard travel before Bessie came out to see me, but I think I can see it through now until I see her again.

November 1935

This is the cruelest lecture tour I ever made. The jumps are too long and the dates too thick. I have had very little opportunity to write, but a great deal of time to think, and one of the most frequent thoughts I have thunk is that I am somewhat of an ass to go out and literally pound myself to bits with such small rewards either in cash or satisfaction. I wonder whether one's book sale is stimulated to any appreciable extent by the author's wind-bagging.

I doubt very much whether I shall ever consent to do a lecture trip like this again. I think the less the public sees of an author the more respect they have for him. Bessie meets me in New York Dec. 12th. Then home.

Can you keep a secret? I've bought Bessie's Christmas present. I got it in Chicago. I looked at one at Shrimp, Glick and Blook's in Boston, but liked this one better. It's a brooch that comes apart and makes two clips. It's got lots of diamonds in it. Won't she look purty?

Upon arriving home Daddy learned that *Cosmopolitan* planned to begin serialization of *White Banners* in March. That would mean he would again be working under the frantic pressure of completing a book while the first chapters were being unrolled to the public. True he had originally promised it for that date, but in the meantime his work had been interrupted to do "Home for Christmas." The lecture trip was his own arranging; but that didn't make the situation any better. He was tired and frayed when he wrote this complaint to Mr. Kent at Houghton Mifflin.

December 6, 1935

I am not going to be pushed into finishing "White Banners" by March. I don't have any funny ideas about myself as a novelist. I know my limitations, imperfections and natural obstacles even better than any of my critics. It's not easy for me to write stories and I'm not going to be jockeyed into the position of doing them in any worse style than they will have to be done in fair and decent working conditions.

However, as usual, after a good night's rest and the soothing company of his wife he calmed down and began to think he could keep everybody happy and meet his publishing obligations. He had a wonderful confidence in his own ability to work night and day, and had never yet let anyone down. Christmas came and went but there was not much time for celebrating. Daddy wrote:

We missed our children, but we gathered around the tree and exchanged our gifts supported by Grandmother and Grandfather Porch. I left them after the festivities and went back to my study. I have managed to get my novel going again very nicely. I was afraid it might be hard to recover the mood, but I am now well along in the seventh chapter. Hannah is being built up into the Gibraltar of strength I hoped to create. Besse likes her.

This was the third winter they had lived in Wellesley Hills, but the last two had been broken by long trips to California. The weather there still appealed to them as strongly as it had in 1927 when they had been so captivated by the sunshine and sea. Daddy figured he could go out again in spite of his book. They wanted very much to take me, the daughter they had left in the frozen north who must need a respite from the responsibilities of two small children. Daddy was sure he could work on the boat and would knuckle down when he arrived in Los Angeles and make up for any lost time. "After all," he said, "I must have a little recreation."

March 14, 1936 [to the Van Vechtens]

Our trip through the canal was very enjoyable. Ever since we have been here in Los Angeles I have been working like a dog to keep up with my contract dates on the story White Banners now being serialized in Cosmopolitan. I have put up about eighty-thousand words, two thirds of the job. I am very tired.

For one entire week I had a painful ulcer on my eye. The same eye that has given me trouble for years. I have practically no sight in it. The doctor here, knowing I was working against a deadline, cured me with a pretty radical treatment. I didn't tell him that I removed his bandage each day after my visit and worked in spite of the ulcer. It is well now. Laus deo!

The movie of "Green Light" will be shown September 1st, they tell me.

Besse and I had planned to drive home, but I now see I cannot spare the time. We'll ship the Lincoln and I'll have to keep my nose to the grindstone from now on to get my stuff out on time. I'll never do this again; it's too hard on me.

In many ways the story is the best job of novel-writing I have done, a bit trickier job than the others and requiring more skill in dialog inasmuch as my leading character is a woman. I wish I might have a chat with you about "Hannah"; I feel pretty well acquainted with her now.

I stayed with them for a few weeks in Los Angeles. Betty came down to be with us, but the family reunion was not as happy as it might have been. Daddy could not go anywhere with us but sat in his room hammering his typewriter until late at night. Mother worried about him, fearing he was driving himself beyond the limits of endurance. When his eye flared up we could not bear to see him working in such pain, but still he kept at it.

"If this is being retired," Mother said, "I wish he'd go back to work."

He promised her he would never allow himself to be caught in such a situation again. If he ever wrote another book, and he doubted he could face the task, he would do it at his own leisure with long periods of rest between.

The weather in California that winter was superb; the same glassy shimmer to the sunshine, brilliantly colored flowers, spectacular scenery. "Imagine all those poor people back East shoveling snow and heaving themselves into their heavy clothes," said Daddy. "We'll always be out here in the winter, Besse; our house in Wellesley Hills will be shut up half the year."

Mother's face went blank as though a curtain had been drawn across it. You could just see her inwardly taking down the pictures, packing her best china, bidding goodbye to the lovely Massachusetts garden, soft and subdued in Easter colors.

Daddy was mentally taking down pictures too. "Why don't you go out and look for a house. Now is the time to buy, they

tell me. It's the sensible thing for us to do." He wrote to
Mr. Kent:

> Besse is suggesting to me that we come out here to live per-
> manently. She and the girls are scouring the landscape for a house.
> There is no dearth of nice places; many of them owned by the
> bank and to be had at half the cost. Some are too big. They took
> me to see a few the other evening. I think I would feel about as
> much at home in them as in the Grand Central Station.
>
> Meanwhile I continue to hammer by typewriter. When this
> novel is finished I shall take a day off.

April 17, 1936 [telegram to Mr. Kent]

HAS COSMOPOLITAN CHEQUE COME   AM BUYING HOUSE   NEED CASH

I had gone home to Montreal and did not see the house they
finally selected. The one I saw which Mother wanted was a
small cozy cottage with flower boxes at the windows and the
rooms arranged so she would not be dependent on help. She
wrote describing the one they bought. "It is very grand. The
grounds and garden are lovely though rather apt to pitch off into
a deep ravine. We will certainly need a full-time gardener.
Goodness knows what use we will make of the tennis court."

The people who owned the house were to stay on for six
months. Daddy and Mother would spend the summer in Massachusetts. They would not go out to occupy their new home until
the following November.

By April they were East again. Daddy could not spare the
time to drive so the car was shipped and he worked continuously
on the train. A letter to Mr. Kent announced their arrival:

> Back today from the golden west. Very tired and dirty. Hope
> this finds you the same.
>
> The last New York photographer who took my picture re-

marked while observing me under his black hood that I looked like Whistler's mother. Can you suggest the services of another?

I enclose a note from a fellow who wants a necktie which I have worn. Shall I send this bird my necktie and go about without any, or shall I ask him if an old sock will do?

June 8, 1936 [to Mr. Kent]

I received my new letters today at Gettysburg College and jolly well earned them too, for it was hot and muggy and my gown became as soggy as an English pudding before they called me up to become Legum Doctorem. Please just call me Legum—the whole of it sounds so darn formal.

I am seeing the end of White Banners. Expect to finish it by the end of the month.

Daddy finished *White Banners* in a perfect pandemonium of illness at home. Families can be a pleasure at times, but when the children come to visit they should at least stay well. In a letter to Tom and Mary Peabody, Daddy described the afflictions which descended upon us that summer.

We got home from California in April. Two weeks later Betty Wilson came romping in from Nevada with a lame back which turned out to be a broken-down vertebra. She had a couple of weeks in the hospital here undergoing all manner of painful clinical surveys. Then they sent her home to us and put her to bed to lie still. She sits up about three hours out of twenty-four. When she does so she is in a steel and leather brace. She has had a nurse in attendance ever since she arrived. Besse came down with flu shortly after Betty came and for two weeks was quite ill. That made two nurses. Virginia Dawson came down from Montreal bringing her two sons, aged four and two, and their nurse. Virginia became ill and was popped into the hospital where she was very ill indeed, requiring transfusions to save her life. She has gone home now sound as a nut, Besse is long since recovered. Betty is making good gains.

Except for the little matters indicated above we have had a

happy and carefree summer. During this general collapse of all my loved ones, I finished my novel White Banners, but I take no pride in the feat. I think that anyone who can write under such circumstances has tacitly confessed that he has about the same emotional equipment as the five-toed alligator of Eastern Tasmania.

The novel will be out on the first of October. It has already been bought for movie purposes by Warner Bros. and will be produced sometime in the late spring. Green Light is under production now at Warners, and is to be released about the middle of October. I am now working on a Christmas story for Cosmopolitan, to be brought out in their January issue. I am doing it in leisurely fashion, for it is not due until September seventeenth, and is only a short piece of about seven thousand words, or so. I also did a little blurb for The Reader's Digest to be published, I think, in the December number. Otherwise, I have been taking my ease like the retired old gentleman I am generally reputed to be by my erstwhile colleagues in the ministry. I'd like to swap jobs with some of those birds for a few months, and give myself a good rest.

October 5, 1936 [to Mr. Kent]

In the book supplement of Herald-Tribune this week there is a Houghton Mifflin page promoting a couple of forthcoming novels in a fine display. This is as it ought to be and I am not desirous of hogging space. But down at the far left-hand corner is a feeble little squeak to the effect that White Banners is now on the market.

This strikes me as an unfortunate way to launch a campaign for a book that is expected to lead the season's procession. Far better, in my opinion, that this feeble little ad should not have appeared at all. I realize that nobody can estimate how much good is actually accomplished by paid advertising, but I consider the psychology of this bad.

Now Mother was packing again. She was to follow the furniture out to California and settle the new house while Daddy made a quick lecture trip across the country. If she wondered why he drove himself at such a tearing pace she didn't complain of it in her letters. "I am potting some of my plants to take out to the new garden," she wrote, "though I doubt if they will live out there. The soil is so different. I hope nothing gets broken this time."

The lecture trip of 1936 was taken with more dignity and pomp than the one of the year before. Daddy was learning to protect himself and put up barriers against the public. *White Banners* was second on the best-seller list (*Gone with the Wind* roosted at the top, unshakable) and *Green Light* was still in demand, even dear old *Magnificent Obsession* was selling well; Lloyd C. Douglas was indeed a famous name.

He obliged his publishers by going to the big department stores and book fairs to autograph his books. He was always very willing to do this and in the days when it had been a novelty to him had written his name on every scrap of paper that was thrust under his nose. Autograph seekers are a curious lot and the inexperienced author may find himself inscribing some amazing things in his books at their dictation. In late October Daddy wrote to Mr. Kent:

The Detroit book fair was a success, I think. The people at Hudson's seemed to feel so. Their auditorium was packed to suffocation. Doctor Victor Heiser decidedly stole the show, making a witty and entertaining speech.

After the performers had all turned their cartwheels, the autographing began down on the lower floor book section. I don't know how many books I scribbled in, but it seemed as if there were a great many. The book people think White Banners is going to have a good season.

Dr. Heiser was tender-hearted enough to consent to autograph everything that came along; so he spent the afternoon writing his name on menus from the coffee shop, and various scraps of paper offered by any old frowsy loafer. I adhered to my resolution not to do any more of that this trip and autographed only my books.

I arrived in Chicago this morning at eight. Hardwick Moseley arrived at ten to fraternize. He took me to Carson, Pirie where I autographed what seemed like five thousand books—though it may only have been four thousand. After lunch Hardwick and I went to Field's where I autographed many, many more. I felt that I could understand the emotions of the arm-less penman, writing names on cards with his toes in a side-show where people bought his products for sweet charity.

Comforting letters from Bessie state that she got Betty back to Nevada easily. Betty has reacted splendidly to the sunshine and hasn't had an ache or pain since her arrival. Zocco also made the journey without grousing. A much travelled dog. A British citizen by birth. Besse will go down to Los Angeles about the sixth or seventh of November and settle the new house. Our goods are expected to arrive there on the eleventh. Apparently my last lecture booking is on the 17th. I shall proceed directly from Minneapolis to Las Vegas. Bessie will meet me there and we will drive to our new Home in Bel-Air.

November 18, 1936
Dearest Bettina,

I finished my last lecture yesterday. Glad you are having so much less pain. I am all a-pip with mad desire to get going to Nevada.

Papa fly!!

13

The House
with the Golden Doorknobs

NOW THAT my parents and sister were definitely settled in the far west I had times of feeling rather abandoned up in the north across the continent from them. I had married into a large clannish family whose ways were often strange to me, and even my little children seemed very Canadian.

But I was not allowed to feel forsaken. I was written an almost daily account of the settling of the new house in Bel-Air and all the novel situations accompanying it. "I can hardly wait until you come out to visit," Betty wrote, "and see what the parents have bought for themselves."

She was with them a good deal. Her back was not improving and one treatment after another was prescribed to relieve her pain. Weary was often away on trips to the hills connected with his mining interests, and Betty, with no children to tie her down, returned to Los Angeles for medical attention. She was a great help to Mother.

They sent me pictures of the interior of the new house. The pictures had been taken by the real-estate people before the former owners had moved out and the big rooms were furnished with elaborate and costly things. The master bedroom was a fancy French boudoir of mirrors and carved wood, lace pillows and shirred satin. Fit for a movie star. I wondered how Mother's and Daddy's slightly battered five-piece mahogany suite, so proudly acquired on sale in Akron, was going to look strung around those handsomely paneled walls.

But I was sure Mother would never part with it. Her bedroom had always been the family meeting place. There we had all gone to find her. Many family conferences had been held on those beds, momentous decisions made; at late hours weary but excited daughters had perched on them to describe a heavenly party to yawning parents. Mother would never let those five pieces go, saturated as they were with her history.

In a letter she told me she had employed the services of an interior decorator. "I'm afraid she doesn't think much of our furniture, although so far she hasn't come right out and said so. She says we should at least have the dining-room table scraped and refinished. But I told her those scratches were made by my little children's feet and were lovelier to me than any antiques she had shown me. One thing she has definitely taken a stand against is that metal lamp you girls have always criticized. I can remember when lamps like that were considered very pretty. Well, I am afraid I must give in, for Betty sides with the decorator. When I get a new one for the piano I will take the old metal lamp up to our bedroom."

She did buy many new things with the help of the decorator, and when I went out the next spring I stood in the hallways marveling at the vistas of charm. But the old things were still there; some covered with new upholstery, some looking a little odd in such grand company, but none disowned.

The bathroom off the master bedroom was a creation of green tile. Mother described it to me: "—and it has two hand-basins standing side by side. Imagine that! I can wash out my silk stockings while Daddy is shaving."

He was very pleased with the glassed-in shower and for a while, until the novelty wore off, gave up the long steaming tub soaks he had indulged in for years against Mother's advice. There was only one drawback to the shower: he complained that the soap often slipped from his hands, requiring him to get down and feel around for it blindly in all the corners. To remedy this Mother got a soap ball strung on a cotton rope for him to wear around his neck. He thought it a clever invention and so economical.

"Look!" He showed it to her one day. "This piece of soap will last me a lifetime. It hasn't worn down a bit."

She examined it. "But, Lloyd, you haven't taken off the cellophane wrapper."

In late December Daddy wrote me a fine long letter, describing from the beginning the real inside story of the new establishment since he had been introduced to it in November.

December 21, 1936

Now, my little daughter, in all my reports of our new life out here I don't believe I have told you enough about Otto, our new man. May I now venture to tell you the whole story?

It seems that while I was on my lecture trip your mama, in addition to unpacking and setting up the household tackle here in Bel-Air, sought counsel in regard to help for the running of this establishment, which is somewhat larger than the one we have recently vacated. (It is true: we do have golden door-knobs on some of our doors—a little vanity installed by the lady who owned the place before us.) It seemed clear that we would need two people employed here, and Bessie engaged a couple: Otto (German born), and Frances, his wife (English), an uncommonly good cook.

I was informed of these matters by letter, but that was all I knew until I arrived in Las Vegas to spend Thanksgiving with the Wilsons.

Next day after Thanksgiving Bessie and I loaded the car and started back to Loose Angels. At one phase of the journey we were riding along, holding hands, saying little, when she said, apropos of nothing which had gone before: "Of course, darling, I tried to make it clear to Otto that we were people of very simple habits, who made no flash, put on no airs, lived quietly in our home with no itch to keep up with Miss Garbo. I told him that."

"And what did Otto say?" I asked.

Bessie hesitated before telling me. "He said, 'yes, madam,' " and her voice quavered a bit.

I tried to comfort her with sweet words and assured her that we would get along very nicely, but I began to be a little nervous over her earnest desire to break these tidings to me gingerly. As you know, your mama is almost entirely without guile, and when she seems to be stalling for the right word it rouses my apprehension.

At length, at the end of a perfect day, we drove into the garage area of our new home, and I made ready to unload the car, as is my custom. It contained among other things (a) six pieces of hand baggage, (b) a large bag of oranges picked up along the road, (c) a large bag of ditto grapefruit, (d) four coats, an armful of books, a haunch of venison, and (e) Zocco. Bessie quietly laid a little hand on my arm and shook her head. Then she softly said, "Otto."

So—I abandoned the car and its contents and we walked to the front door where Otto bowed us in, took our coats and hats, and we presently heard him sneaking stealthily up the back stairs with the baggage which he unpacked. He hung everything up and stowed things in bureau drawers and put the empty baggage in the storeroom. Then he appeared at the living-room door and said with dignity, "Dinner is served." And so it was.

Of course you know that I am just a plain and simple country boy. I never had any advantages until we drilled that oil well in Willett & Colby's back lot. I am not accustomed to having people fag for me. This is the first time in my experience that I have had a man waiting on me.

The thing is that I am getting used to it. Some features of it are still a novelty, but you would be amazed if you could see the ease with which I am accepting my new lot. Bessie takes to it all like a duck to water. I have no concern about her.

Otto brings up the morning paper and lays it at my door. He turns on the early morning fire. He draws the evening curtains. He gets out the car when I want to use it, and when we want him to drive he shows up in a spick uniform. I never thought the day would come when a uniformed chauffeur would drive any of my family about in style. This afternoon Betty was going downtown to meet Bessie who had gone downtown earlier. Otto, in full panoply, helped her in and mounted to his place with a flourish. As they drove off I—standing in the doorway, open-mouthed with amazement which I have not yet been able to overcome—was unpleasantly adieued by your sister, who through the window gave me a haughty look, accented by a prolonged and raucous Bronx cheer.

Every evening after Otto has served the coffee in the living room, he scurries upstairs and turns down the beds. When we arrive there at eleven everything is hospitably waiting for us. My pajamas are neatly spread across my bed, and my slippers, primly side by side, are awaiting the arrival of my pretty little feet. They sit there righteously smug and dignified, as if they too had joined up with Otto to make a sissy out of me.

Of yore, I was accustomed to wearing my nice clean pajamas a whole week if I wanted to, and it was nobody's goldurned business. Now I sit on the edge of my bed in the chilly morn and wonder how many days I have worn them—and wouldn't Otto think me untidy if I didn't chuck them in the laundry bag. He grabs up a shirt or a collar the instant I take it off and makes haste to tote it off to the discard. Thus I am wearing a clean shirt every day, to the considerable anxiety of my Scotch soul.

Before this regime set in I was in the habit, as well you know, my daughter, having accompanied me often on these excursions, of prowling out to the kitchen about midnight for a bottle of beer and a piece of cheese. I can't get away with it any more. I tried it once. The house was very quiet and I thought Otto had long since retired, so I tiptoed carefully to the kitchen, but when half-way across to the refrigerator he put his head in and caught me. I felt no end guilty and ashamed. He asked me what I was doing there and I confessed that I had only come for some beer and cheese and crackers. He waved me out and I left with dispatch. Presently he came to my study with my requirements on a silver tray.

I have an old lounging suit which your mama made me and in which I have written three best sellers. It once was pretty, but is no longer so. The pants have taken a lot of sitting: they are ample of paunch, baggy of knee, shiny of seat, but I like them and work better when I have them on. The other day I decided I would wear them while doing a little spot of composition. But half-way down the stairs I met Otto. He was very neatly dressed and his appearance put me to shame. I crept back to my room and hung the suit in the closet. I then wrote to Mr. Kent and told him that if they had any authors at Houghton Mifflin who might benefit by wearing these enchanted pants I would gladly send them on.

I try to see this business through with as much dignity as I can generate. Yesterday I resolved that I would be pretty stiff with Otto and let him know that I am entirely familiar with valets, chauffeurs, and suchlike things. He came to my study door, stood at attention until I reached the end of a typewritten sentence, and said, "The car is in the drive, sir."

Very haughtily I replied, "Thank you, Zocco."

Now why the devil I should have called him Zocco at a moment when I was desperate to reinstate myself in his esteem, I can't explain on any other ground than that there is a devil in me which requires exorcism.

Day or two ago we had our Christmas packages ready for mailing and Otto said he would take them all to Westwood and get them off. Naturally I was pleased, but a little perplexed too for all through the years I have relied upon this shocking experience of standing in line at the post-office, hot and weary and loaded to the ears with packages, as the annual penance I might perform to expiate my sins and reduce the term of my residence in purgatory.

However (such has been my moral slump since coming under the influence of Otto) I welcomed his suggestion. When he was ready to start I thought to go along with him and take Zocco, who needed a manicure for he has been biting his nails lately. I decided to get into the front seat with Otto and be his chummy little friend, but he fixed me with a reproachful stare, opened the door to the tonneau, and stood at attention. Zocco and I popped in chastened of spirit and tried not to attract too much attention as we rolled into the ritzy purlieus of Westwood; for at heart Zocco and I are democrats even if we didn't vote for Mister Roosevelt.

This, then, is all there is to be said at the moment about Otto. If anything of further interest turns up I shall let you know.

By the turn of the year Daddy and Mother were beginning to feel quite at home in Bel-Air. Nothing could change their way of living—even a manservant and a home situated among the handsome palaces of movie stars did not affect the simplicity of their lives. They found near neighbors who were quite normal people, happy to chat over the garden wall about the problems of garbage disposal and the seasonal insects which invaded the houses.

Sometimes Daddy wrote describing parties they had been invited to on the strength of his reputation.

I am afraid I can't tell you who our host was. He may be an actor or he may be a producer, and again he may be nobody in particular, but he gave the party and it was attended by fully a hundred people, very few of whom we had ever seen before. Bessie and I stood together trying to guess who some of the people were, but without much success for we're not very well up on the movies.

There was a big fat man whose name was Glick or Glush or something. He took me in tow and led me about from one screaming group to another introducing me as Mr. Russell. I saw no reason why I should raise any objection. I think I even told several people myself I was Mr. Russell so as not to embarrass my convex friend.

They were happy enough to skip the limelight when possible. There was plenty of it at places where Daddy made speeches or at parties where guests had been invited especially to meet Mr.

and Mrs. Douglas. The novelty of adulation wore off, but it is never unpleasant to be surrounded by admirers if the flattery is laid on with some intelligence (a very little intelligence will suffice). It must have given Daddy a good deal of satisfaction to wake up in the morning and realize that somehow he had become a famous man (and late in life too when most men were putting in for harbor), pleasant to lie and think that now he could indulge in some of the good things: pictures and rugs, a handsome car, a house with golden doorknobs.

But that house saw more worry and unhappiness than any of the modest little parsonages of the years behind. Many happy days were spent there, but sickness came again and again and nurses trod the graceful stairway and whispered in the halls.

In January Daddy wrote to Mr. Kent:

> I wired you yesterday about Betty's operation. She has come through in splendid style. It will be some time—two months or more—before the actual results of the operation are demonstrable, but she is doing as well as anyone could at this phase of her surgery. We have had a rather trying time here for a week or more. Betty was in so much pain that her case became really acute; nurses on full time, heavy opiates. Just between ourselves I have a feeling that this diagnosis might have been arrived at some time ago. My little girl spent eight months of tedium and pain receiving treatment for a benign cyst which turns out to be tuberculosis of the spine.
>
> Now you might think that anyone condemned to spend two months on her stomach would probably decide that she would be far better off dead, but I found that Betty has been rigged up with small adjustable pillows under her shoulders in such a manner that she bears no weight on her neck or chin. She moves her head from side to side occasionally. Her leg—where they took the piece of bone for her spine—is not causing her much pain.
>
> We do not worry. Betty has been relieved of the quite dreadful pain in her back. I shall carry her your love message tomorrow.

Alas! I have not yet finished my Easter editorial. Too much of a worrisome nature has detained me. I think I can get down to it tomorrow.

February 23, 1937 [to Virginia]

We have enjoyed your letters these past weeks and when they come we hurry in to town to read them to Betty at the hospital. They are going to turn her over on Sunday. Now I don't want to seem to be bragging about my relatives. God knows they have their faults. But this Wilson woman who has been lying flat on her belly for six weeks without one single yip of complaint deserves honorable mention along with St. (Arrows) Sebastian and Ste. (Fingernails) Clothilde. I know very well that I couldn't have done it. I would have taken poison.

You wrote a few weeks ago that you couldn't fix yourself in bed at night—being obsessed by Betty's discomfort. I believed you, but wished you hadn't said it. Pretty soon I began waking up in the night and would lie flat on my nose as long as I could bear it— sort of votive offering to appease the gods who are definitely psychopathic with an active sadism (take this up with Howard).

I was much amused by Howard's observations that most lecturers don't know what they're talking about, and if they do they aren't interesting. I think he hit the whole problem of lecturing right smack on the button. Give him my sincere applause and a kick in the pants for being so analytical regarding the type of lecture that I, myself, emit.

Sorry to hear you are all bedevilled with colds up there. I do think that Montreal is one of the coughingest, handkerchiefingest, sniffliest cities between the North Pole and Pawtucket, Rhode Island. Sometimes I found myself in a street car in your town. On these occasions I invariably had to hold on to a strap, swaying like a decayed corpse on a gibbet in a wild November gale. The strap was always clammy with heaven knows what, and the pestilential air seemed to be a saturate solution of every known disability that could do havoc to (a) the turbinates, (b) the bronchia, (c) the incus, (d) the stapes, (e) the hammer (to say nothing of the whiffle).

Now will you kindly take a large handkerchief and go about among your beloved offspring and blow their little noses. Sit on the edge of Dr. Dawson's bed and smooth out the lines of worry and care.

Soon you will be leaving to come to us. We will be sitting on the curbstone waiting for you. *Don't forget your ticket.* If you postpone your trip by one single hour I'm going to spank you on your arrival.

February 24, 1937 [to Mr. Kent]

A publicity man from Warner's was here yesterday. Said that "Green Light" had opened at The Strand in New York on Friday and was playing to packed houses with long strings of customers waiting to get in. Also that the picture was showing in Miami with the same sort of success. This, coming from Hollywood, is to be taken for what you think it is worth; probably subject to slight discount. Hollywood loves discounts.

Mr. DeVoto of the Saturday Review of Lit wrote me asking if I would do a review of James Hilton's new Novel "We Are Not Alone." I replied consenting: adding "We are not alone in our belief that we are an indifferent novelist and probably an incompetent critic, but we will do our best." Mr. DeVoto gave a sour review of "Green Light" and I am surprised that he should turn to me for a review of Hilton. However this gives me an opportunity to attempt to counteract the belief among the sophisticates that I can't write anything but sentimental sludge. I am going to give myself to this job with considerable zeal.

Betty continues to improve. In a few days they will turn her over on her back. After that she will have much more freedom of movement. We go down to the hospital every day which is a considerable journey from Bel-Air.

I am now comfortably settled in my new library-workshop and shall have difficulty explaining to myself or Besse or you why I shouldn't get to work. I have been giving some diligent thought to the new novel.* My first task will be the painstaking composition of an intensive character sketch of the doctor who is to shoulder this story.

* *Disputed Passage.*

It is warm, muggy and wet this morning. During the last long cold snap Besse knit a little green sweater for the chromium dog on the radiator of our car. I do not feel that this added materially to our popularity among the Native Sons.

Mr. H. O. Winkler, Secretary
Bel-Air Improvement Association
Los Angeles (24), California

Dear Mr. Winkler:

This is in acknowledgment of your current encyclical on aesthetic values in Bel-Air, together with lively admonition concerning the proper timing and placement of old cans, bottles, and miscellaneous garbage as related to local glamor.

Until now it had been my unhappy observation that the public servant, whether a salaried careerist or a dutiful amateur, is a singularly humorless fellow who views his trust with an air of morbid taciturnity. However genial in his private life, his official obligations weigh upon him until his formal utterances are peevish and punitive. On occasion his proclamations are shockingly sadistic—as in the case of our annual Assessment for Street Lighting which states that if the bill is not paid within 30 days our property will be sold at public auction, and that we will be billed for the ad announcing this sad event. All Public Servants of this feather are, in my opinion, a Pain in the Neck.

This is to say, then, that your sprightly letter persuades me that there is still hope for this once humor-loving nation which—for too long—has had but infrequent occasions for amiable mirth.

But you are never going to get the garbage cans put forth and recalled at designated hours by any such bait as you have provided in this charming letter. As for ourselves, we have resolved to paint our Receptacle de Garbage red, white, and blue, and place it on a pedestal beside the gate, in the hope of evoking another communication on this subject from our esteemed Secretary.

Again thanking you for restoring our faith in popular government, and felicitating you upon the adroit manner in which you have called the community's attention to a somewhat delicate problem, I am

Appreciatively yours,
LLOYD C. DOUGLAS

March 2, 1937 [to Shirley Smith]

The other day I was called over to the Warner lot to pose for some pictures with the cast of White Banners. We did one of those teasers which advertise coming plays. I had always felt that when I got too old and stupid to write novels, perhaps I might get some work in the movies, but I have changed my mind about that. As a movie actor I am the assistant button-polisher for the King of Siam. Not infrequently have I felt like an ass in the course of my long and lean career, but never have I been at so great a disadvantage as under the blinding lights and loud injunctions of Hollywood.

March 12, 1937 [to Mr. Kent]

I have been making some progress in drafting the principal characters for my new novel. It offers a fine opportunity for observations of all sorts. I want it to be a warm, human document with a spiritual flavor, but I sometimes fear that the theme I have in mind is too much like the themes I have already dealt with. Some things can't be said too often, but I am afraid people will get tired of me if they find I have only one string to twang.

Betty is to be brought home today from the hospital. A nurse will come along with her. Virginia is here to divert her and we are having a joyous family reunion. Virginia starts home on the thirtieth and I will go with her until she drops off at Topeka, Kansas, to see her grandfather who is not well. I shall proceed to Boston to see about our house in Wellesley Hills. The agent says there is water in the basement. I am not surprised to hear it. Real estate may be a good investment for experts, but is unsafe for amateurs of whose society I am the president and entire Board of Directors.

May 12, 1937 [to Mr. Kent]

Sorry to have been so tardy. After a couple of days in New York I went to my mother's where I had word from Bessie that she was en route to Topeka where her father was very ill. I went on to Topeka and the good old Dr. Porch had died before my arrival. Besse and her mother and sister went to Springfield for the interment and I came on home. Now I am ready to begin work on the novel. I have thought a good deal more about it and laid in a supply of medical books selected for me by a neurologist and a bookseller with a lot of nerve too in the making out the bill.

Upon my return I found the royalty report which I thought was very good. It had recently occurred to me that I had spent so much money this year on houses and such that we would probably have to go without food through the chilling blast of a California winter.

Reassured on this point I had chicken livers for breakfast, this morning, as usual.

I have thought a good deal about a name for my story, but nothing has turned up. In a little while I shall be sending you some samples of my composition.

June 5, 1937 [to Mr. Kent]

Very murky here for some days: morning mists and evening fogs that might be called rain if they occurred back in Indiana where the people speak a blunt dialect.

The new story is moving along. I have read what I have written to Besse and Betty and they think the story gets off to a good start. I wish I could get the girl into the plot a little earlier, but I don't see how this can be accomplished. Doubtless the movies will think of some way to remedy this when it comes to them. I can only let the reader know she is on the way by declaring at the outset that the young man has firmly resolved to be a bachelor for the sake of his science.

July 14, 1937 [to Mr. Kent]

Finished the sixth chapter. I have found a scrap of Whitman verse which fits my theme admirably and I think I would like to have it on one of the introductory pages.

"Have you learned lessons only of those who admired you
and were tender and stood aside for you?

"Have you not learned great lessons from those who braced
themselves against you and disputed the passage with you?"

Were this to be done I think a nice title for the book would be
—Disputed Passage.

You might give this the benefit of your thought.

Tomorrow morning Bessie and I are going on a little vacation
for a couple of days. We will drive down to Laguna and stop
for the night, returning Saturday. Mrs. Porch, Besse's mother is
living with us now. She is rather frail and we don't like to leave
her alone with the help for more than a few days at a time.

I shall be shipping you my finished copy about Tuesday. Please
feel free to criticise and offer suggestions. I have made no effort
to have the medical-surgical episodes checked over by an authority. I think these incidents are sound and accurate, but I shall
take pains to get an expert opinion before considering the job
complete.

Did I tell you that I am on the point of buying a little three-
acre ranch in the country near here. Oranges, lemons, figs, chickens, guineas, geese and a large deficit.

July 30, 1937 [to Betty in Las Vegas]

We are missing thou. We know your long-suffering husband
is joyous to have you restored to him, but our institution is lacking in excitement without you. We do not know when or where
to look for things to belch forth on the radio. Breakfast is too
calm and peaceful these days. Haven't you got some teeth that
ought to come out? We would be happy to see you for a day
or two.

We have got a nurse for Grandmother Porch. She is pretty
frail and requires a lot of little services. Besse was always afraid
to leave her.

All our days are alike now. Nothing entertaining goes on. All
the rivers run into the sea and the sea is not full. The thing that
hath been is the thing that shall be. The dog chaseth his tail and
doth not overtake it. All is vanity.

Write to us often, darling. We are just two old people quietly
going to the grave with nothing ahead of us but a hell of a lot
of work on this next novel.

The novel *Disputed Passage* was thirteen months in the writing. It appears to have had more discouraging setbacks due to
editorial criticism than any of Daddy's books since *Magnificent
Obsession. Cosmopolitan* had not definitely contracted for it, and
as the chapters came in they expressed through Mr. Kent their
dissatisfaction with the general plot. The chief objection was
lack of action. Again and again the chapters were returned for
more spice, more love, more adventure. Daddy mopped his
brow, but attempted to oblige. For a minister who was trying to
wrap up Sunday sermons in a jacket of fiction it was a difficult
thing to be required also to contrive one tense situation after
another to keep magazine readers on the hot seat until the next
month's issue was on the newsstands.

But Daddy earnestly desired to write good stories as well as
inspirational ones. The handling of words had always been a joy
to him and in his sermons and articles he had written prose of
which he had been proud. But his experience was in the essay
field; in fiction he often found himself floundering. His characters had so many important messages to impart that their personalities were apt to be ready-made and their adventures cut
to fit the theme.

All the criticism came through Mr. Kent who served as a
bumper for many years between Daddy and various editors and
agents. Ira Rich Kent was a very dear and loyal friend. Daddy's
letters to him were full of the gripes of authorship and Mr.
Kent's answers were always soothing and encouraging. Sprinkled
throughout their correspondence, among discussions of the book
in progress, were comments upon the state of the nation, always
a complete weather bulletin, and reports of the health and doings
of their families.

September 3, 1937 [to Mr. Kent]

I shall be sorry, of course, if Cosmopolitan finds my story too unexciting to use. I do not know how I could make it more of a shocker without re-writing it completely with some other characters and another theme. I agree that it doesn't involve any hair-raising crises calculated to pull the reader out of his pants or make him afraid to go downstairs to put the cat out.

The fact is that Disputed Passage contains about the same amount of incident that was to be found in Magnificent Obsession. Burton tells me they want my stories chiefly for their philosophy. The thing that has sold these stories is not their capacity to shock people but to steady them. As I recall Cosmopolitan fretted all the way through Green Light because there wasn't enough happening. Well, I'm not writing shockers and if they want my stuff they'll just have to make up their minds that it's that kind of stuff.

I have been going through some very painful dentistry lately to relieve a bad case of neuritis. Besse's mother is gravely ill here with a heart attack. The house is starchy with nurses. We had expected to go east this fall but that is now quite impossible.

November 21, 1937 [to Virginia]

The days slip by pretty fast. I have done a thorough overhauling of my new novel. There were a lot of long arid stretches of talk in which my characters didn't do as much business as pause to swat a fly or take another chaw of terbaccer. The story is much improved in clarity. It's on its way now to be a pretty decent novel (for me). I can't expect you hard-boiled sophisticates to think very highly of it. The critics will say it's just another sloppy little appeal to sentiment, but I tried to keep my people from crying as much as they did in White Banners.

Grandmother Porch seems to be improving. It wouldn't surprise me if she got up and went at it again. I always did like her very much; now I am discovering where our Bessie gets her poise and stability. The nurses are competent, but the fact is we have had nurses under our feet, in our hair, in our trouser cuffs almost continuously for eighteen months, what with Betty's long illness. They eat with us, are inescapable.

Four nights last week we went to Grand Opera. Interesting experience, but rather trying if you do it steadily for a number of nights. The spectacle of a fat man who has been justifiably killed with a poison dagger, rising up—after everybody had believed and hoped him safely dead—to yell to high heaven for forty minutes from his couch of pain, takes heavy toll of us old fellers who go in so thoroughly for realism. I'm for having these dead heroes embalmed immediately after the tragedy, and then we shall see whether they can get up and stagger about the stage shrieking and beating their breasts until all hours of the morning.

Yesterday I went through all manner of clinical examinations. It may not result in any good to me but may stake the doctor and his wife to a trip to Honolulu which is a very nice thing to do.

We can hardly wait until you come for the promised visit. Betty will come down too and we will make some trips up and down the coast.

December 1, 1937 [to Betty]

It's the help's night off. The Goddess is in the kitchen broiling a steak and getting splashed with expensive grease. Any moment I shall be summoned to carry out the lettuce with the extra-heavy Roquefort dressing.

I am going to send you a little cheque as soon as I get some money. At the moment—I regret to say—I am broke. We have had high expenses and no income for a long time and if we aren't financially down to the huckleberries I am the Author of My Day and the former Pshaw of Persia. We aren't missing any meals yet, but we are treading softly. If you haven't a better bank account at this moment than I have you may find yourself a-settin' by the window where the card says NO VISITING.

December 9, 1937 [to Mr. Kent]

Thanks very much for the impressive cheque. With this item tacked to my 1937 income I may contrive to salvage a small proportion of my 1938 income from the Income Tax Octopussy.

Regarding the book—you say in your letter it is too early to have the heroine kissed in the first encounter. But—dammit—you didn't even want her kissed at the next encounter. All I gotta say is you stopped too long with the "Youth's Companion." I strongly suspect you won't be able to wangle that kiss away from the Cosmopolitan even if you sent a sheriff after it.

January 7, 1938 [to Virginia]

We are now looking forward eagerly to your visit. If you can get yourself going a little earlier than planned, pop along. The Mother and the Father will be looking down the railroad track for the little daughter.

Local News Items

"Mr. Douglas, the retired clergyman living in Bel-Air went to Hollywood this afternoon and had a Turkish bath and massage. The old gentleman is quite vigorous for one of his years and was able to climb into his car without the assistance of his invaluable man, Otto, who accompanies him everywhere, brushes his teeth and warms his mittens.

"Word has been received here that Mrs. Howard L. Dawson, final product of Mrs. Douglas and her husband, the retired clergyman who is said to write religious tracts, is packing up to visit her parents in late February. Mrs. Dawson has been known to forget her tickets and money when setting out on long trips. It is to be hoped she will bring everything this time, including a top-coat.

"Mrs. J. Weldon Wilson, of Las Vegas, Nevada, is expected in a few days as the guest of her mother, Mrs. Douglas, the well-known gardener of Bel-Air. Mrs. Wilson is coming down to shop in our marvelous stores, being much in need of a tin washtub."

January 18, 1938 [to Mr. Kent]

I see your point concerning the lack of action in my story. Of course, Cosmopolitan wants action and more action. But then they tell me they want my stories because they embody a philosophy.

I want to please them, but I can't undertake now to throw this story away and write another one in which there is a succession of shipwrecks, earthquakes and assorted disasters. It isn't that kind of a book. I can't write that kind of a book. I never thought I was a very good novelist, but such success as I have had can be explained on the ground that the 'thesis' is the thing—rather than the action.

For good or ill the novel is rapidly drawing to a close. I think five more days will finish the job.

January 27, 1938 [to Betty]

This is the help's day off and Bessie came through with a wonderful steak which was almost too much for Papa, many of whose teeth are down in Doctor Wallace's safe and not recoverable before tomorrow.

Yesterday we up n'bought the ranch and all. It is a sweet little square of four acres with a nice view of the mountains. There are two dozen big walnut trees, lemons, a water lily pool and a sort of hula-hula picnic hut with a thatched roof. No other buildings on it. The ground is very fertile. This will give me something to play with and I hope to get some out of door exercise. It looks now as if Bessie and I will have to give up the European trip we had planned for this spring. Mama Porch's last backset warns us she is likely to have these spells often. Two nurses again for the past week. She is a gallant old girl and is so anxious to be of no bother that it is pathetic. But I think we might as well decide that we're not going to Europe. I don't like to give up the idea for I've had my nose to the grindstone for a long time and I'd like to have a change of scenery.

Nurses are nice people, but I've been looking at them now for something like twenty-months off and on.

This little place in the country may help to occupy my mind when I've finished this novel. I've had more repairs to do on this book than any I ever wrote.

Last night I made a dinner speech before the Women's Athletic Club which was the worst speech that was ever made in the world. It took Bessie quite a long time to get me cheered up about it. I have one more to make this spring. After that the fellow who hooks me into any kind of speech regardless of the occasion or price will have to get up so early in the morning that he might easily be Queen of the May.

Buy yourself a bottle of ink and write to Poppa.

March 9, 1938 [to Mr. Kent]

I finished the revision of Disputed Passage this afternoon and, if I do say it myself as shouldn't, it's a good book. Now I am going to take a holiday. Both the girls are here and we are all going to celebrate by taking a drive to Coronado where we will spend the night, going on to Encinada for a few days. The weather is fine—bright and clear.

I have not been able to spend much time on my new ranch, but now that I am free again I expect to go out there and see to some pruning of the trees.

I am very anxious to hear how Cosmo likes Disputed Passage.

April 12, 1938 [to Mr. Kent]

Besse and I have just returned from a six-day trip in celebration of our thirty-fourth wedding anniversary. I found your letter awaiting me with Burton's comments.

While I do not relish the thought of wading in on a revision demanding such a considerable amount of hard labor, I am forced to admit that Burton's criticism is sound, and I suspect that the novel will be very much stronger if I act upon his good advice.

I agree with him there wasn't the one outstanding figure in this story which my readers have come to expect. Dr. Cunningham had a chance to become that figure, but I pushed him back because I wanted the girl to be Beaven's inspiration. Apparently the girl failed. I thought Disputed Passage was a good book. It now appears that it isn't and must be done over.

I shall set to work tomorrow on the revision and push it along as fast as possible.

I have lost a few tail feathers.

May 29, 1938 [to Virginia]

I finished the revision of my novel last Wednesday, feeling that the story had come to a neat and satisfactory conclusion. It is a bigger book now—fatter too, running to 144,000 words.

Now that this over-long job is off my hands I have a carefree sensation such as I have not enjoyed for some time. I have been at work at that book for about thirteen months and am pretty tired.

I must stop now and make self pretty to ride in the country with my spouse. We are going out to the ranch to watch the pouring of the cement for the basement of the little house out there.

Grandma Porch seems much improved in health these days. We expect to sail in late June. Date of our return from Europe is still open. We may come back in time for Christmas in Montreal.

May 30, 1938 [to Mr. Kent]

We are now getting close to the time when Cosmopolitan will either have to fish or cut bait. They will soon be getting the revised script. This will be the final revision. I have appreciated their criticism and have made an effort to comply with their suggestions, but I'm not going to revise the story any more.

I am sorry it has taken so long to get this into your hands, but I did not want to make a hurried job of this revision and take the chance of having it pitched back again.

Besse and I have had to cancel the sailing we had planned and will not try to put off for France until the middle of August. Last night my mother-in-law, gallant old soul, had a bad flare-up with her heart, and today the house has been over-run with docs.

I get so tired of nurses in the house; in your hair, in the soup, in your pockets, on the stairs, at the table; telling you to exercise more and eat less or you'll bust, reciting sad stories of fine old men who failed to walk fifteen miles per day and had a stroke of paralysis.

This, then, will be all. I shall knock off and walk in the garden.

June 17, 1938 [telegram to Mr. Kent]
RETURN FIRST NINE CHAPTERS BY AIR   WILL START REVISION

July 7, 1938 [to Mr. Kent]

The revised script of Disputed Passage left here by air express Monday night and it may be assumed that Burton has his copy by this time. There is an ironical flavor to the title of this work, seeing how many disputed passages have been found in it by editors and publishers. I hope we may have early action on this matter now as it concerns the magazine.

Now that the novel is off my hands *for the last time* I am enjoying my freedom. The little house at the ranch is nearing completion. A friend of ours presented me with fourteen baby ducks. We couldn't take them to the country—nobody out there yet to be responsible for their care, so we put them in the little service pen back of the garage. They have been getting out of their pen on an average of twice a day, requiring the combined efforts of the family and help to beguile them back to their quarters. A favorite hide-out is the muddy ravine back of our grounds. I get so mad at those ducks I could kill them. I mean to when they are big enough to eat.

Peculiar weather here: densely foggy until noon, hot as blazes until four P.M., chilly evenings. Nobody likes it, not even confirmed Californians.

September 27, 1938 [to Mr. Kent]

The dispatches of the last three or four days make it very certain that Besse and I would be very foolish to go to France at this time. It is still within the range of possibility that Hitler may back down, but even if he does and the thing temporarily blows over the people will be in a grand state of jitters. So we have definitely given it up. At the moment we are figuring on a leisurely cruise down the South American coast as far as Buenos Aires. We may be gone two months.

Mrs. Porch is recovering from a bad fall, but we feel it is safe to leave her with her nurses. Betty is near enough to drive down if anything serious turns up.

November 10, 1938, en route to South America
[to the Thomas Peabodys]

This is a neat and clean little ship. Our fellow passengers are nice people and we are having a good time. We hobnob with the captain, slightly disadvantaged, however, by being seated at his table where we can't very well crab about the food—which is dreadful. Meats, potatoes, eggs, everything has been in cold storage so long that it has decayed without becoming a health menace until warmed up in the frying pan.

December 14, 1938 [to the Peabodys]

I ate something a couple of weeks ago down in darkest Chile that was intended for somebody else, and by the time we got to Buenos Aires I was at least fatally if not a little sicker than that. All I saw of Buenos Aires during our eight days there was from the bathroom window.

January 7, 1939 [to the Peabodys]

We are glad to have seen South America. It is something that everybody should do once. But no sensible person should ever think of doing it again. At least not until he has been everywhere else twice.

January 10, 1939, New York City [to Virginia]

I understand that you think you are going to have twins. My observation is that every expectant mother thinks she is going to have twins, and as her time draws nearer to the fulfillment she talks of triplets, quads and even wonders if she might nose out Mme. Dionne for the All Time. I, being somewhat psychic (see press reviews of my novels on spiritual matters), have a hunch that you are presently to bear one child, a girl, who will look like you. I hereby stake off a claim to spoil this child as thoroughly as can be accomplished by a senescent and doting grandparent.

We are in the same suite we occupied when you came to see us in October. This morning we had our breakfast in our room and Mrs. Douglas said to her husband, "If I were to go around in a dressing gown covered with big blotches of food and torn at the pockets and torn at the armholes would you think it was very pretty of me?"

So after Bessie had left I sneaked over to Fifth Avenue and bought a new dressing gown. When I told the clerk (a very remarkable fellow as you shall see) what my name is, he said— awestricken—"Not the author of Green Light!" And I softly purred and murmured wormily, "Yeth." Well, after that they wanted to sell me the whole store, leading me from department to department hoping to send me out with nine thousand shirts they couldn't sell to anybody but a celebrity. Fortunately I had very little money on my person.

Letter from Mr. Kent today says the advance sale of Disputed Passage is in excess of 45,000. He says the New York Times is doing a good review and prominently placed. I am glad about this for I would rather get a good review from them than almost any of the other reviewers.

February 1939, Bel-Air [to Mr. Kent]

I noticed our book is still at number 3. It seems to be moving along nicely out here. I have not progressed beyond the thinking stage with "Doctor Hudson's Journal." Can't seem to settle down.

Betty Wilson is with us again to take some treatments for her arthritis. She is a little discouraged over her condition which is not to be wondered at. She has been in poor health for so long that her patience and fortitude are at a low ebb. Our main occupation just now is to devise brightening distractions for her.

March 1939 [to Mr. Kent]

I received a letter today as follows: "I am an orphan and my girl is an orphan and we have no money and we want to get married. There is no one to help us but you."

I get letters at the rate of about two dozen per week from high school students. Typical request runs as follows: "My high school teacher has assigned me the task of doing a paper on the life of an author. I have chosen you. Please send me information about your life and works and an autographed picture."

Everyday somebody sends me tidings of a life story which I may easily mill up into a wonderful novel. They inquire at about what date may they expect their share of the proceeds. Verily I have come to believe that I have a chemical affinity for nuts, cranks, goofs and assorted brasses.

April 12, 1939 [to Mr. Kent]

We laid my mother away yesterday in a country cemetery half a mile away from the old Cassel place where she spent most of her youth. Many old friends came. It was not an occasion for grief, but reverence. My mother in death seemed very much at peace and rest. I was glad.

April 30, 1939 [to Betty]

Montreal is still gay and festive from the Royal Visit. They are not taking down the bunting and crowns and purple banners until after Vic's birthday—the 24th.

The new baby boy is a fine specimen of genus homo—much black hair. He is to be named after me. Looks like Howard more than anyone else to date.

May 2, 1939, Bel-Air [to Mr. Kent]

I am now seriously at work on Doctor Hudson's Secret Journal. When we bring out this next book I think there should be a publisher's preface. In that you might mention the astonishing number of letters that came from every state of the Union and Canada to the author concerning Magnificent Obsession. Prominent among the queries in those letters was, first, "What page of the Bible was it that Mr. Randolph carried in his wallet?" Second, "Is the complete Journal of Dr. Hudson available?" This book then would be the answer.

June 25, 1939 [to Mr. Kent]

Composition is running along smoothly and rapidly considering how frequent have been the interruptions these past days. Besse was hauled off last Saturday for an emergency appendix. It proved to be a routine affair; she is regaining her strength, is already tired of her hospital bed and anxious to be home.

Murky and foggy today much to the discomfort of Betty, whose arthritis responds to the weather. Now that the entire family is in bed but me I am treading softly. Did you ever know a family that underwent more repairs. Verily, we are an unhealthy tribe.

July 1939 [to Virginia]

Our Bessie gains a little more strength each day. She is reading Archibald Marshall's The Squire's Daughter and replies to most of my questions with a dreamily detached "Humph." Recent word from Betty sounds more encouraging. She thinks the heat (110°) is good for her.

The new book is moving along splendidly, nearing 40,000 words now.

I am sending you a magazine to which I have recently subscribed. Perhaps you will be able to understand it. I am getting to be an old man now; lots of things I might have grasped at thirty are elusive. In the case of this literature enclosed there are long stretches of the story which are so far over my head that I can't identify them with the naked eye. You should be able to find sustenance here for you are young and strong.

The caretaker at the ranch has set another lapful of pheasants under the cornish hen. Constance, the cow, continues to eat her head off and look reproachfully at any one who comes to milk her.

We have about put off our trip to Honolulu. We have had an unusual amount of expense lately. Then too, the Poppa can't hope to be writing lucrative books forever. Someday the people will say that they now know everything the Poppa knows. I am going to be sixty-two in a few weeks. As a popular novelist I shall some day soon be a crotchety old man with a lot of chickens.

August 1939 [to Mr. Kent]

I have completed Doctor Hudson's Secret Journal. The last lap required eleven unbroken hours of intensive work. It was under strong momentum at the last and I couldn't stop.

The finished job, including the preface and foreword run a little over 84,000 words, so I have not let you down in your prediction about the book.

I have had three days off since June first. I suppose I shall now feel—for a little while—like the old cow who lost her calf. I am always restless and bewildered for a while after I have finished a long job which has required undivided attention.

I hope you will like this book. It has about torn my insides out.

September 1939 [to Mr. Kent]

I am nearly swamped with work, trying to get four addresses in shape to deliver in Washington DC. I tried to persuade them they didn't want these speeches. Nobody is thinking about anything but the war these days, especially in Washington. The lectures I was going to deliver would be pretty tame fare when served to an audience wanting a commentary on European affairs dished up hot and garnished with hand grenades. But they have held me to my agreement.

Besse and I leave here by train next Sunday, shipping the car to Louisville. I have a speech in White Sulphur Springs and then we will drive to Williamsburg. I have promised Besse I would take her there.

I am glad you and Cosmopolitan are enthusiastic about my proposal to do a string of stories centering about the character of Dean Harcourt. I can be ready to start on them after the first of December when I return from my lecture trip.

If Cosmopolitan want to see all the stories before they contract for them it will mean they can not begin publishing before next June. I shall not be busting any of my harness in a frenzied endeavor to have them all under their eye in sixty days. Tell them for me that "Life is real, life is earnest, and the grave is not its goal."

This will be all now. I'm going out to the ranch. Constance is expecting a calf, we think.

September 29, 1939, Williamsburg Inn [to Betty]

We have had a wonderful drive through beautiful country and interesting old towns. It's been a Godsend to Besse who is feeding her soul on antiques.

Sent you a Smithfield ham yesterday. These hams are as tough as Satan unless you boil them before you bake them. Boil it all day, bake it all the next day, slice it paper-thin and use your sharpest set of teeth. They have some hams down here that were taken from one of the hogs that jumped over the precipice on the occasion of the miracle of Gadara.

Marion Hunt says nothing of ours was hurt in the big storm. She wired: "Constance is living in the chicken house." I wonder what Western Union thought of that.

I've seen so many relics lately that I'm beginning to view everything with a glazed eye. Saw a painting yesterday of a whole family in which everyone looked exactly alike: father, mother, James, Lucy and the baby. They had a dog that looked precisely like the rest of them. The only difference between James and the dog was the elementary fact that James had no tail. Later: Today we visited a gallery in which Mrs. John D. Rockefeller, Jr., has amused herself by assembling a lot of folk-art of amateur painters. I studied these with great care and am reproducing some for you from memory. I can assure that my drawings are as good as the originals.

October 1931, Washington, D.C. [to Mr. Kent]

I am leading a very active life now. The lectures are being well received and well-worth doing. Paramount Publicity man is with me setting up interviews with papers, broadcasts, etc. They would have me running around in circles. I wish Besse were here. She has been so sweet and tried to act as a buffer between me and the usual bunch of bores and cranks who like to buzz around anyone whose name happens to be mentioned in the local papers. At the moment she is en route to Rochester to meet Betty at Mayo's clinic. We hope to know what must be done to make Betty well. We are holding our breath. This thing is getting serious.

I have thought up plots for the first two of the Dean Harcourt stories and a third is nibbling at the hook. It may have the makings of a nice novel.*

---

* *Invitation To Live.*

November 1931 [telegram to Mr. Kent]

BETTY TOLD TODAY SHE MUST HAVE ANOTHER SPINAL OPERATION
INVOLVING LONG SANITARIUM CONVALESCENCE SHE RETURNS LOS
ANGELES FOR SURGERY   LECTURE ENGAGEMENTS SUCCESSFUL BUT
AM INEXPRESSIBLY WEARY.

December 1931, Bel-Air [to Mr. Kent]

I haven't settled down to work yet. I needed a few days to get acquainted with my wife and daughter, the ranch and the neighbors. There has been a great deal of mail. Letters and criticism of Doctor Hudson's Secret Journal are satisfactory.

Betty went gaily into the hospital today and will be operated on tomorrow morning. We are fortified by the hope that this time the surgery will be successful. Surely this courageous child deserves to be well and strong again.

Christmas Night 1939 [to Virginia]

Our thoughts have turned often this morning to you and your home. Your telegram came a little while ago. We enjoyed Howard's sally about "Silent Night." Well, it was just a bit too silent around here last night, but we didn't mope. We trimmed a tree in the upstairs hall so Grandma Porch could see it from her bedroom, and then listened to Christmas carols on the radio until, having harked to the Herald Angels about nineteen times, we decided to go to bed and read.

Four tough-looking burglars showed up at about eleven o'clock and sang "Gentle Jesus, Sweet and Mild" on our front steps. Besse didn't want me to go to the door for fear they might come in and rob us, but I put my nose out long enough to hand the biggest one a dollar bill. Then they stopped right in the middle of a pious yelp and ran off to the next house.

For some days I have been filling a stocking which Bettina handed me before she left for the hospital. It turns out to be one leg of a pair of giant tights and the task of stocking the stocking has been no small matter. We took it over yesterday afternoon. Betty was in high spirits. The room was stuffed with flowers and gifts from far and near. They took the stitches out of her back yesterday and she was glad to have that over. Her pain is very much relieved, but so it was after the last surgery. Well, time will tell; we can do little but pray for her recovery.

I will stop now and let your little mama finish the account of our Christmas doings. I hope next year I can take her to Montreal. She would so love to spend a Christmas with her grandsons. It's a pity we live so far apart.

14

Verily, We Are an Unhealthy Tribe

I DON'T KNOW what ails this institution," Daddy wrote. "Everybody gets sick. Even the dog has been sick."

It did seem as though the house in Bel-Air had far more than its share of illness. Grandmother Porch, very frail and needing a nurse, lived an upstairs life at all times. When she had one of her frequent attacks extra nurses were called in and flickered whitely about the house.

Betty was undergoing her second long hospitalization. The doctors at Mayo's had found that the grafted bone in her back had broken loose and it was necessary for the entire thing to be redone. Daddy and Mother greatly feared that Betty would never be well again. It had been so long since she had been without pain.

During one of Grandmother's brushes with death Aunt Glen had come out from Topeka to see her mother and was herself taken seriously ill and operated on at once. When she was well enough to return to Bel-Air she brought nurses, and for a few weeks the house was a complete hospital, the kitchen a scene of hourly battles.

There was a time when I dreaded to open their letters; it seemed there was no end to the afflictions which could be heaped upon my poor family. Daddy gave up trying to be cheerful about it and wrote long paragraphs describing the gloom of the house. "I might as well tell all," he concluded. "I am going through a siege of the most wicked dentistry. Perhaps I shall be relieved of the pain in my shoulders when it is over. The little mama is well but carrying a pretty heavy load of care and anxiety. On top of everything the poor thing has had to listen to my squawks this past week. Enough to drive her crazy."

Throughout all this confusion he worked steadily on the series of stories he was doing for *Cosmopolitan*. These stories, although independent in plot, all revolved around the character of Dean Harcourt, the Episcopalian rector who had first appeared in the novel *Green Light* and spoken the words of the religious theme that ran through that story.

, *Green Light* had been very successful. The many principals in it had acted out their problems to satisfy the plot, but the strength of the book lay in the personality of the benevolent, ever-approachable Dean. Many readers believed there was such a man. Letters came to Daddy beginning, "Dear Dean Harcourt," and others asked where they could find him to discuss with him their difficulties. Clearly the Dean filled a vast human need and it was not necessary to look far for material to work into stories in which he might advise and comfort the perplexed in spirit.

Simply, these were sermons, but the usual battle went on between Daddy and the editors over the plots of the stories themselves, which tottered along under the weight of the texts. Again more love, more action, less talk were demanded. Daddy wrote to Mr. Kent who was, as usual, the intermediary in these exchanges:

> Dean Harcourt is a unique figure. I know more about him and how he should be treated, and what manner of incidents will be most compatible with his dignity, serenity and poise, than anyone else.

Even the illustrator got into the discussions. The *Cosmopolitan* editor wrote:

> Mr. Jackson is enthusiastic about the first story, but he begs you with tears in his eyes not to dress your lovely Barbara in black for a spring issue. He asks may he dress Barbara in white?

In all six of the new Dean Harcourt stories the solution of the problems brought to him by the characters in trouble was based upon the resolute faith that there is a shepherd who looks after his children, and that the world is moving onward and upward no matter how imperceptible its progress. One must have a strong conviction that this is true to be able to write realistically enough to convince others. Daddy barricaded himself in his study each day, leaving on the other side of the door the tall black headlines shrieking of violence and inhumanity—and his personal worries and fears. His greatest concern was for Betty. Only recently in the Kent-Douglas files did we discover what he really feared in those days.

> Betty is in her thirteenth week at St. Vincent's. Tomorrow she is to be brought home in an ambulance. Her nurses will continue on duty. She is to remain in bed for three months more at least. For about six weeks her temperature has risen a little every afternoon. One suspects difficulties in the chest, but the doctors have found nothing there. Betty retains her optimism, is almost gay, breaks our hearts with a joyousness over a situation that strikes me as being pretty serious. What may be going on in her own mind is impossible to determine. She may be in secret despair. I know *I* am.

At the same time Daddy wrote to me describing Betty's condition, but with no such pessimistic intimations. However there is one paragraph that shows the struggle he was having to maintain his belief in the ultimate good of all things.

> I have spent most of my time now for five months in the company of Dean Harcourt. Often it has been beautifully said that

the Dean is just like me. This is enormously incorrect. The Dean thinks everything in the world is wonderful. I think the world is in a terrible mess. The Dean can think what he likes. I envy him his sublime confidence. But I have times of thinking what a confounded impudence it is of me to invent a character who pretends to have a ready-made solution for these evil times.

The war news last night was very depressing. France has been putting up a great fight, but it looks now as if the Germans have her outnumbered, and, as far as military strategy goes, outsmarted. It is too too bad. Makes us sick. It is hard to believe that things have come to this dreadful pass. Seems like a bad dream.

Nineteen-forty continued to unroll its disasters abroad, and within the walls of the house in Bel-Air trouble was not over. Daddy wrote to Mr. Kent:

For some time I have not been as well as I should have liked. My indisposition began with an excessive thirst which kept me fairly busy all day. I drank everything, anything, by the gallon, firkin, flagon, hogshead. During this time my eyes and teeth seemed to require constant attention. I lost eleven pounds last month, nine more this month.

I thought the dental surgery had probably thrown me out of balance and tried to talk myself out of the idea that I might be getting sick. We've had so much sickness this year that I couldn't get the consent of my mind to admit I was in trouble. I kept all this from Bessie. The poor darling has had about all she can bear. Her mother has been so low lately and the house stuffed with nurses and doctors. But yesterday I saw that she was fretting about me so I went to the doctor and told him I thought I had diabetes. He examined me and said it was so. They are putting me into the hospital tomorrow with a view to discovering how much insulin I must take. I do not know how long I must be there. Verily, we are an unhealthy tribe.

Later he wrote to me describing his "new way of life."

In case you are interested and even if you are not I shall tell you about my new disease. You can't just have diabetes and hang a sign on the door warning away visitors; you have to do something about it every day. The procedure is somewhat as follows. I arise about six-thirty in the morning, go to the bathroom where I keep my cute little laboratory. First we put a small quantity of cool tap water into a graduated test-tube. This is not difficult. Then we find some urine. I needed no special instruction on how to accomplish this. We now put eight drops of urine into the test-tube, drop into the solution a small green pill, and lay a little white pill on the metal plate below the test-tube which is firmly fixed in a bracket. This is the hard part and that is why only very intelligent people catch diabetes.

We then set fire to the little white pill which begins to burn with a pretty flame. Now we sneak down to the refrigerator for our bottle of insulin. We have a dainty oblong pan in which our hypodermic syringe lies in a bath of alcohol. We put the syringe together and draw up the required amount of insulin into the barrel. Now we are ready for the crowning act. We begin to hunt around on our little legs for an area not black and blue from previous jabs. With cries of delight we fall upon a virgin tract and polish the field with alcohol. We stick ourselves, push the plunger and there you are.

This act of stabbing oneself with a needle required at first a bit of resolution, but we have now overcome that temporary squeamishness. It is an act that flavors a little of suicide, different from complete self-destruction in degree only.

Now we can pack up our trinkets and have done with the thing for the day. We have a smug feeling that we are a brave fellow. Insulin is supposed to make people bright and witty, but it hasn't had that effect on me. Perhaps my doctor hasn't given me the witty kind. I must see him about it.

Mother seems to enjoy my disease. She spends hours doing the mathematics of my diet. At this moment she is out in the kitchen weighing out morsels of food for me. You can see that diabetes is an occupation as much as a disease and it really takes two people to make a success of it.

Although the war news went from bad to worse, the affairs in the Douglas household improved as spring came on. Dean Harcourt sent every month his messages of hope and comfort to *Cosmopolitan* and his convictions had been borne out in the many personal trials of his author. Aunt Glen recovered and went back to Topeka, Grandmother survived yet another of her attacks and was able to sit by the window again and work crossword puzzles, Betty surprised even her doctors by the healthy appearance of her X-rays and was at last permitted to go back to her long neglected husband to continue her convalescence. Daddy settled down to be a diabetic with no more comment than in an occasional letter: "I started my day as usual with a squizzle of insulin."

It was wonderful to know that Mother was relieved of the burden of worry she had borne for so many months. She had stitched endless tapestries as she sat by hospital beds, and stools and benches decorated with her handiwork had mushroomed up all over the house. Now she and Daddy were able to get away again for overnight drives; up the coast to Santa Barbara or down to Coronado where they stayed at the old hotel known by us as "Ye Olde Fyre Trappe." Daddy wrote me a letter from there on one of their trips:

> Remember the fun the four of us had when we stayed here two years ago? I shall never forget the expression of alarm on your face as we traversed the extended balconies of the old hotel, noting the abundance of ropes, fire extinguishers, buckets, ladders, coils of hose, etc. You thought I had exaggerated when I gave you a forecast of this hazard, and the hotel's bland confession that there was a certain element of risk.

In the afternoons when Daddy had finished his work for the day he and Mother often drove out to their little ranch. As a financial investment this property had not been a success. Daddy figured the fresh eggs they brought home cost him about ninety-three cents a piece, and the fryers were proportionately high. But one must pay something for the quality of freshness, and it also gave them a place to go on their little outings. Daddy wrote:

> Things are beginning to look quite lovely at the ranch. Friday Besse and I spent the whole day there. She planted some flowers; I planted corn and beans, dragged a hundred feet of hose for miles over the ploughed ground wetting the orange trees and shrubbery.
>
> I got hot and peeled off my shirt. Frank, our new caretaker, was stripped down to the waist and I envied him the ventilation. Gosh! but it felt good to be out there half-naked, close to Nature, under God's lovely sun. I hadn't realized that God's lovely sun could do so much damage. You should see me now. The top of my head is about to come off in one large flake. Besse has to help me put on my clothes and take them off.
>
> "Poor Frank" I said last night, thinking of him out there alone with no wife to help him. But Besse just snorted. "Frank was brown to begin with, not pink like you."

Concerning the chickens Daddy wrote to Burton Garling-house:

> I have been learning quite a lot about Psychology in my recent association with chickens. I find that in a group of ten adult hens, there is always one hen, who by mental superiority or physical prowess arrives at leadership. One of the important perquisites of her office is the right to peck any of the other hens. No. 2 hen can and does peck any of the other hens except No. 1. This protocol is observed down to about hen No. 7. Below that rating hen No. 6 pecks No. 9 and 10. But herein is the mystery!—No. 1 hen does not peck any hen below No. 7. Indeed she is considerate of the lower bracket hens and occasionally pauses after the eleven o'clock service to inquire after the little chicken that had the pip.

Concerning the cow he wrote to Mr. Kent:

Constance, our cow, is about to have a calf in a few days. I think I have previously advised you to that effect. Virginia told her boys about this blessed event and little Arthur has asked the privilege of naming the calf. We all agreed to this and Virginia writes that Arthur—after considerable deliberation—has decided to name the calf "Miss Thompson" in honor of his teacher. Should it occur that this name is unsuitable we will call the calf Mr. Thompson.

By June the Dean Harcourt stories were completed and it was planned that when all had been published in *Cosmopolitan* the six would be brought out in a book to be called "Appointments with the Dean." A letter from Mr. Kent intimated that this title might be improved upon. "It would suggest to many," he wrote, "extremely unpleasant interviews with the disciplinary officer of a university." Daddy answered:

Last night I had an inspired moment and the title for our new book was handed me. It was at a banquet down-town where I spoke to 850 men—leaders for boys' groups in this area for YMCA. Bill Rogers—son of Will Rogers—was toastmaster; asked me what I was going to talk about. It was the Pygmalion idea that runs through these stories. I said, "I'm going to talk about making things come to life," and added, "an invitation to live." So if you will consent we will call the book,

INVITATION TO LIVE

Hope you will like it. I think it's just right.

The book came out and did well. Many letters poured in daily, expressing appreciation. In response to one letter in which a reader pointed out in criticism that all the characters benefited in the stories were privileged, well-heeled citizens, Daddy answered:

I appreciate your letter of the 28th and admit that your criticism is entirely sensible. It happens, however, that the poor and forlorn have been receiving an immense amount of attention from novelists in these past few years.

It seems to me that the large majority of contemporary fiction has been diligent to invoice sympathetically the trials and tribulations of people who live narrow lives painfully tramping out the grapes of wrath in their wine press of poverty.

I am not negligent of their need or indifferent to their distress. It has seemed to me however, that there is room for a type of novel that dealt largely with more or less privileged people living normal lives, and if worried, anxious about other matters than where their next meal is coming from.

You will doubtless say to me, "Yes, but these poor people have moral and spiritual problems which deserve as much attention as the ethical needs of the Episcopalians."

I admit the truth of this comment, but I still think I am working in the alley where I feel most at home and therefore can do the most good.

The professional critics, while deploring the many coincidences used by the author to bring his characters under the influence of the benevolent Dean, admitted that in a world where all seemed wrong it was pleasant to read of one where sweetness and light ultimately triumphed. The bells of the Dean's church chimed each Sunday, "O God, Our Help in Ages Past, Our Hope in Years To Come"; it is the message that rings so clearly through all the Douglas stories and, however phrased, cannot be scorned.

With the publication of *Invitation To Live* a period in Daddy's literary career ended. He would have been amused had he heard anyone speak seriously of the periods under which his novels fell. He never considered himself a literary figure and was embarrassed if introduced as one. In fact it is rather pathetic to note how often in the bulk of his correspondence over the years he apologizes for his stories. Betty and I would never have thought of classifying his books into groups if we had not read a very scholarly article in the *American Quarterly* by Carl Bode, Professor of English at the University of Maryland. The article was entitled, "Lloyd Douglas: Loud Voice in the Wilderness." In it Professor Bode does not dwell upon the literary style of the Douglas novels, but feels they should be examined for the light they cast upon the popular mind. He says, "To know Douglas' novels is to understand our country a little better." He groups the books under three general periods: the first, the professional books for ministers; the second, the modern theological novels; the third, the two historical novels of biblical times.

In his article Professor Bode points out the gradual change from the modern scientific approach of the early books to the traditionalism of the ancient scene and mysteries of the miracles which color and support the last two novels: *The Robe* and *The Big Fisherman.*

> Douglas' concept of the ideal man of God . . . changes throughout the course of his literary career. To begin with in *Magnificent Obsession* and its immediate successors, he is the physician. No St. Luke, he is a brisk and thoughtful healer. . . . Half of the novels that Douglas wrote in his middle period have a doctor either as the main character or as a god from the machine. . . .
>
> In his slow swing toward traditionalism, however, [he] introduces the character of Dean Harcourt. In this dignified but kindly Episcopalian churchman Douglas avoids the things that repelled him in the nonconforming ministry but comes back to a professional ministry nevertheless. Dean Harcourt is supposed to be primarily a man of God, not a psychiatrist. Douglas introduces him in *Green Light* and makes him the central figure in *Invitation To Live*, which was the last novel to appear before *The Robe.* . . . The trend toward tradition continues in *The Robe* and *The Big Fisherman.* . . . The neat, ready answers and the clever stratagems of the earlier novels are gone . . . in Jesus himself, Douglas develops his ultimate conception of the shepherd.

Professor Bode's description of the gradual change of philosophy in the Douglas novels is quite in accord with Betty's and my discreet observations concerning Daddy's personal religion. It was characteristic of him that his own faith and beliefs were matters he could not discuss with his daughters. To people who wrote and came for advice he gave the benefit of his solemn convictions. But Betty and I never fell into such discussions with him and he doubtless thought they would bore or embarass us. He had brought us up to be lighthearted and amused by the capers of life. That side of his nature was the one he turned to us.

So often in my youth I marveled as I looked at him in the pulpit, earnest and dedicated. "Is that my own father?" I would ask myself in wonder. He hid that self from us because he sensed we wanted it that way. One time and once only I questioned him about his beliefs. He told me that as a young man he had passed through all the stages of rationalizing and doubt, but of one thing he had always been convinced. "There is a plan," he said, "be confident of its integrity."

The years had brought him much happiness and little sorrow, but he had many opportunities to see the troubles of others. In a world upset by wars and violence it was quite true he became dissatisfied with the slick manner in which he had been solving the problems of mankind. If he were to write another book Jesus Christ would be the adviser; faith in the faith of our fathers, the hope. Ivy and moss were beginning to creep back upon the walls of his church.

15

The Robe

O NE DAY in the early fall of 1940 among the usual pile of fan mail, came a brief letter to Daddy from a lady in Canton, Ohio. She wrote: "As I was reading in John of the Crucifixion how the soldiers had cast lots for the seamless coat of Jesus, this was my thought: what might have been the reaction of the Roman soldier who won the coat? Did he wear it? Is there any legend about that man?"

I was not there when my father read that letter, but I can see his face quite clearly as the modest words written by the little Ohio saleslady rose from the paper and struck him. It was probably the same expression that transfixed him so long ago at the dinner table when Betty matter-of-factly suggested he use his Sunday sermon in the novel he was trying to write. From time to time these things happened to Daddy. He did not consider them lucky windfalls. He seemed to think they were answers, and the look I speak of as so characteristic was one of overwhelmed gratitude.

When he hit on an idea himself after hours of brain-combing he would rush out and spread the good news through the house, bouncing in his eagerness to be congratulated. But on the occasions when something was handed to him quietly from an unexpected source he was curiously reluctant to talk about it.

However, Hazel McCann's suggestion did not crash over him

at once as a full-bodied novel, unfolding and unfolding upon itself the pageant of ancient Rome. In a long letter to Mr. Kent giving his opinion of the government and the international situation and their current business affairs, he added this postscript:

I am working on the idea of a ten-thousand word story distinctly appropriate for the Easter Season. At first I thought it might make a good Easter editorial, but as it develops I see story material. At the scene of the Crucifixion the Roman soldiers conduct an informal raffle for Christ's robe. The soldier who wins it produces much hilarity later, in the barracks, by putting it on over his uniform. Everybody laughs but the new owner who is suddenly sobered, takes it off quickly and stores it in his locker. He gets out of the service and goes up through Galilee, alone and on foot, the robe hidden in his sack. He visits such places as Capernaum, Cana and Nazareth and has conversation with people who knew Jesus. It has the makings of a gem of a little story, giving promise of great usefulness for Easter thought. I'm going to give it the best I've got for the theme is too good to be handled casually.

In November he wrote to Mr. Kent:

The story idea I spoke of to you hastily in a postscript the other day is beginning to take shape. It has immense possibilities, I think. What I want to do is to get it ready as a short story for magazine publication at the Easter season for 1941. Then I shall begin the job again with the expectation of making a full-length novel of it. I wish I might have a long talk with you about this project for it is important. If the thing is done at all it will have to be done well. It will involve a considerable amount of research.

December 17, 1940 [to Mr. Kent]

I have been giving much careful thought to the story I expect to work on as my next project. It now becomes increasingly clear that any attempt at a short story would be a distinct disappointment to us all, ruthlessly burning over a very valuable piece of property. I think we had better give up the idea of an Easter story for Cosmopolitan. As I envisage this job now it is much too important to deal with in the manner I suggested. If this novel keeps its present promise it will be far and away the best thing I have ever thought of. Perhaps you can explain this to Cosmopolitan so they will not be expecting the Easter thing.

I am itching to get into it; a bit frightened, more than a bit humble, first time I have really been scared in the face of a new job since I wrote the Obsession. I feel I am not big enough to do this thing as it ought to be done, but I'm going to try. I'll be handling some pretty high-powered stuff. Here's where the mouse labors in the hope of bringing forth a mountain.

And what happened to Hazel McCann? People always want to know when they hear of her part in the story. Mrs. McCann recently sent us a copy of the letter Daddy wrote her in November of 1940.

Dear Mrs. McCann,

I am deeply appreciative of your letter of October 28th. Almost every day I hear from someone who thinks he or she has found a good idea for a story, and I am always grateful for the cordiality and interest implied by these donations. But not often have I had an idea handed to me which seemed to have large possibilities.

Your notion about the possible story of the seamless coat which a soldier won in a lottery at the time of the crucifixion is indeed a very inviting theme and I am thinking seriously about it. It would make a very pretty magazine story for Easter.

It was very kind and thoughtful of you to give me the benefit of this luminous idea and I shall try to do a story on it that will fulfill your expectations.

A new book of mine, *Invitation To Live*, has just been published. I want you to have a copy of it and am sending it today.

With all good wishes and sincere regards, I am

Faithfully yours,

LLOYD C. DOUGLAS

"And was that all?" people ask us, thinking of the enormous clamor the book made when it finally came out two years later. Betty and I have a huge scrapbook which Daddy's secretary made, devoted to newspaper comments about *The Robe*. On one of the early pages there is a long interview cut from a Canton, Ohio, paper and headed with a big picture of Lloyd Douglas sitting in a chair and smiling at a lady who sits beside him. She is smiling too, but not at the camera, as most ladies would, but at the man. She seems to be twisting a handkerchief in her lap and her expression, too, is a little anxious, but she does not seem conscious of her own importance on the occasion. She looks at the man beside her in unconcealed admiration.

When *The Robe* finally appeared it carried these simple words on a page inside the cover:

Dedicated with appreciation
to
Hazel McCann
who wondered what became of
The Robe

From the first moment of its inception the idea of this book seized him as no other project had. The great possibilities of the story spread in broad avenues from his center theme the more he thought upon it, and at times he would have to fight down a sensation of being engulfed by the very magnitude of what he was attempting. He had always yearned to write a life of Christ, but considered it had twice been done with a perfection he could not hope to approach. However, he felt that the actual teachings of Christ had never been sufficiently emphasized by the Christian church. Much time and scholarly thought had been put into the study of the miracles; learned men had long been expounding upon the more abstruse texts of the New Testament; but the simple, kindly lessons of the Master preached in the fields and by the lakes of Galilee were too often forgotten amid the pomp and ceremony of the church.

We remember Daddy frequently saying in his sermons that the churches dwelt too much upon the birth and death of Christ. He said, "People for centuries have been reaffirming in the Apostles' Creed their belief in Jesus Christ, who was born of the Virgin Mary, suffered under Pontius Pilate, was crucified, dead and buried." It seemed significant to him that in that creed the years of the Lord's ministry were given only the space required by a small comma.

Now in the story of the crude, homespun robe lay an opportunity for him to take people back to the quiet summer days where, without altar or stained-glass windows, Jesus spoke to his flock.

Daddy was consumed with thoughts of the new book. Before, it had been possible for him to lay aside his work when he left his study, but now it went with him into the garden, sat in his chair when he played gin rummy with Mother at night, and lay beside him in his bed. At the typewriter it often eluded him. "I am working today in my second chapter, but not doing very well," he wrote. "Had to brush my teeth too many times, get drinks of water, sharpen pencils."

He gradually collected quite a sizable library of books concerning Rome and the life of the times in which he was working. In his letters to us he was apt to impart odd bits of information. "Did you know that the ancient Romans—even our Better People —slept in their clothes, merely tossing aside the toga when they went to bed? That they rarely washed their faces in the morning? That their slaves made so much racket it was impossible for anyone to sleep after sunrise?"

Before beginning the book Daddy wrote out a complete synopsis of the plot for the enlightenment of his publishers who were not quite sure what manner of tale their popular author was now venturing upon. Although this outline was closely followed throughout the two years of labor, Daddy often found himself surprised by characters who casually wandered into the story and seemed loath to depart. He wrote to Mary Peabody:

I had an odd experience yesterday. A small company of people in the andronitis (lobby to you) of a Greek Inn were getting acquainted. I knew all five of them very well, but they hadn't known one another until I brought them together. Everything was proceeding normally when a tall, young brunette came in at the door and sauntered toward them. I was quite taken off my feet for she had no reservation in the story. But she kept coming toward us. I watched her with interest as she moved across the page. A matronly woman reached out a hand toward her and said, "This is my daughter, Theodosia." Just like that. Now I don't know what to do with Theodosia; the house is full. I have made no plans for her. She is pretty, but a bit audacious. I've sent her out to the swing. I am now wondering whether to bring her back, or let her swing and send someone out to talk to her, or take her myself down to the duck-pond and drown her. My job this morning is to think up something for Theodosia to do. I hope she behaves herself for this is a nice story.

By January of 1941 the novel was going forward on the strength of its own momentum. In Daddy's letters to us he reported its progress more as a participant than as one contriving the events. The realization that he was steadily approaching the time when he must witness the Crucifixion depressed him. "I dread it," he wrote.

I worked all day very hard. I have decided to end the fifth chapter at the close of the trials. The crucifixion is in the next chapter. I hope it doesn't get me down. I shall be glad when that part of the story has been told.

And when he finished the sixth chapter he wrote wearily to Betty:

Well, at long last, as good King David saith, I have finished my sixth chapter. It was a tough job. I feel as though I had been through a long spell of illness. I am glad I have finished with the grim part of the book.

During the early months of composition he and Mr. Kent wrote frequently of the serialization of the novel in *Cosmopolitan*. Daddy was considering the demands of instalment publication.

Of course from the standpoint of the magazine the sooner we dive into the main action the better. It has been my observation that magazines want about everything packed into the first installment (which is impressively played up with pictures and preferential position) after which the succeeding installments are progressively pushed back, whittled down, and used mainly to prop up the advertisements.

But this time I am writing a book; not a magazine serial, primarily. I am not going to agonize over the problem of cramming the whole thing into the first 20,000 words. This story must lead the reader gradually to the point where he is mentally and emotionally ready for the strange events in Galilee. Otherwise you have only the old, old story told in the old, old way. It's been done that way quite often enough.

What you say about avoiding anachronisms is a sensible warning. It will be easy to make shocking mistakes. Let us do the best we can; there will be many places, no doubt where a meticulous historian might have a fit. I bear him no ill-will, but if he has fits he will have to see a doctor. For example: the sober fact is that Gaius was acting regent (under weary old Tiberius) a few years earlier than the time I have assigned to him. At this distance I don't think it makes much difference; at least it doesn't to me. If any Ph.D. revolts we can refund the price of the book or substitute a better one.

However, Daddy went to great pains to make the book as accurate historically as possible. He checked with students of the period over many details. His heroine he had planned to call Augusta, but was told by an authority that the name Augusta was given only to women of the imperial family. She became Diana. He wrote to me in October:

A recent letter from Dr. Harris E. Kirk suggested that a statue of Epictetus on Mars Hill is not very well timed, Epictetus having been born in 60 A. D. He proposed that I change Epictetus to Epicurus which makes everything hotsy-totsy and does not require any alteration of the surrounding landscape. I wrote him that he should at least admit not many celebrities get a statue twenty-five years before they are born.

The toil went on month after month. The old complaints appeared in his letters. "Your aged father is working very hard . . . pain in my left shoulder from sitting too long in one strained position . . . I sit humped here over my typewriter. . . . This novel, like the poor, we expect to have with us always." He began to worry about the paper shortage, wondering if he would have enough to see him through his job. Then he wrote:

Today I was lucky enough to buy six boxes of typewriter paper. With this hoard in my cupboard I don't ever need to end this novel. I can keep on writing until the world comes to an end.

In March he planned a little break. I was going out for my yearly visit and Betty, entirely recovered from her back trouble, was to be there. It would be the first time for some years that we had been together when the presence of her pain had not shadowed our pleasure. Even on the trip to Coronado two years before we had all known she was holding herself against the jolts and bumps of the road. This reunion was to be entirely joyful, and weeks before Daddy and Mother were writing to us of their plans. To Betty:

Time marches on; it will not be long until the reunited original family will be making the welkin ring. You and your frozen-toed sister will be met by the Boy Scout Band and a large chorus we have secured from Aimee Semple McPherson's temple. I queried Howard Adams today about a house in Palm Springs that might be had for a week; a house with a high wall and huge gobs of sunshine pouring in. Then we could take our meals where and when we pleased with breakfast in our own kitchen, and a slave to come in and make the beds and kill the cockroaches.

Did you read Pegler's ode to Mussolini in the Times this morning? Nothing left to be said on that.

Letter from the little sister today says she will get away on time notwithstanding the three moppets have chicken pox. She has become a skier of great renown now and can almost stand up on her new skis without leaning against anybody. She talks more about her fetching costume than the actual mileage she has hung up. Howard, it would seem, has retired from his practise, and is now skiing for a living. He is, we hear, very competent, very graceful, beautiful.

Bessie is out paddling about in the garden trying to snag some flowers for the dinner party we are having tonight. Poor dear has had some painful work done on her teeth. Our dentist ought to send nembutal capsules with his bill. Oh well, I've only got nine teeth left.

Grandmother Porch is better again, sits up for a few hours, but this last illness has taken a good deal out of her, I fear. She seems very frail. Love to your miner. Tell him I hope he finds a great big nugget the size of the State house.

That family reunion was marked by rain. Day after day it came down in torrents, so heavy that it hammered on your bare head painfully when you dashed through it from cover to cover. We four went to Palm Springs and spent a week in the desert bungalow Daddy had engaged. The plaster walls soaked up the rain and exuded an earthy chill on our side. Our bedrooms were built around a little patio and to get to them at night we had to scurry briefly through the open. However, we had much to say to each other and huddled cosily around the fireplace talking . . . talking. "Doesn't this remind you of the summer we spent at Carmel?" Daddy asked. And it did in more ways than the damp and the brightly burning logs suggested. In spite of the fact that Betty and I were married and our interests deeply invested in things apart from our parents, when we all got together that second life was quite forgotten and we became young girls who have never left home.

Toward the end of the Palm Springs holiday Mother developed a painful tooth. "It's probably the rain," she said, "but I think I had better see the dentist." When we put her on the train she was distressed to leave us. "Don't say anything funny till I come back," she said.

But she didn't come back the next morning or the next. Her tooth was infected, she said when Daddy phoned, and required treatment. That worried him so we cut short our holiday and went home. We found Mother upstairs in her bed. When we went into her room she had the covers up over her face and hid from us. "I don't want you to see me," she wept, "my face is too horrible."

Betty and I crept away, but Daddy sat on her bed and murmured to her. He told her he didn't care how horrible she looked, that he loved her and always would love her and insisted upon seeing just how badly her face was swollen. He took care of her himself for several days until the swelling in her face went down. Nothing had wrung his heart so much as when she had hidden from him. "My wife has been sick," he wrote to Mr. Kent. "She is a pathetic little creature at times."

Betty and I too, found ourselves becoming increasingly protective toward Mother. She was sixty-two and her pretty face was no longer young, but in a shy childish way she seemed younger than we and far more innocent. With Daddy shut up in his study working so many long hours of the day she was alone a great deal. She had several devoted friends and a few outside things interested her; the International Institute was dear to her heart. In a letter to Mary Peabody Daddy wrote:

Besse is taking me to the International Institute for dinner tonight. We will have candied mice, buttered worms and grilled breast of Pekin cat.

But for the most part Mother puttered about her house, spending much time with Grandmother, who lay in bed too frail and deaf to notice a great deal, and working in her garden. She liked to be on hand when Daddy finished his book for the day and came groaning and stretching from his study to look for her in her bedroom or out in the little lath house where she potted her plants. Always she had kept herself ready for the time when the three she loved wanted her. When we were children and came home from school we went at once to her room and rarely found her missing. It was as though she had built her life around the thought: "When they come to look for me I must be there."

She hung on every word I had to tell her of her three grandsons. That winter I took out to Los Angeles some movies Howard and I had taken of the children. They were as dreadfully bad as inexpert photographers could possibly make them. Long stretches of the film consisted of figures who seemed to be moving slowly through a submarine forest. When Mother was better and able to come downstairs Daddy rented a projector and I ran the pictures while my family sat expectantly in the dark, letting out from time to time little yelps of recognition. "That must be Johnny," and "Is that Bunny in his carriage?"

I couldn't say for sure.

Then briefly a clear space would flash across the screen and we would see the children's faces. "Ah," Mother would sigh, "there they are."

When we turned on the lights again Daddy said he thought the show was very good. "Full of mystery and suspense," he said, "though I never did learn who committed the murder."

The family reunion came to an end. Betty and I returned to our homes and Daddy and Mother settled back into their old routine. The work on the novel plodded on. Daddy wrote: "My book is getting longer all the time and I have still about twenty dollars worth of paper left." Often in the afternoons he and

Mother went out to the ranch and strolled about checking up on the series of caretakers who came and went: some good, some very bad. "Miss Thompson has had a calf," he would write, and, "We now have rabbits: Mama rabbit, Papa rabbit, and five little ones whose names we did not learn."

They had times of being quite social, went to parties and gave pleasant little dinners which Otto served with much ceremony. Their guests were friends from the East who were wintering in California, or met at the Bel-Air Garden Club; and sometimes they entertained the more sedate members of the movie colony. Irene Dunne, Arthur Treacher, Fay Bainter and others who had appeared in the filming of Daddy's novels came for dinner at times when I was there. They wrote of a wide variety of other interesting people they had met and entertained.

Several times they made hurried trips across the continent when Daddy had to fulfill speaking engagements, but for the most part they stayed at the old grind and chapter after chapter of *The Robe* was handed to Marion Hunt to type and send on to Houghton Mifflin Company.

Two years is a long time for one's publishers to keep shouting enthusiasm over a manuscript they are receiving in small batches month by month. After all, they have other books and other authors skimming the cream from their fine cries of joy. Publishing houses should employ one special man whose sole job is to keep inventing fresh phrases of delight to be dealt out in regular doses to authors at work. Perhaps they do. Perhaps some writers work without this lubrication of praise, but Daddy had always needed it. In the thick files of HMCo., LCD letters, which they have very kindly given us, are sprinkled queries: "What do you really think of this stuff I am sending you? So far I seem to have the cheering section to myself."

Although enthusiastic support always came in answer, one feels their reservations; but one man of Houghton Mifflin Company foresaw the immense possibilities of *The Robe* from its early days and wholeheartedly expressed his convictions to

Daddy. Hardwick Moseley, at that time sales manager of the Chicago district, wrote him in 1941:

> *The Robe* is going to be a great book. It will sweep the country in the tradition of the great American bestsellers. It will sell long after the copyright has expired because it is a magnificent story told in the simple and universal feeling for values of the greatest story in the world from which it drew its inspiration.

Daddy answered:

> Your warm encouragement is deeply appreciated. That sort of stimulation is a mighty fine tool to put in the hands of a writer while he is still at work on a project.

His letters to us during these many months generally began with an account of his progress in the book, followed by a bulletin upon the weather, the sins of the incumbent caretaker at the ranch, and the general health situation, winding up with a long and snorting diatribe in the style of Grandmother Douglas on the political scene. When he took an active dislike to a public figure he deprived his name of a capital letter and varied the spelling to the serious disadvantage of his dignity. "And this," he would conclude, "is what I think of the international mess. If there is anything you don't understand just ask me and I will gladly clear it up for you."

Cosmopolitan magazine continued to put off contracting for the serialization of the forthcoming novel. Their editors felt they should see the entire manuscript before accepting it, lest religious developments be objectionable to some of their subscribers. As time went on Daddy cooled to the idea of letting this work come out in any magazine. He wrote to Mr. Kent.

> More and more I doubt the wisdom of attempting a magazine serialization. It would cut the story to pieces. As for the money, the government would take almost all of it away from me.

As the novel neared completion the publishers became excited and pressed for a definite date. But this time Daddy refused to be hurried.

I have your [Mr. Kent's] letter this morning in which you inquire about a probable date for publication of The Robe. Your query is quite in order and I wish I could say with any degree of confidence that this novel will be in your shop bright and early on the first day of May. But it would be unfortunate if, with any publication date in mind, I should finish it in haste.

The composition of the three or four chapters I have been working on these last weeks has required a lot of thinking. I am not attempting to present photographs of New Testament stories, but rather portraits. However I felt the necessity of adhering as closely as possible to the traditional narratives, and this task of claiming a novelist's liberty, while keeping one's eye on the text, has slowed my pace considerably. I thought I was thoroughly familiar with all the "Galilean" material, and there need be no detaining problems of research, but I have been obliged to proceed with caution every step of the way.

I think my nineteenth chapter is going to induce many people to re-read the Acts of the Apostles. I had thought I was fairly well acquainted with this treatise, but was amazed to discover a large number of conflicts in its chronology; so many, indeed, that on one occasion I felt free to make another of my own.

Whenever I have been obliged to make a direct quotation I have employed phrases from the text. Example: in Simon Peter's prayer, after his release from prison I dissected the language out of one of Peter's Epistles so that no one could say I had put words into his mouth that he wouldn't have spoken.

Well, enough on that. You will doubtless have heard conflicting reports about a recent air-raid out here. It was quite a spectacle, plainly visible from our southern windows. Twenty searchlight beams converged on one spot for half an hour while anti-air guns riddled the sky at that point, with exploding shells. The detonations were constant and heavy, a Fourth of July pageant on a colossal scale. At our safe vantage we were more interested than

scared, though it did give you a squeamish feeling to see the war
flung into your own front yard.

Let me advise you that I, too, am an air warden, having custody
of a key to the switch box down at the corner where I can turn
off all the street lights in Bel-Air. I have a tin hat and a whistle.
Have they given you a whistle?

April 29, 1942 [to Betty]

A bright idea for my novel dropped in upon me three days ago
and I am carefully tooling it into my 22nd chapter. One of the
chief criticisms leveled at the old book Ben Hur was the charge
that the hero, having become thoroughly sold on the divinity of
Jesus, never did anything about it. He engaged in a chariot race
with a pagan (symbolic of War) and beat him by a neck, but as
for his exemplification of his new-found Christianity, he didn't
come through. I have been in the danger of stumbling into the
same pitfall. Now I have decided to go with Marcellus for a
few weeks out into the open country with a clear chance to do
something for the poor people; very little of indoctrination, very
much of humane helpfulness. The book needs this, and I am giving
much thought to this phase of it. The story is moving to a close.
I never felt better in my life. The thing unfailingly keeps me
buoyed up so that I feel no fatigue.

A few days after he wrote that letter Grandmother Porch
died. She had lain for weeks paralyzed and unconscious. It had
been a long, long strain, especially for Mother. "This winter
of anxiety has taken a great deal out of Besse," Daddy wrote.
"Each day I see her a little quieter. I hope now that her mother
has been mercifully released she will be able to pick up some
strength. She has no resistance."

Betty and Mother took Grandmother back to Springfield,
Ohio, to be buried with Grandfather and her people. Daddy
wrote to Mr. Kent:

Besse and Betty have gone back East for Mrs. Porch's burial.

The house seems strangely quiet. For five years we have had nurses starching up and down the stairs; I almost miss them.

I am working on the last chapter of The Robe. Very sad things are happening. I am tired.

At two-thirty this morning I was phoned out of bed by a "Yellow Alert." Fifteen minutes later I got a "Blue" which put the old warrior into his pants and boots, flashlight and whistle. After stalking up and down the street in the bright moonlight for a while, feeling pretty warlike for an aged civilian, information came that I could go back to bed.

In the early summer of 1942 *The Robe* was finally finished. Daddy went back to Boston to confer with his publishers, who were in a high state of excitement over their new property, and then, gratified and happy, he returned to Bel-Air to enjoy his rest.

I am now a gentleman of leisure, sitting quietly in my patio under my vine and figtree while my sweating slaves in Boston do all the work.

This morning I did a little pencil work, after reading the report of the new income tax demands, and I figured that from the proceeds accruing from my new book I shall be able to keep $6.92 for myself. This sum—come March of 1943—should be sufficient to purchase two nice lamb chops for Bessie and me.

The Robe appeared on the bookstands the sixteenth of October. It went to the top of the best-seller list in mid-November and remained there, as number one across the country, for eleven months. It stayed on the best-seller list for four years. The book has been translated into eighteen languages and the regular sales up to the present time are well over two million. It would be hard to compute how many people have read the book. One reporter wrote in a review: "Among my close friends I know of six who own copies of *The Robe,* and on enquiry I find that these six copies have been read by at least sixty-four people."

Not long ago a lady proudly showed Betty and me her copy of the book. In the back were the signatures of all the people who had borrowed it. They covered two pages and were crammed into the corners.

The Robe preached to a mighty cathedral, and its author had the satisfaction of knowing that his words had sent thousands to their Bibles and thousands who had never before turned its pages sought the scriptures with awakened interest. A professor and dean of letters in a big university wrote Daddy: "I have read the book and resolved to do something about it—try harder to be a Christian. Whoever rises from prayer determined to be a better man—his prayer has been answered."

On the whole *The Robe* was treated with respect by the critics. From reviewers who represented the great yearning public the praise was almost reverent. The more sophisticated critics stroked their chins and admitted that one could not very well ignore the importance of a book which had met with such an immense response from rich and poor, educated and uneducated. From one of the most jaded critical pens of our land came this weary tribute—two years after the book was published:

> It is time for this department, which did not mention *The Robe* when it first came out, to take cognizance of Dr. Douglas. I have procured a copy of the book and gone through it and what I have found is rather surprising. Instead of the usual trash aimed at Hollywood and streamlined for the popular magazines, one is confronted with something that resembles an old-fashioned historical novel for young people.

Letters of appreciation poured in written on every kind of paper from lined pages torn from exercise books to heavy bond handsomely engraved. Professors of religion endorsed it gratefully and hardheaded business men wrote that they were buying the book in wholesale lots to be distributed among their employees. In every mail there were begging letters too: hospitals wanted new wings, universities new libraries, churches thought it would be nice if Lloyd Douglas donated an organ or steeple to their building. Daddy got a little cynical at times with his fan mail and said it seemed as though everybody in the country needed an operation and thought he should pay for it.

But the sincerely appreciative letters which came from people who had no axe to grind, who just wished to say how much their personal lives had been enlarged by reading the book, made up for all the cranks and nuts who wrote pages of moonshine. The most satisfying letters of all came from soldiers, many of whom wrote from their stations directly at the front. They spoke of being in foxholes, or crowded barracks or aboard destroyers in dangerous waters. Many others wrote from hospitals or prison camps. This rather touching letter came from a boy in a hospital in England:

Dear Sir,

To one who has just come back from facing violent death and knows that in a very short time he will again be at the front, the reading and digesting of The Robe comes as a great comfort.

It wasn't the fear of death that worried me so much—it was the fear of "not living." And there is a difference. I'm young, I have a lovely wife and a child that will be born soon, and I love life itself. I want to live very much.

But so did Marcellus.

I don't pretend that I face death as bravely and calmly as Marcellus did, but the reading of your book has strengthened me immeasureably. My thanks to you, sir.

This came from France:

Dear Mr. Douglas,

I found The Robe (Armed Forces edition) on the boat which carried me to France on D plus 1. I started reading it sitting on my life jacket with my back against the bulkhead (you're not supposed to sit on life jackets). I immediately lost interest in everything else. Once a friend came around and asked me if I knew we were being shelled. Then I heard three shells come over. I carried my life jacket and book around to port and continued my reading. I'm not trying to sound heroic, I'm just trying to show the power of The Robe.

I finished reading the book in France in a ditch by the side of the road while we were waiting to advance across the Douse River and join the fighters and engineers who had gone ahead. It was a great story and I was certainly hungry for it. When we finally went into the battle I moved under a simple, Christian cloak: if God wanted me to die that was all right with me, if he only wanted me to lose a leg that was all right too, but I wondered how my wife would feel about it. If he wanted me to come home whole that would be fine because that meant he had faith in my ideas and work and wanted me to live a good life.

Thank you for writing The Robe. I enjoyed it and it made me think.

This letter written from Torino, Italy, came to Daddy in 1947 when he was ill and grieving. It did much to make him feel that his work had been worthwhile.

Dear Mr. Douglas:

I am an Italian student, and I have just left Rome where I've been living during the war. My home was right over the Catacombs of St. Callisto, and there I had the occasion of hearing your name. It was on June 5, '44, while American tanks along the old Appian Way were ironing towards Rome. The men of a small unit came to visit the catacombs. I guided them. They were the first American soldiers I met, and I was finding it somewhat difficult to understand their broad accent; nevertheless we fraternized immediately.

At the end of one of the dark galleries, some slabs of marble were fixed on the wall with old Latin and Greek inscriptions and old Christian symbols. When I pointed out a fish, and nearby, the word IXOUS, one of the GI's said: "That's the fish of The Robe." He put down his helmet on the pavement of the gallery, of

trodden tufa sand, and there, at the light of some candles and military flashlights, at fifty feet underground, started telling us the
story of The Robe. So I made acquaintance with Marcellus. When
we got out, it was dark—about 9 o'clock—all around Rome the
glare of artillery fires was flashing and shells flew invisibly hissing
above us.

Since then I have heard hundreds and hundreds of times—at any
time we met a fish carved on a slab of the catacombs—your name
and the title of your book.

And many times, walking up and down the wonderful Cypress
Avenue which has at one end the view of St. Peter's dome, at
the other Cecilia Metella's gigantic tomb, under a starry sky, I
imagined your Marcellus or Marcipor starting from the busy
highway (the old Appian Way, running along the ground of
the Catacombs) and coming down the cypress drive as far as the
old caves.

Excuse me my boldness. I imagine myself to be just one of the
fellow workers of Marcellus in the melon-fields of Arpino.
Kindly excuse my bad English which has been picked up from
conversations with GI's and occasional readings.

After the publication of *The Robe* Daddy was really famous.
Such fame as he had had before seemed a mere whisper to the
terrific clamor the sound of his name now called forth. When
I went home to visit I could not get used to it and marveled at
the calm way Mother and Betty accepted their roles in the
general tumult. In Canada Daddy was well known, but people
didn't stagger and clutch at me if I mentioned him as being my
father. He had written to me of the burden of his fan mail, but
I was astounded when I actually saw a day's load. I gaped like
a country cousin at the waiters who scurried forward when
we entered a restaurant, and the crowds who pressed for autographs at places where Daddy spoke. "How does it feel to be
famous?" I asked him, as he had been asked so many times by
foolish women.

"Now the little daughter mustn't spoof at the poppa," he
said, and stuck out his tongue at me. But I wasn't teasing; I

really wanted to know. I concluded he didn't know himself. He was just the same. He never took himself seriously. He still had the same silly experiences every time he stepped outside the house and told them gleefully when he returned. If he was recognized and fawned over in places where he was known he was still ignored when he passed himself off as the general public. In a letter to me full of accounts of speaking engagements and dinners in his honor he made this confession:

> What you say about your inability to bowl them over with your grandeur when you appear in shops, garages, hotels, etc., finds me in a responsive mood. For this has been the attitude of the public toward me all my life. I seem to make a pretty favorable impression in a letter and on the telephone, but when I show up personally they wait on everybody else and then clump in small huddles to converse with one another until I crawl into their midst and squeak mousily of my needs. They look me over with disapproval and direct me to the rummage counter. If I meekly suggest that I might be interested in something a little better, they take me for a shop-lifter, and a bald-headed man with bow legs and a bow tie follows me closely to see that I don't slip off with a silk-lined bassinette tucked down inside my pants.
>
> Blessed are the meek for they shall inherit the earth. If they ever get it, that's the way it will have to come—by inheritance. We meekers aren't in it with the tin-lunged, elbow hurlers. We'll just have to wait in patience until things are handed to us (and then somebody will have to show us how to plug it into the wall).

That same winter Daddy wrote to Burton Garlinghouse concerning a shopping experience in which he had faced the shortages of war.

> Speaking of shoes—and also of Iowa—on March 21st I spoke at the University of Iowa. The day had begun with six inches of snow, but under the pleasant influence of the first sunshine since last September, the snow melted by 2 P.M. into a dirty slush, curb deep. I had brought no overshoes with me. Now, feeling

the urgent need of rubbers, I cat-footed to a shoe store hard by the hotel and asked for some. The clerk regarded me with a sour grin.

"Live in United States?"

I nodded childishly.

"Had you heard there was a rubber shortage?"

I admitted I had heard of it, but thought there might be a few pairs left.

He shook his head, but at this juncture a shaggy old clerk slipped up and whispered something about "that there one pair."

My man turned to me and said, "We do have one pair."

"What's the matter with them?" I asked.

"Well, they're a little large," he said.

"Let's see 'em," said I, with ostentatious bravado.

The rubbers were brought and presented to me. Clerks left their customers sitting in their socks and gathered around. I stepped into the rubbers. They were, as the man had said, a little large. They showed signs of having been stepped into before, probably by some of the biggest feet that ever followed a plow.

"I'll take them," I said. "I've got to have rubbers."

They brought the morning edition of the Des Moines Register and Leader and crumpled up sixteen pages for ballast. After we had packed the first eight inches of the forecastle I found that I could keep the overshoes on, provided I did not lift my heels off the ground. In this interesting condition I slid out into the slush and proceeded to a radio station where I was billed to coo on a soap-opera program. I do not think I am an abnormally sensitive man but I am not accustomed to being followed on the street by strangers who are about to strangle with suppressed laughter.

At the Radio Station the overshoes refused to go upstairs so I left them at the entrance, feeling pretty sure they would not be molested. I skated about in them throughout my stay in the city bringing joy to many persons who appreciate the more elementary appeals to humor.

Next day I left on a very good train for Chicago. I pushed the rubbers as far back as possible under my chair in the club car hoping the porter would not find them. But he found them and carried them out. When I debarked onto the platform the over-shoes were sitting on my two pieces of luggage. A woman was saying to another. "Let's wait 'till he comes out. He must be gigantic."

I tried to give the rubbers to the redcap, to leave them in the taxi; I tried to give them to the chambermaid and every bellhop who came up to my room. When I checked out I left them in a far corner of the closet shelf, but when I connected with my baggage at the taxi stand, there they were. At the station I had an inspiration. I checked my rubbers at the parcel window and then I took the claim ticket and tore it up into small, precise squares as I marched—bright-eyed and unafraid—to my train.

During that winter of 1943 when *The Robe* was making its brilliant debut, Daddy's life was crammed with speaking engagements and public appearances in big cities all across the country. He wanted Mother to share with him all the adulation and excitement of his position and she longed to enjoy the travel, the parties and the crowded schedule and convinced him that she was well enough to stand it.

I met them in New York for a brief whirl of engagements and I had never seen Mother so gay and vivacious. "She certainly has kept up with him every step of the way," I thought. As always she turned to him constantly, but her personality shone in its own light. Perhaps she thought he didn't know what an effort it was every morning for her to get to her feet and face the events of the day, but he confided to me: "I don't think your mother should be banging around like this. However she insists she's having a good time. The poor darling deserves a little fun after all the months she's sat around while I was working. I haven't the heart to send her home."

In the spring they went back to Bel-Air and Mother did not give up until the last day on the train. Then she was suddenly very sick. She recovered but it was the beginning of the end. One little thing after another put her to bed. Daddy wrote: "I lifted your mother in my arms this morning and she cried out in extreme pain. I had broken her rib. What can be the matter with her?"

They put her into the hospital and the X-rays showed that some sort of deterioration was taking place in all of her bones. Daddy wrote to Betty's husband:

Weary, I'm scared about Bessie. I'm afraid she has something that will keep her from getting well. She will come home this time in pretty fair condition. She will stay in bed for a week or two and then get up and go out in the garden. But then she will twist an ankle, or sprain a wrist, or worse, something will happen to her back which they say looks unhealthy in the pictures. I am afraid of that day when she knows she has gone to bed for keeps. I dreamed last night that I was trying to get her into a hospital in Chicago with many obstacles and detainments. I woke up weeping and utterly spent. I have stood by so many bedsides and a hundred graves and glibly offered soothing words, but now I can't take it. I know now how shallow my slick and easy comfort must have been when offered to others.

My beautiful Besse is going to suffer; it is the history of these things. I can't bear it.

We did not tell Mother what her real trouble was. For a year Daddy and Betty tried to keep her from going anywhere alone without letting her know they were watching her constantly. When I went out to visit in the spring of '44 it seemed hard to believe she was ill of a disease which any minute might cause a bone to crumple and throw her into excruciating pain. She was frail but had never seemed prettier to me.

The loveliness of spring and the blossoming of the garden were her delight and our sadness. I came upon her one afternoon standing in the living room at the deep window, looking out at the fruit trees which were a froth of pink bloom. "Mother," I said, "let's have a man come and take some pictures of you in the garden. It's such a perfectly beautiful spring."

Her hand went up to the curtain and she grasped it tightly. When she looked at me my heart went sick, for I thought I saw the color of fear in my mother's eyes. "How queerly you all speak of my picture," she said slowly. "Daddy has asked me the same thing. And Betty too. Doesn't my family think there will ever be another spring?"

It was miraculous that week after week she was able to go about with so little discomfort. Daddy watched her and waited for the dreadful collapse which the doctors warned him might come at any time. He kept his secret from her by inventing all manner of plans for the future and was pleased when she appeared to share his interest.

Ideas for a new book were beginning to tease him and his publishers were enthusiastic when he wrote of attempting an autobiographical novel of his youth in Indiana. But the project did not take fire with him. In June he sent an impulsive telegram to announce that he was beginning work on a story of Peter. It was to be called *The Big Fisherman*. In a follow-up letter to Mr. Kent he wrote:

Perhaps you were surprised (maybe a bit disappointed) by my telegram reporting a new idea for a book.

I daresay it is the unusual success of The Robe and the very considerable amount of laudatory mail that comes in daily from all directions that has kept me fast in this First Century mood. I have tried to tug loose from it; have made a conscientious effort to retool my industry for work on Indiana in the Nineties, but it's no good. I'm still back there in the Near East, about the time of Christ; can't think about anything else.

There is a certain warmth and humanness about Peter which has endeared him to the Christian mind. He is impulsive, passionate, volatile; capable of sudden valors and dismaying weaknesses.

I have been talking to Besse about it. She feels I am right. The more I think about that post-pioneer Americana the less business it does with my emotions. It all seems so trivial in comparison with this more important work.

Later in the month he wrote of his progress:

> My new book ambles along and I am able to lose myself in it
> for a few hours each day. However Besse's condition is so con-
> stantly on my mind that I find it difficult to push aside my
> anxiety.

Then one morning it happened. Mother fell to the floor in
the bathroom and her back was fractured. She was put to bed
and never was able to turn by herself again. But science has
wonderful inventions and her life was prolonged for many
weeks. All that summer and through the fall she lay there quietly,
afraid to move lest she bring on the torment. Daddy suffered
every spasm with her and so tuned to her spirit was his body
that in a short time he became too crippled to walk or even move
his fingers. His was a mysterious illness entirely associated with
hers. A nurse wheeled him to her in the guest room for a few
hours each day and he sat by her bed watching her fading,
fading.

The anguish broke him. One night they carried him off to the
hospital with pneumonia and it seemed his death would come
before Mother's: his in a cold white sterile room, hers at home
without his hand to hold. All their married life he had taken care
of her as though she were a child. A single day apart had torn
them and when they met again they clung together like two
flames. That they—so long in love and dependent—should be
separated in the time of their greatest need for each other was
tragic. I remembered Daddy's letter written on a lecture trip
in 1935:

> I put Besse on a train and I boarded another for Chicago and
> all night long we were rushing away from each other as fast as
> we could go—a dreadful situation if there ever was one.

And that is the way their love story in this world ended:
he was in the hospital struggling with needles and oxygen tanks,

she lay in a darkened room waiting for him to come back. "Lloyd," she called out sometimes in the night. When we went to her she looked beyond us to the doorway, but no one was there.

"How is he?" Mother would murmur when Betty and I came back from seeing him.

"He's getting better," we would tell her.

"And am I getting better?" she would ask.

We begged her to believe that she was. We dreaded to see her frightened.

Then one afternoon the hospital nurse tiptoed into Daddy's room and laid her hand on his thin shoulder. He was lying on his side staring at the plaster wall. "She's gone, Dr. Douglas," she whispered.

He didn't move, but she heard him give a deep sigh.

16

The Big Fisherman

MOTHER DIED a few days after Christmas in 1944. Daddy was not able to leave the hospital until May—five months later. The arthritis which had seized him during the summer of her last illness reduced him to a pitiful wrack of bones. The big genial, rosy man was no more and never returned, although his humor and boyish enthusiasm often spoke from the drawn lips of the frail, elderly invalid he eventually managed to become.

For weeks he lay helpless in bed while the acute pain seared through all his joints. Minor afflictions came to plague him: corneal ulcers and infections. Through it all he seemed apathetic, showing little interest in helping nature or his doctors. One thing he was determined upon: he would never go back to the house in Bel-Air. He insisted that Betty put it up for sale and accept the first offer that came along. "You and Virginia take what you want and then dispose of everything else—everything. Turn the key in that house and give it to strangers."

Betty did as he asked, although she kept many of his old things: the intimate little trifles he was used to seeing in his study, his working table and chair, most of his books, hoping that the time would come when he would be well enough to sit at his typewriter and interest himself again in *The Big Fisherman*.

It was an unhappy time for her to be alone. She divided Mother's linen and silver and china, came upon her fancywork with the threaded needle caught in a stitch, decided what to do with boxes of love letters from Daddy and cards which had come with their wedding presents and notes congratulating them on the birth of their babies. There was a pile of saucers of which the cups had all been broken—wedding gifts. "It was a crime to use them for everyday," Mother told us, "but we were too poor to buy others." Betty hadn't the heart to give them away after Mother had packed them so carefully from parsonage to parsonage through all the years. They were divided and now they rest on our top pantry shelves until some unsentimental young person shall come upon them and cry, "Look at these old saucers! What a clutter." At last all was disposed of and the house with the golden doorknobs knew Lloyd and Besse no more. All that was left was a lonely sick old man in the hospital.

Daddy slowly improved and took more interest in his recovery. His first letter—dictated—was to Hal Seeley, who had recently lost his wife.

> Well, dear friend, all things come to an end. It is our common lot apparently. The seeds of these tragedies are indigenous to our life. Sometimes it happens that after having spent many years of a relatively happy existence, everything tumbles to pieces at once. You have had more than your share of bereavement in recent years. And you have my heartfelt sympathy. I shall not suggest that you be of good courage; that would be an impertinence. You will have attended to that.

As he grew stronger the routine of hospital life irked him more and more. No doubt he was a difficult patient, being a man who had never enjoyed waiting. Fortunately he was able to entertain his nurses as well as provoke them and they bore with him. In March he dictated this letter to Mr. Kent:

> Had I written to you as often as I have thought of you in these past weeks you would have had a daily letter. Now at the risk of being tiresome I shall tell you what I do with my time.

I wake early and am ready to meet the morning nurse when she comes on at seven. We have a lot of small but necessary chores to do, then I am put into my pajamas and slippers and handed my cane. I slip gingerly off the edge of the bed and shuffle slowly and uncertainly to the bathroom. Then I return to my blanketed chair where I wait for my breakfast to appear. The breakfast and Dr. Chapman arrive at the same time and one of them cools off while I exchange light bandinage with the other. I then await the arrival of the lady who does the physiotherapy on me.

I am not sure whether you met her when you came out to visit me. She is a very pretty, amiable, gentle-voiced person who looks as if she wouldn't hurt a fly. But no wild animal with a brass collar and three rows of teeth could do more damage than she is capable of in these physiotherapeutic engagements. She carefully takes me apart, finger by finger, toe by toe and lays all my various disarticulated members on chairs and tables while she manipulates my sore shoulders. You may have learned as a child that the human shoulder is rated as a ball and socket joint and when in proper order revolves at high speeds. One notices this especially in baseball pitchers. Well, my shoulders were originally geared like that in days which I find hard to remember, but since my illness the cartilage has worn thin and the juices have dried up, and to say it hurts like hell when she moves my arms is to say nothing about the matter at all. However at long last, she becomes exhausted in her endeavor to slay me. She carefully gathers up the disjecta membra and puts the pieces together again as well as she can recall their former relationship.

It is noon by now and the barber comes up to shave me. With ruthless abandon he takes me by the ears and throws my head around, not unlike the antics of our president when making a fireside talk.

It is time now for me to get up again. The nurse goes out to the pantry and gets an old wheel chair into which I am fitted and we journey down the long corridor to the elevator and thence upward to the roof where, on sunny days, I sit muffled to the ears while she does a jig-saw puzzle furnished by my daughter. I find the most comfortable occupational therapies are those undertaken by one's nurse.

The nights are long and lonesome. I am bedded down about 9:30 with plenty of straw, two nembutal cartridges and a shot of Dilaudid (a benign sedative which many liars say is not habit forming). I wake promptly at 12:30 and find the room dark and cheerless. The elderly nurse who comes on duty at eleven has settled into a couple of chairs and is having a nap. I lie with my thoughts until I am no longer able to bear them, then I moan a little, more and more audibly. She does not stir. Finally I yell "urinal" and she comes at full gallop, having a stake in that enterprise.

The doctor thinks that at my present rate of progress I may be out of here by May. In that case Betty will drive me to Las Vegas where I will stay at a ranch until the new quarters they are building for me adjoining their home are ready.

I am beginning to have thoughts about my novel again although I do not have the strength to do much more than think about it. I feel quite dedicated toward it now. For some reason I have been kept alive through these long ghastly months; it may very well be that I am to finish The Big Fisherman.

In May Daddy was able to leave the hospital and was taken by ambulance to a ranch located about ten miles south of Las Vegas. It was a cluster of pleasant bungalows around a center dining room. The buildings were shaded by a grove of trees, and beyond in all directions lay the hot desert rimmed with a ruffle of mountains. He wrote to Hardwick Moseley in June describing his new life.

The Big Fisherman is rolling along now. I am able to work about three hours a day on it. The job will be my salvation, distracting my attention from my physical infirmities and my unspeakable sorrow. The story opens in Arabia and so closely does the country there resemble the view I have here from my window that I need only turn my head to write an accurate description. History too has been generous, even to the point of confirming a lot of things that I had fully intended to say whether true or not.

The dry desert air here is supposedly friendly to people with arthritis and I am beginning to feel the effects. I still get about with the agility of a three toed sloth, but I contrive to dress and undress myself and my four typewriter fingers are released from the rigidity in which they were frozen for a while. I call them my Four Freedoms. I claim that people who use all their fingers in typing are sissies.

I have brought Bertha Kraft, my morning nurse at the hospital, along with me to help me get used to doing for myself. She gives me my daily deep muscular injection of liver extract. Bertha says people can do that for themselves, but I am squeamish about tackling the job. The needle is about the size of a four-penny nail. She is going back to Los Angeles in a week and then I shall be stuck with it, william-nilliam.

This ranch has accommodations for only ten people and it is always full. All the inmates are females except myself, who am probably neuter. They are sitting out their six weeks Nevada residence requisite to divorce procedure. Most of them have an authentic talent for autobiography. Indeed I now know more about some of them than I know about myself.

From what they tell me the typical story is something like this: all was hotsy-totsy for the first eighteen years of comparative poverty. Then Henry got to making money by the potful, met a blonde, and has now invited Mama to go out to Nevada and get herself a nice big divorce. They are well-meaning, gentlewomen, but I must say that if any of them were suing me for divorce I should be much too chivalrous to contest the litigation.

You might think I would be terribly bored here in this place where nothing happens but the desert (which was formerly viewed by me as an appalling stretch of itchy gravel and sagebrush, inhabited in its more fertile areas by rattlesnakes and lizards) has begun to take on pastel shades in the post-sunset hours and I am seeing things that had previously escaped me. Even so, do you not think that Las Vegas is an odd place for an elderly prophet to spend his last days?

It is two o'clock and as dry here as an Economics lecture. A hen on a neighboring ranch yesterday laid a poached egg. No, no—not on toast. You expect too much.

November 1945 [to Hal Seeley]

You will be glad to know that I am now contentedly installed in my new apartment in Betty's home. The dear girl and her husband, my devoted friend, have spared no pains to make this place beautiful and convenient. They trucked all my dunnage in from the Ranch one day last week and next day brought me in to find everything in its place; books in their shelves, all my little household gods strewn about, pictures on the wall, as of my former life.

I have always had some convictions about the difficulty of two or more generations getting on nicely under the same shingles. Not that they might quarrel, but that the interminable politeness required is likely to be hard on the personnel's pituitary.

However I hope this may work out all right. Betty's husband and I have a good deal in common and she has been my prop, my salvation during these past months.

I have my nurse, Bertha, back with me. She is a very competent young woman, a good companion, knows when I want to be entertained and when I want her to shut up and let me alone. I sent for her a few weeks ago because my diabetes, which for some unaccountable reason deserted me during my days in the hospital (probably feeling it had picked my carcass clean) came galloping back recently attended by all the well-known symptoms, faulty vision, unquenchable thirst and a general listlessness not to be arrived at except via diabetes or membership in the C.I.O.

Now I have begun the old insulin routine again, fitting back into the habit groove as neatly as if I had never left it. Sometimes I think I must be a very remarkable fellow to be entrusted with so many woes. If it be true (see Holy Writ) that the Lord loveth those whom he chasteneth, I should feel flattered.

However I have no notion that the Lord has singled me out for target practise. I just say to myself, "Now you have arthritis and diabetes." I'm a cripple, but I never did walk very much—just from the door out to the car. Almost any sort of legs will do for that. I am thankful I am able to get about at all and can still put in a few hours daily work on my book. Simon Peter is really a grand fellow—if I do say so myself.

One of the things I am trying to do in this book is to trace the building of a great soul from seeming meager materials. To do that adequately from a dramatic standpoint I have to postulate a young Simon with some pretty gaudy weaknesses, though I do not think I have taken many liberties with the Gospel record, which certainly doesn't bother to flatter him. It isn't quite as serious a job as making a silk purse out of a sow's ear, but the Simon of the fishing fleet and the St. Peter of the cathedral window are separated by quite a lot of railroad track.

Another motive of my book is to emphasize the universality of the Gospel. Simon, in Galilee, is a narrow-minded Israelite. The Jewish-Arabian girl, Fara, typifies the problem of a polyglot, polychrome civilization in desperate need of salvation, equipped to answer the heart-yearnings of all tints and tongues.

Now with the Jews and Arabs raising the devil with each other in Palestine my story has unusual timeliness. The morning headlines furnish me with food for thought.

You ask my opinion of the atomic bomb. No doubt our use of it saved many American lives, and, from a military standpoint, was justified. But now we are stuck with it.

We have always been the Moral Mentors of the World, or thought we were, and said we were. Now we have abdicated from that position. The old hymn we used to sing—"From Greenland's Icy Mountains," sounds funny now. Listen.

> Shall we whose souls are lighted
> With wisdom from on High
> Shall we to men benighted
> The lamp of life deny?

WHAM! CRASH! WHEE!

I'm not saying we shouldn't have used the A. Bomb. I'm just saying that we're on a pretty hot griddle now. It was mighty clever of us to have invented the thing, but it might have been more clever if we hadn't. But—I'm no statesman. Maybe it will turn out for the best.

In November of 1945 Daddy's old friend and adviser, Mr. Ira Rich Kent, suddenly died of a heart attack. So many of his generation were dropping out, and each death seemed to lay Daddy mentally low for days. Of Mr. Kent he wrote to Ben Ticknor of Houghton Mifflin.

> I am going to miss our valiant old friend. I shall be lonely without his counsel and comradeship. As life goes on the many open doors through which we passed into seemingly indispensable friendships quietly close, one by one. I am increasingly aware of this. I remember my mother's remark—in her late eighties —that nature softened one's dread of death by making one too lonely to want to stay here any longer. When the most and best of one's friends put off for foreign parts there's not much to be had by tarrying.
>
> Rich and I often discussed the probabilities of a Future Life without arriving at any conclusions worth documenting. Well, he knows all about it now. I hope they give him something to do that will require a blue-pencil. How he did love to make little sentences out of big ones.
>
> As you know I have been sending Rich a copy of each chapter of my book as I finish it. I think you will find that Miss Rodenheiser has nine chapters to date. It would please me if you would read this partial script and tell me how the story impresses you. Don't be reluctant to make suggestions.
>
> In spite of the many interruptions I must count on due to my frail health I think I can finish the job by July of '46. That would leave a four year interval between The Robe and The Big Fisherman, which is about right. The spacing of one's books is important. If they come out too fast one's regular customers say, "Gosh— I haven't read his last one yet!" If one waits too long, the customers say, "What? I thought the old guy was dead!"

Progress with *The Big Fisherman* was slow. The desert winter with its rains and winds did not improve Daddy's arthritis. Often for weeks his fingers were too crippled for him to use his typewriter. He had never learned the trick of dictating except for short letters; it was necessary for him to be completely alone before his ideas ran freely. In May he wrote to Hal Seeley:

> About Christmas time I had something of a physical slump. I had to send to Los Angeles again for Bertha, my nurse, and she has doctored and massaged me back to form. I am now able to sit up at my machine and hammer away again on The Big Fisherman who is in trouble and misbehaving himself, for he is a tough guy, not having yet encountered the Lord. Yesterday Peter was so distressed in mind that he drank a lot of heady wine—to which he was unaccustomed—and got himself thoroughly drunk. Whether this episode will win the approval of the Pope is a question to be viewed with some apprehension. But if Peter, after long and prominent discipleship, could be weak enough to deny that he so much as knew the Great Galilean, surely no one can be much shocked if—before his regeneration—he should have imbibed recklessly.
>
> I have now finished ten chapters of the novel and have the next fourteen pretty well laid out in my mind. My nights are restless and I have plenty of time in the stilly watches to organize my work.

The summer of 1946 Daddy spent with Bertha in Hot Springs, Arkansas, trying the baths and massage, hoping for some relief from the unceasing pain of his arthritis. At first his letter were encouraging and he wrote long amusing descriptions of the steam rooms and the people he met there and in the hotel. "No one recognizes me in my new shape, but those who see my name hurry up for autographs."

The hot baths left him apathetic and he reported that he was too listless to do much work on his book. He wrote to his publishers suggesting that some one come out to encourage and stir him up. "I need a few burrs under my saddle," he said.

Mr. Henry Laughlin, the president of Houghton Mifflin, came

in answer to this request and they spent several days together —Mr. Lauglin listening attentively while Daddy outlined to him the entire story of *The Big Fisherman*. When he finished he realized that the story he had told was much deeper, and better than the one he was writing.

As Mr. Laughlin was departing Daddy announced to him that he had decided to rewrite the novel completely from the beginning, that he now saw the possibilities of a much finer book. The publisher was overcome with horror.

"Oh no," he protested. "It's splendid just the way it is. There's no need to begin again. Keep on; it's fine."

Daddy shook his head. "No, Henry; all those chapters must go in the wastebasket. I now have a far better book in mind, thanks to you."

Mr. Laughlin returned to Boston anxiously wondering how he was to report to his confreres the results of his trip.

Daddy wrote to Betty and Weary:

> I am going to do a thorough overhauling on my book. It will take a lot of courage, but I see so many places where it can have added strength and interest if re-written. The time factor is negligible in comparison to the quality factor. If The Big Fisherman does not appear until the fall of '48 nobody is going to be hurt. The Arabs and the Jews will still be fighting, the statesmen of the world will still be confused and the people will be just as afraid of practising the Golden Rule as they are today.

In July Daddy and Bertha decided they had had all they could stand of Hot Springs. The massages seemed to leave him lamer than ever and the humidity did nothing to elevate his spirits. He wrote to me:

> The weather here is foul. The old-timers say this continued damp is unusual, but it has been my experience that the weather is always unusual where I am. Arkansas is a funny place. Sometimes I get the sensation we are not in the United States at all.

Some of the cars are so ramshackle that it says ARK right on the license plate. The people have been nice to me, but it is too damp here for one with my trouble. I feel quite sure that I shall never be saw in Arkanseen again.

During 1947 Daddy's letters record with equal attention his progress with the novel and his arthritis. He was determined to see the end of both of them. In spite of all the setbacks which hindered his work, repeated ulcers on his eyes and lameness in his four good fingers, he seemed always sure that this too would pass and he would get back to his typewriter. On the way home by air from Arkansas he and Bertha encountered a heavy storm. In a letter describing the attempts of the plane to land he wrote:

By this time most of the passengers were scared out of their britches. All but me. Bertha confessed once we were on dry land that she too had been terrified. I said, "You needn't have been. You were with me. I must finish The Big Fisherman. My reservation in heaven was cancelled once before for that reason. Stay close beside me and you will be all right." And such faith has Bertha in my pronouncements that she accepted that as a verity.

The work did not move quickly, but all his hours were spent thinking upon it, and little by little the chapters were completed. He wrote to me:

I hope I have not misled you about my recent output of literature. It doesn't bulk up heavily, but now that my eye is improving I am able to sit at my typewriter for longer hours each day. The revision of the novel is completed and I am back at the place where I left off and proceeding into new territory.

The long winter is ended and Jesus is about to return to his public speaking and all the dramatic events involved in the summer career. I have made a discovery while exploring certain episodes in the New Testament. Notwithstanding the fact that Galilee had four seasons, well-defined, the Gospels have no climate. No mention is made of winter, or snow, or the obvious fact that great crowds could not assemble out of doors for almost half the year. It gives me a chance to have a lot of people rained in on one occasion.

I have been reading a great deal of exhaustive comment on the Bible all my life, but I have never heard anyone say that the New Testament has no climate. True, there were a couple of bad storms on the lake, but apparently no one was much inconvenienced by weather on land. Ginger, next time you see my friend Dr. Norwood, ask him what he thinks about that.

June 1947

Things are looking quite a bit brighter. My left eye is practically free now of the troublesome infection; and my right eye is slowly mending, though the vision is badly damaged. My general morale is better. I worked all forenoon on the Fisherman and had a good time. This promises to be a thought-provoking chapter. Simon wishes that Jesus had a little more spunk. If he was only six feet-two and would stand up and tell old Rabbi Ben-Sholem that he could jolly well go chase himself, Simon would have been delirious with joy. Alas, alas! Jesus had both hands full of power and could do whatever he liked with it, but would let almost anybody impose on him for the sake of peace—It is indeed a very delicate and debatable problem, as anyone knows who knows Munich; but in a book like this it is important to be honest even at the risk of raising questions we can't answer. If Christianity won't work, it is high time we found it out. And if it will work, we'd better try to put it into practice.

That summer Daddy decided to go to Los Angeles to try the gold treatment for his arthritis and for a while his letters were full of the details of the experiment.

July 1947

Dr. Boland explained the risks one takes in following the gold treatment and suggested that I take a few days to think it over, but I told him that time was of the essence, that I was content to proceed without further delay. Whereupon he excused himself and came back with a tall syringe full of solid gold.

Now if you think that the "gold" treatment involves no more effort on the patient's part than the mere offering of a rump for hypodermic puncture once a week you have much to learn about the enterprise. This is a full-time occupation. The man won't give you the gold unless you promise to work at rehabilitating your moribund muscles by certain painful and tiresome exercises. To wit: listen, please.

At 7 A.M. Bertha wakes me and helps me into a tub of hot water where I steam for five minutes. Back in bed for twenty minutes while she give me a shot of the good old insulin. Then she slowly counts while I do a long string of muscle flexings to strengthen "the legs."

Patients of long standing (or sitting) come to be regarded impersonally, nurses referring not to "his legs," but "the legs." And as he gradually becomes more and more torpid I think they refer to these appendages as "its legs." But this is an idle digression.

Then I do an exercise playfully known as "climbing the wall." Stand erect at right angles to the wall, raise your arm until your hand touches it. Climb with your fingers up the wall as far as your rheumatic shoulder joints will let you go, then climb slowly down again. Five times, please, for each arm. No fudging, no cheating. That will do. Now you may sit down and hurt like hell for an hour.

August 1947

I am working every day on the novel and making good progress. I have had unmistakable evidence that the arthritis treatments are beginning to operate. Dr. Boland seems delighted.

Last night I took the steps down into the grill without any assistance. Very showy performance. My appetite is not much improved. We had lobster which Bertha seemed to enjoy, but which I thought tasted like long white strips cut from an old hot-water bottle. Not as good as some hot water bottles I have had.

I have now become the repository for a great deal of precious metal. There may be more gold in Fort Knox, but not elsewhere except in me.

September 1947 [to Mary Young, Montreal]

So glad to have your letter this morning. It sounded like old times. I must reluctantly confess with you that it is difficult for any intelligent person to evade the feeling that the world, if not conclusively gone to hell, has pushed off to a good start in that direction. Some of that feeling, my pet, is inevitable to our advancing years. After sixty the world seems to be in a devil of a mess, whether in 1947, 1066 or A.D. 37. We must keep this fact in mind.

I suppose it is just as well that I wrote Magnificent Obsession and Green Light when I did. One burns a lot more carbon now when documenting one's optimism. Verily the world is in a hell of a mess. However it has been in messes before and bumbled on, scared and scarred, but still ambulatory. The physicist is frightened but the historian is not. The physicist fears that the world is about to be destroyed, but the historian knows better. We are en route from the jungle to paradise, with less than half the mileage covered. If the whole thing blows up now nothing means anything, nothing makes sense. We must hang on to our faith that God is intelligent.

January 1948 [to Hardwick Moseley]

As you see I am back in Las Vegas with my family and my own things again. Bertha is still looking after me and I have kept the poor girl pretty busy lately twenty-four hours of the day. The flu which has laid me low for some weeks is clearing up now and I wish I could say the same for the weather. It has been raining here for the past forty-eight hours. All persons afflicted with rheumatiz and allied disorders have been kept indoors and seasoning their vittles with aspirin. Fishing on the Sea of Galilee has been unprofitable; nothing much to be had but large-mouthed, speckled tripe.

March 1948 [to Hardwick Moseley]

I have finished the twentieth chapter, probably the most dramatic thus far. The twenty-first (the denial of Peter) will be very brief. There is little doubt in my mind now about my ability to finish the job by the middle of July. From here on the composition should proceed rapidly.

The weather here is foul, not fit for man or beast. Every day and night we have gusty gales that send clouds of desert dirt into the house. The old timers say they have never seen the beat of it. I am anxious to get back to Los Angeles where one has only the smog and dampness to contend with. However my arthritis is not too bad. I am so absorbed by my work that my infirmities don't seem to matter.

May 1948 [to Virginia]

Getting along deep into chapter 23 but didn't get much take-home copy out of this day's work. I have been sticking at this thing so constantly—day and night—that I feel jaded. Doubtless my infirmities have something to do with it. Also my wakefulness at night. There isn't enough diversity in my program. My days are as alike as the Dionne sisters. I wish I could go to a circus.

August 12, 1948 [to Virginia]

It begins to look as if we might have a book completed pretty soon. I finished the 28th chapter yesterday. It is full of excitement and surprises. Some of the surprises surprised *me*. They just dropped in on me as a Heavenly Gift. This morning I tinkered with the beginning of the 29th chapter. I did not put up much copy, but made a fairly comprehensive outline of the incidents involved. It will not be so difficult to write. I should be able to finish it by the end of the week. The final chapter, the 30th, will be only a thousand words. If nothing turns up to detain me I should complete the job by a week from today. I hope so; for I have been at this thing so long that it has nearly worn me out. I am getting tired of the steady grind, day after week after month after year. I am glad you have liked the chapters we have sent you recently. I think the pace has been kept up pretty well. I have been getting about what I wanted.

August 21, 1948 [to Virginia]

I finished The Big Fisherman today at noon—thirty chapters, 226,000 words.

I am very weary, very happy, very humble. I feel sure that I had help from The Outside.

Publication will probably be made on November 9th. All the manuscript but the last two chapters are already in type. I feel like a boy out of school. Your sister has helped and now applauds. I do wish you were here, darling, to celebrate with me. Your frequent letters have cheered me. Too tired to write more today.

Daddy's mental depression during the last weeks of work on the novel alarmed Betty and she went down to Los Angeles to be with him. His extreme exhaustion had thrown him into an almost mystical state and he talked a great deal of Mother, a thing he rarely did in these days. When the last word of the book was typed for the last time he called Betty to him. "It's finished," he said wearily. "Do you think Bessie knows I've finished?" He thoroughly expected to creep to his bed, pull up the covers and die, now that his work was completed. Betty was so anxious about him that she wrote to me: "It makes me laugh when I listen to them arguing whether the book is to cost three-fifty or three-seventy-five. This book has cost a man's life."

But by the time *The Big Fisherman* was published in November Daddy had come up from the exhaustion and depression that had enveloped him and was taking interest in the book's reception. Its arrival had been so long awaited that the advance sales were enormous and it figured on the best-seller list even before the date of release. As with its predecessors it soon went to the top of the pile and remained there for many months. The reviews poured in and Daddy had plenty of time to peruse them.

December 1948 [to Betty]

One would think, by the generous outgivings of this pen, that it was full of prune juice. All fountain pens hate me, as do many reviewers.

Bertha and I dawdled for 2 hours over the breakfast table,

reading a large batch of mail. She read me the press clippings you sent, and you would have been amused and gratified to have heard her indignant snorts when she came upon something a little less than flattering to Poppa's opus. Bertha is sputteringly partisan and allergic to sour comments by reviewers.

But all things considered—I think these clippings are pretty good. It is not to be expected that these hard-boiled, jaded cynics will be unanimously fulsome in their praise of a religious story written by a retired old parson. The sales are huge.

As you doubtless notice by this labored writing I am very lame. I'll be glad to be back with my own family. I'm tired of hotel life. Seems to me the cooks here aren't very good. You remember the note they sent up with the dinners listing the pieces of valuable silver to be returned? Last night, after tackling a dried-up dinner I added to the kitchen inventory—"six leather-bound French fried potatoes"—and returned them with the other museum pieces.

I am discontented, probably because no work is driving and diverting me. I have too much time to think about my infirmities. Bertha brought her little typewriter down for me to use while mine is in the shop, but it runs like my Uncle Perry's manure spreader and is much too stiff for my lame hands.

This morning I had a letter from the famed Indiana Society of Chicago asking me to be principal speaker at their annual dinner. How I wish I could go. That would be just my dish. I would have much much fun.

The huge scrapbook containing reviews of *The Big Fisherman* is interesting and revealing. As always the more intellectual critics reviled the colloquial language and everyday aspect of Bible characters who had been taken down from their cathedral niches and examined as ordinary mortals. Those who were repelled by having their Gospel translated in 1948 found no good in the book and ignored its message; others gladly stepped into the mood and joined the crowd seeking the man Jesus. The review from *John O'London's Weekly* says:

One can almost feel the hot dusty roads of Palestine filled with thousands of pattering, sandalled feet, hurrying to catch a glimpse of Jesus.

It is interesting to note how the criticisms from England, New Zealand and Australia emphasized the story's dominant message and dwelt upon it in their discussion of the book. One wonders if their closeness to the threat of disaster made them more resigned to accept the compromise of the story's conclusion: that if peace is to be had it must be within oneself.

Several thoughtful American critics wrote with regret that the closing pages of the book seemed sad; that *The Robe* had ended on a note of optimism for the future of mankind, while *The Big Fisherman* seemed to express a doubt that men would ever cease to cheat and hate and kill. Some wanted more assurance than the simple words of Jesus, "The Kingdom of God is within you."

In the article in the *American Quarterly* quoted earlier, Professor Carl Bode sums up his discussion of Lloyd Douglas' books in these words:

> As the times have changed, so has Douglas' philosophy. At forty, when he began writing books, he displayed in his ministerial manuals the brisk but conflicting ideas of a modernist minister. In his novels of the 1930s the philosophy is one of doing good for the sake of improving one's personality, with material rewards following consistently if "quite incidentally." In his two novels of the last decade, the emphasis has shifted. In a time of life-and-death struggle, the spiritual rewards of good have been stressed. The goal has become not this world but the next.

Daddy's changing viewpoint undoubtedly was influenced by the stress of world upheaval, but also a contributing factor was his age, his illness and bereavement. What man cares about improving his personality at the age of seventy-one? From that pinnacle his pronouncements are less inclined to be concerned with such trivialities; he looks with the naked eye upon the vast question of life hereafter.

Few critics in reviewing *The Big Fisherman* seemed to know that it was written by an elderly man suffering acutely from arthritis. They mentioned that it took five years to write the book, but they didn't know why it took so long, how many days were spent by the author unable to bear the pain of his crippled fingers striking the keys of his typewriter. One reviewer reports in passing that Simon Peter seemed to be unusually concerned and annoyed by the weather; when it rained he was depressed and moved stiffly, when it was hot he was listless. Again and again in LCD letters of those years one comes upon the line, "The weather is foul today."

Age shaped *The Big Fisherman* but its conclusions are no less valuable that they come from a man who had lived beyond his three-score and ten. One looks to the old for assurances concerning the verities of life; their experience gives them authority, the beliefs to which they cling in spite of vicissitudes can give us comfort.

Daddy had an abiding faith in the survival of Christianity. In the closing paragraphs of *The Big Fisherman* he imagined these words to be the note upon which Peter ended his life: "Tell them that the Kingdom will come, but they must not expect it to reign now—except in their hearts. The world is not yet ready to receive the king."

To a young man who wrote in 1950 questioning Daddy upon the fate of the church he answered:

I am so glad you wanted to confide to me your perplexities and I only wish that I might be in a position to solve your problems for you. Sometimes we all grow very much discouraged about the outlook for organized Christianity. But I think a good medicine to take for that is to remember that the Christian church has weathered a good many storms; it has been through plagues and famines, wars and persecutions again and again these past centuries. If it is true that the only forecast we can make is predicated upon the past, I think there is ground to hope that Christianity will not only survive but continue to be—with all its imperfections and frailty of leadership, the greatest power for good in the world. I ask you to share my own belief in the divine character of the church. The fact is that if the church had not had a divine origin it could never have survived the clumsy and inept human leadership it has so often had.

If one takes the writings of Lloyd Douglas as a declaration of his beliefs over the years one can trace the gradual change in his viewpoint concerning the divinity of Christ. As a young man he was disturbed by the miracles and earnestly sought reasonable explanations for them. In his early novels any contacts with a divine experience appear mysterious and dream-like, leaving the reader to judge for himself. In *The Robe* the hero Marcellus is described as being a skeptic until late in the book when he says, "I believe." But in *The Big Fisherman* Christ is depicted as a divine figure at all times. The miracles are told as facts needing no explanatory postscripts. It would seem the author of that book at last himself believed.

The immense popularity of the two religious novels is surely some sort of a comment upon the spiritual decisions of a generation. Whether the endorsement is wistful or based on solid conviction, it merits the attention of students of our times.

Professor Carl Bode seems to have given much thought to the phenomenon of Lloyd Douglas' success. In an article published in the *Christian Century* he suggests interesting possibilities.

The novels are themselves a testament to his religious experience. They picture indirectly the working out of his own private religious dilemma; they show the way he found an answer to it years after he left the professional ministry to concentrate on didactic writing. In Douglas' own apparent conversion we may even have the expression of a more nearly universal one.

Time To Remember

DADDY LIVED two years after the publication of *The Big Fisherman*. For a short time his mobility was partially restored by benefit of the drug cortisone and he was able to take a last trip back East to New York.

In my country-fed imagination New York has always been an enchanted city. I was always happy to have an errand there and would spend a few days in bug-eyed admiration of its highly advertised splendors. This trip has cured me of my hallucination. The town is full of hurrying people—faceless. I don't know them.

After he returned to Los Angeles he never again attempted to leave his apartment and became more and more resigned to his bed. His arthritis had cooled off, but the results of all the various treatments had taken a toll of the rest of his body.

The miracle drug does all that is claimed for it. My arthritis is much improved. But my diabetes! Perhaps that young Danish Prince was right in his surmise that it were better to bear those ills we have than fly to others we know not of. Another miracle like that would put a lily in my hand.

In an effort to get his mind off his infirmities he began to write his memoirs. That was the direction his thoughts took during the long hours. His father and mother, his little brother Clyde, and all the experiences of his childhood came back vividly, and with great effort he managed to spend several hours a day at his typewriter. Bertha would secrete herself in the bedroom until his breathing became noticeably painful, when she would come forth and lead him back to bed and his oxygen mask.

Chapter by chapter he wrote the story of his youth, interspersed with frequent digressions upon a wide variety of subjects: the merits of the old family stove compared to central heating; modern education, the weather, funerals, the government—anything that came to mind and all viewed at long range. More than any other of his writings this last book reads very much as his friends knew his conversation; salted with humorous anecdotes and colored by personal opinion. He deals tenderly with his childhood, seeming to have forgotten how as a young man he bitterly resented its frustrations. His father and mother are understood and appreciated. He looks back and sees that life was good. *Time To Remember* the book was called and in it he laid his last thoughts.

Betty and I were with him the month before his death, but we left with no particular foreboding that the long, long illness was drawing to a close. Bertha phoned us in Las Vegas before I had started East and asked us to come back. "Your father wants to go to the hospital," she said. "He thinks it is the end."

We went to him at once and arrived late at night. He was sitting slumped on the edge of the hospital bed, his feet on a chair. "You were good to come back," he said. We could not bear it that he should feel grateful to us for anything, but what we really felt we could not say.

He took our hands. "This is it," he told us, and he seemed thoughtful, but not at all afraid. When he lay back on the bed he closed his eyes and sighed. "I'm happy," he said.

After that he smiled when we took his hand but it was as

though we reached to him from a distance; his lips moved but he was too far away for us to hear.

A few months before he had written to an elderly friend:

> I shall be willing to settle for Eternal Rest. I am weary and shall be wearier yet when the time comes to be off and away. I don't want to march in white-robed parades or sing in a Celestial Choir. I want to lie down in peace to sleep. God will stay awake.

He lived a long life and was many men, but always his desire was to help people realize their nearness to God. He was a preacher from the beginning to the end. Although his theology changed with the changing years his basic faith remained the same. The parting words he said to his congregation in Akron, Ohio, held the heart of his beliefs and all his novels stand in these words:

> I have taught you that humanity is on the way up, by the grace of God, toward some exalted destiny.
>
> I have told you that we can add length to our earthly days through altruistic service, that whatever may be the nature of our future life we know enough about this life to be assured that men do not quickly die and leave no trace who in the quest of the Christian ideal have contributed something of their hope and faith and work to the generation in which they lived.
>
> I have taught you that belief in a life beyond this world is consistent with orderly thought. It is inconceivable that God would endow us with this eternal hope and disappoint us in the end with death.
>
> These things have summarized my creed. I have tried to make them clear to you. Doubtless I have failed sometimes, but that was not because they were hard to believe, but only because they were blunderingly stated.
>
> I go away with deep affection for you, and I pray that God's blessing may be with you, everyone, through all the coming years.

12-22